# MYSTERIES AND GLIMPSES OF KASHMIR

THE AUTHOR

# MYSTERIES AND GLIMPSES OF KASHMIR

**Mohammad Yasin**
**Madhavi Yasin**

**RAJ PUBLICATIONS**
R-115/2, Model Town-III,
Delhi-110009

**Mysteries and Glimpses of Kashmir**

**First Published 1996**



ISBN-81-86208-03-8

*Laser Typesetting By* :
Ideal Printers
2/11, Roop Nagar, Delhi-110007
Ph : 2910909

*Printed at :*

*Published By :*
Smt. Poonam Goel
For RAJ PUBLICATIONS
R-115/2, Model Town-III,
Delhi -110009
Ph. : 7136455

# CONTENTS

**To The memory of
our parents**

वेदाहमेतं पुरुषम्महान्तं आदित्यवर्णम्

# Foreword

For many years the late Professor Mohammad Yasin and his wife Prof. Madhavi Yasin worked in Kashmir on a broad spectrum of topics relating to the culture, history and philosophy of this unique valley. These are now brought together in the form of a book. Although some of the articles are rather dated, they do represent collectively a valuable source of information and insights on a variety of areas which I am sure will be of interest to scholars and the general public alike.

3, NYAYA MARG
CHANADKYAPURI
NEW DELHI-110021

Karan Singh

# Preface

Present work is a set of articles by late Prof. Mohammad Yasin and myself. It presents the history of Kashmir from Ancient to modern times. Part I (A) and (B) contain the papers of Prof. Mohammad Yasin and Part II contains my papers. About Part I (A) Prof Yasin says:—

Kashmir is the land of bliss. There is not a single nation in the world that does not hear about Kashmir on any one day and there is not a single person on earth who does not wish to travel to Kashmir. G.T. Vigne wrote in 1842: "Kashmir will become the focus of Asiatic civilization; a miniature England in the heart of Asia... and, presenting as many attractions, it will become the *sine quo non* of the oriental traveller, whether he be disposed to consider it as the *Ultima Thule* of his voyage, or a resting place whence he may start again for still more distant regions." Vigne's prophecy has literally come true with this much difference that Kashmir has become the heart of the globe not that of Asia alone and it is both, the first milestone and the destination.

Kashmir offers many known attractions—its gardens, snow-clad mountains and glaciers, springs, lakes and peaceful and sublime resorts. But Kashmir offers something more.

Kashmir is heaven on earth and so it also abounds in "heavenly mysteries".

The purpose of this brochure is to introduce the readers to these mysteries and mysterious beauties of Kashmir which have generally escaped notice. A visit to Kashmir is a must and if already visited a second visit is a necessity to have a complete picture.

It was Mirza Ghulam Ahmad of Qadian (1835- 1908), the founder of the Ahmadiyah Movement in Islam, who for the first time wrote his treatise "*Masih Hindustan mein*" in 1899 A.D. and pointed out that Jesus Christ did not die on the Cross nor he ascended to Heaven alive. Instead, Jesus went over to Kashmir, died a natural death and is buried there in Srinagar.Mirza Ghulam Ahmad told a truth but his religious zeal blurred the real issue. The Mirza used this discovery to demolish Christian doctrines and to establish his own mission. Beliefs and sentiments, facts and arguments, were inter-mixed with the result that nothing was proved convincingly and the scientific world did not accept anything.

Mufti Muhammad Sadiq of Shahpur developed the thesis of Mirza Ghulam Ahmad further and published his "*Qabr-i-Masih*" in October 1936. This is a laborious work and the author tries to prove that the Bani Israel (i.e. the Jews) were the early settlers of Kashmir.

Khwaja Nazir Ahmad of Lahore compiled his monumental work "*Jesus in Heaven on Earth*" in 1951. The thesis of Mirza Ghulam Ahmad and Mufti Muhammad Sadiq, has been further developed. The work is well-documented and contains an exhaustive bibliography on the subject. But the original sin was committed by all these writers when they mixed religious belief with hard facts of history. They invited criticism from all quarters–the Christians were all out to defend their faith, and the Muslims, in general, could not accept Mirza Ghulam Ahmad as the Promised Masih.

Following in the footsteps of their leader the Ahmadis have brought out a large number of booklets and pamphlets to propagate this thesis. In Kashmir, Abdul Aziz Shora, editor "Roshni", Srinagar and Dr. Aziz Ahmad Qureshi of Kashmir Civil Service, jointly brought out *Sipahr-i-Haqaiq* or *Hazarat Isa awr Isayiat* in 1953-54. There is nothing original in the book. It is entirely based on "Jesus in Heaven on Earth" of Khwaja Nazir Ahmad. Abdul Aziz Shora independently brought out a small booklet "*Masih Kashmir mein*". It simply gives unchecked and unanalysed references quoted by Khwaja Nazir Ahmad.

In 1957, Dr. Aziz Ahmad Qureshi compiled his "Asrar-i-Kashmir. The author has verbatim drawn upon Mirza Ghulam Ahmad's *Masih Hindustan mein*, Mufti Muhammad Sadiq's *Qabr-i-Masih*, and Khwaja Nazir Ahmad's *Jesus in Heaven on Earth*" though he claims himself to be the originator of this thesis. He also proclaims himself as the prophet of the age (*Imam-i- Zaman*). Where facts and arguments fail, he takes refuge in the garb of *Kashf* (Divine guidance or revelation). Maulana Jalal-ud-Din Shams, Ex-Imam of London Mosque, brought out his "Where did Jesus die ?" in 1959. The book may be regarded as the abridged edition of *Jesus in Heaven on Earth*.

We have not involved ourselves in religious controversy. Our approach is purely historical. We are concerned only with the physical presence of Jesus Christ outside Jerusalem and his earthly remains. Other facts like Kashmir being the Land of Promise, the Tomb of Moses and the Tomb of Mary, serve as the background to highlight the main thesis about *Rauzabal*.

We have not discovered any new facts except the correct rendering and translation of the passage in the *Bhavishya Maha Purana* which has been wrongly understood and translated by Khwaja Nazir Ahmad and all other subsequent writers. They read *Ishputram* (the son of God) as *Yusashaphat* and make it *Yuz Asaf* whereas *Ishputram* in itself is the most conclusive proof.

We have drawn our information mainly from Khwaja Nazir Ahmad's book, *Jesus in Heaven on Earth*. But all the references have been carefully checked. The greatest drawback of Khwaja Nazir Ahmad's book is that the references are not correct, the citation is faulty and the bibliographical data are neither complete nor exact. We have only tried to present the thesis in a more scientific and logical manner. What has been written in this brochure needs further careful and through study uninfluenced by religious leanings. We feel that there is some basis to make a start.

I take this occasion to thank Dr. Karan Singh for his ungrudging help, whenever I asked for it. In spite of his busy schedule he took out his precious time to write 'Foreword' to the book.

I thank Dr. Kapila Vatsayan, Director, Indira Gandhi National Centre For The Arts and Shri P.N. Haksar, Chancellor of J.N.U.

I thank Prof. Ravinder Kumar, Chairman ICHR. My thanks are also due to Dr. T.R. Sareen, Dr. Raj Kumar, Dr. P.K. Shukla, Dr. P.K.V. Kaimal and Shri P.N. Sahaya, of ICHR. I also thank Ms Neeru Gadhia of the C.S.L., New Delhi.

I gratefully thank Shri R.C. Tripathi, Adviser, Planning Commission, New Delhi. I thank Dr. S. Sarkar, Director General, National Archives, New Delhi.

I thank Janab Mahmud-ur-Rahman, Vice-Chancellor A.M.U. for his kind consideration towards me. I thank Prof. Irfan Habib, Janab Asghar Ali Engineer and Prof. Aparna Basu. I thank Dr. Rajendra Prasad, Director, Ramayana Vidyapeeth. I also thank Dr. P.N. Chopra, Editor, Sardar Patel Society, New Delhi and Dr. (Smt.) Prabha Chopra. I thank Shri D.V. Batra for his care towards me.

I thank my parents late Shri Radha Krishna Tewari and late Smt. Lalita Tewari, whose debt I shall never be able to repay. I thank Shri S.C. Prasad and Smt. Asha Prasad for all the troubles they take for me. I also thank my brother Shri Ashok Tewari. My thanks are also due to Shri N.C. Mahajan, Smt. Indu Bala Sharma and Kiran Hura of NMML, New Delhi. I thank Shri J.N. Vohra, Shri J.N. Fotedar and S. Virender Singh.

I am thankful to the publishers for publishing the book in recorded time. I am grateful to Sri P.K. Goel and Smt. Poonam Goel for their keen interest in bringing out the book.

M-I, Sector-25, Madhavi Yasin
Jalvayu Vihar
Noida-201 301

# ILLUSTRATIONS

"All over Central Asia, in Kashmir and Ladakh and Tibet and even farther north, there is still a strong belief that Jesus or Isa travelled about there ... there is nothing inherently improbable in his doing so."

—Jawaharlal Nehru

(*Glimpses of World History*, 2nd Indian ed., p. 86 )

# Part I
## (A)

# 1

# RAUZABAL

Jesus Christ died on the cross. Devout hands took his body down from the cross and laid it in a tomb on the Friday evening. He rose from the tomb on the following Sunday. After an earthly sojourn, during which his disciples saw him on several occasions, he ascended to heaven. He now sits on the right hand of God as an intercessory between man and God. Jesus is alive in heaven.

But in mohalla Khaniyar, Srinagar, Kashmir there is Rauzabal, a tomb, where Jesus Christ is said to be buried.

Facts, sometimes, appear more unreal than fiction. There is no denying the truth that Jesus was put on the cross. What happened next? From here we have different stories. Those who hold that Jesus is buried in Srinagar say:—

**I.** That Jesus Christ did not die on the cross.

1. Jesus prayed to God to save him from the death of an "accursed of God"—the death on the cross. His prayers were heard (Hebrews, V : 7).
2. Jesus did not remain on the cross for more than three hours. He was removed from the cross during the day-time (Luke, XXIII : 44, 46).
3. One could live on the cross for days together though in that horrible condition (Dummelow, *Commentary on the Holy Bible*, p. 717; William Hanna, *The Life of Christ*, III : 328, 329; Stroud, *On the Physical Cause of Death of Christ*, pp. 123, 124). The very purpose and object of crucifixion was not the direct killing and immediate death. It was a torture that continued for three or four days. The death was partly

caused by hunger and thirst, the vicissitudes of hot and cold or the attacks of revenous birds and beasts and in others was designedly accelerated by burning, stoning or breaking the bones.

4. If persons crucified were :

"taken down in time and carefully treated, recovered and survived"

(Ibid, p. 55; the instances are cited by Paulus, *Exeg. Handb.,* 3b : S. 781; Wiser, *Bible Realworteb,* I : S. 672; Hass, S. 144).

5. Jesus was crucified on Friday. Saturday is the Jewish Sabbath. In view of the approach of the Sabbath, "executions lasting until late in the afternoon were impossible" (Sifre, II: 221; John, XIX : 31).
6. The body of Jesus had to be removed from the cross, in any case, before nightfall (Deut., XXI : 23).

**II.** That Jesus was brought down alive from the cross.

1. The bones of Jesus, contrary to the prevalent practice, were not broken as "they thought him to be dead" (Renan, *History of the Origin of Christianity,* Book I : 246; John, XIX : 36; cf. Ps. XXIV : 20).
2. Jesus, who only appeared to be dead, had in fact fallen into a comatose state. He was "only in a syncope" (Farrar, *Life of Christ,* p. 421).
3. The other two culprits (thieves) who were crucified along with Jesus were still alive when taken off the cross. (John, XIX : 32).
4. Jesus had strength enough to utter a loud cry about the time when he was taken down (Matt., XXVII : 46; Mark, XV : 34).
5. When "one of the soldiers struck his spear into the body (of Jesus) in such a manner that it passed over the hip and into the side... from the insignificant wound followed blood and water (a sure sign of life).... a wound in a dead body flows nothing but a few drops of thickened blood" (*The Crucifixion by an Eyewitness,* p. 71; John, XIX: 34, XX:27; *Ency. Biblica,* Art. *Cross,* col. 960).

6. The body of Jesus was delivered to his friends and sympathisers and not to his enemies (John, XIX : 38).

**III.** That Jesus was placed inside a new tomb in a private garden and not in any common burial ground; he was *alive* though with wounds.

1. The tomb in which Jesus was laid was sufficiently spacious and airy and belonged to Joseph of Arimathea, a secret disciple and a friend of Jesus (John, XIX : 38; The Gospel of Peter, II :28; Mark, XV: 43; Luke, XXIII : 51; *The Jewish Ency.*, IV : 250). After the alleged resurrection, Joseph Arimathea was arrested and the Jews attributed to him criminal purposes in that he had been in secret association with Jesus" (*The Crucifixion by an Eyewitness*, pp. 109, 110.).

2. After Jesus' body was placed in the sepulchre the Jews came together to Pontius Pilate and asked him: "Command, therefore, that the sepulchre be made sure until the third day, lest his disciples come by night and steal him away, and say unto the people. He is risen from the dead. So the last error shall be worst than the first" (Matt., XXVII : 64).

3. His wounds were treated with "the herbs which were useful in such cases" (*The Crucifixion by an Eyewitness*, p. 66). "Nicodemus spread balm in both nailpierced hands" (Ibid., p. 75). "The Myrrh and aloe wood were reduced to powder and inserted between the bandages which were wound fold upon fold" (Dummelow, *Commentary on the Holy Bible*, p. 808).

4. The constant application of *Marham-i-Isa* or *Marham- i-Rosul* (the Ointment of Jesus or the Ointment of Prophet) to the body of Jesus healed the wounds and caused the blood circulation freely in the body. Numerous oriental medical treatises state that this ointment was applied to the wounds of Jesus when he was taken off the cross (*Cannon of Avicenna,* Vol. V, Discourse No. II on Ointment and Plasters).

5. To avoid suffocation the "neck and face of the body were doubtless left bare" (Dummelow, *Commentary on the Holy Bible*, p. 808) and the tomb in which Jesus was placed was not filled in or covered with earth though demanded by the Jews. Only a stone was rolled over the sepulchre (*The Crucifixion by an Eyewitness*, p. 75).
6. Pilate, the Roman Governor, appears to be sympathetic towards Jesus (John, XIX : 12).

**IV.** That Jesus "rose alive" from the tomb, out of the jaws of death.

1. The tomb of Jesus in Palestine is empty (Eusebius, *Vita Const.*, III : 26).
2. Jesus appeared to two Marys, who embraced his feet (Matt., XXVIII : 9).
3. Jesus directed his disciples to proceed to Galilee, about one hundred and fifty miles from Jerusalem (Ibid., 10).
4. Jesus appeared to James and Paul (I Cor., XV : 7-8).
5. He appeared to his disciples and drank and ate with them (Luke, XXIV : 33, 36-43).
6. He paid a secret visit to his disciples eight days after (John, XX : 26, 27).
7. Jesus appeared in Galilee (Matt., XXVIII : 16-20; John, XXI : 1).
8. When Jesus appeared to his disciples, "They were terrified and affrighted, and supposed that they had seen a spirit" (Luke, XXIV : 37). To dispel their doubts, Jesus said : "Behold my hands and my feet, that it is I myself : handle me and see; for a spirit hath not flesh, and bones as you see me have" (Ibid., XXIV: 39).

**V.** That it was a natural and perfectly human life and body subject to physical and organic laws.

1. Jesus showed to his disciples "the print of that nails" in his hands and his side (which was thrust with spear) (John, XX : 19-20).

2. Thomas put his finger into the print of nails and thrust his hand into his (Jesus') side to make sure that it was a corporal body and not a spirit and that the body was not transfigured (John, XX :25, 27).
3. Jesus himself told to those who came with Peter : "Take, handle me and see that I am not a bodiless phantom" (Andrews, (*Apocryphal Books of the Old and New Testaments : Gospel According to the Hebrews)*.
4. Jesus consumed earthly food and allowed himself to be touched (John, XXI : 12, 13).
5. Continuance of the marks of the wounds, the human speech, the acts of walking and breaking bread are incompatible with a heavenly corporality.
6. Jesus did not appear to his enemies. A Divine Being resurrected from the dead should have no fears.
7. The removal of the stone from the mouth of the sepulchre clearly shows that Jesus got out of the tomb in his earthly body.
8. The Gospels do not provide any positive proof of the resurrection of Jesus Christ.

**VI.** That the ascension of Jesus is rendered unbelievable.

1. Mark and Luke contradict one another, Luke also contradicts his own earlier statement in this regard (Acts, I : 3).
2. There is no agreement among evangelists about the time, date and place of ascension.
3. A palpable body which still had flesh and bones and ate material earthly food could not have been qualified for a celestial abode because Jesus himself has declared that life in heaven was not earthly (Matt., XXII : 29, 30).
4. If Jesus,after resurrection, took earthly food for the sustenance of his earthly body, he must be doing the same in heaven after his ascension.

5. Not possible for an earthly body to liberate itself from the laws of gravity as to be capable of an ascent through air without any aid or agency (heavenly or otherwise).

**VII.** That Jesus did not ascend to heaven. He only migrated from Jerusalem.

1. When afraid for his life Jesus used to take shelter in mountains in unknown places (John, VI : 15, 20; X: 39, 40; Luke, VI : 12).
2. Finally he went to the mount of Olives or Gethsemme (Matt., XXVI : 7; Luke, XXII : 39; Mark, XIV : 26).
3. There was a "white house" on the top of the Mount of Olives, the edge of which is regarded the point of ascension (Edersheim, *The Life and Times of Jesus, the Messiah*, I : 148).
4. He took leave of his disciples and started climbing on the Mount Olives, "while engulfed in the clouds, Jesus went into this house" (Ibid.).
5. Heavy clouds, as often happens in mountainous country, came low and their mist gradually engulfed him.
6. The olive trees on the Mount also screened him.
7. By the time the clouds lifted, Jesus reached the summit and crossed the ridge (*The Crucifixion by an Eyewitness*, p. 124).

**VIII.** That Jesus could not disclose his real identity in Palestine and preach there.

1. He was a hunted man. The Jews wanted to "slay him" (John, V : 16; VII : 19). He was all along aware of this danger.
2. Persecuted, tortured and tormented,both physically and mentally, he did not have the heart to stand another betrayal and second trial. After all he was a human being.
3. After his alleged resurrection he appeared in disguise (Mark, XVI : 12).

4. Jesus had his migration in mind. He had explicitly told: "I go my way, and ye shall seek me, and ye shall die in our sins; whither I go you cannot come" (John, VII: 21).
5. He gave repeated warnings and clear indication of his intended journey to a far off land (Luke, XIII : 33, 34; XVII : 22, 23, 26; Matt., XXIII : 37-39; John, VII : 35; XIII : 33).

**IX.** That Jesus migrated from Jerusalem and went over to Kashmir.

1. Canonical Gospels are silent about the life of Jesus from his birth up to the twelve years of his age, "the day of his showing unto Israel" (Luke, II : 40).
2. Jesus is again in picture in the thirtieth year of his life. The life up to thirtieth year is unknown.
3. A Russian traveller, Nicholas Notovitch, gives the details about the formative period of the life of Jesus in a book called "*The Life of Saint Issa*" (New York, 1890), written on the basis of some ancient memoirs in the library attached to the Buddhist monastry at Himis (Ladakh).
4. What did Jesus do during the first thirty years of his life? He is not mentioned in Palestine during this period except once at the age of twelve. The only answer is that he was not in Palestine. The obvious inference is that he was out at some other place in some other country. He left Jerusalem after the age of twelve.
5. Jesus, thus, knew the routes and topography of some other countries other than Palestine.
6. In *Kanz-ul-Ummal* it is reported from Hazrat Abu Huraira that God guided Jesus to go away from Jerusalem lest he should be identified and further persecuted (*Kanz-ul-Ummal, II : 34)*.
7. "Jesus was like unto the Holy Prophet (Muhammad). He and his mother, Mary (as a result of Jewish persecutions) had to migrate from Palestine and leave for a far off country and he went from country to country" (Ibn-i-Jarir, *Tafsir Ibn-i-Jarir at- Tabari*, III: 197).

8. "And we made the Son of Mary and his mother a sign, and we gave them shelter on lofty meadows and spring" (The Holy Quran, XXIII : 50).
9. Travelling by night, resting by day, he reached Nazareth and went to the Sea of Tiberias (John, XXI : 1-2).
10. "Since the Jews falsified the Prophet, they turned him out to the city, Jesus and Mary set out and went to Syria" (*Rauzat-us-Safa*, I : 134).
11. Jesus reached Nisibis (Magdonia) in Mesopotamia, about nine hundred miles from Palestine between Syria and Iran (Ibid., I : 132 : 133).
12. In Nisibis, "people tried to kill him (Jesus) and he ran away" (At-Tabari, III : 197; *Rauzat-us-Safa*, I : 149).
13. Afraid for his life he travelled incognito and even changed his name to Yuz Asaf.
14. The present custodian of Rauzabal holds a decree granted to his ancestor Rahman Mir, son of Bahadur Mir, signed and sealed by five Muftis (judges) of Srinagar dated 11th Jamadi-us-Sani, 1184 A.H. (1766 A.D.). This document establishes three facts:–
    (i) That the holy shrine of Prophet Yuz Asaf was "regularly visited by all, high and low". "Nobles and ministers and kings and high dignitaries and the general public", came "from all direction to pay their homage" and made their "Offerings".
    (ii) That during the reign of Raja Gopadatta, Yuz Asaf did come to Kashmir.
    (iii) That he lived, preached and died in the valley, and is buried in mohalla Khaniyar in Srinagar.
15. It is obvious that Yuz Asaf could not be a Hindu, a Muslim, or a Buddhist. He was not an Indian. He was entrusted with and performed a prophetic mission.
16. The documents (in Tibetan and Pali languages) in the possession of the Buddhist monastry at Himis (Ladakh) "tell of the days that He (Jesus) passed in Leh where he

was joyously received and where He preached" (Merrick, *In the World's Attic*, p. 215).

17. The German diaries of Morovian Mission, Drs. Marx and Francke, located in Leh, also speak of the days Jesus spent in these parts (pp. 118, 119).

X. That Yuz Asaf and Jesus Christ are one and the same person.

1. Mulla Nadiri, the first Muslim historian of Kashmir, who wrote in Persian, says that during the reign of Raja Gopadatta (About 49-109 A.D.) "Hazrat Yuz Asaf having come from the Holy Land (*Bait-ul-Muqaddas* i.e., Palestine) to the holy valley proclaimed his prophethood". It was during this time that Sulaiman, a Persian, was deputed to repair the cracks in the dome of the temple at Shankracharya (*Takht-i- Sulaiman or Koh-i-Sulaiman* i.e., Throne or Mount of Prophet Solomon). Sulaiman, the artisan, inscribed on one of the stones of the flankwalls enclosing the stairs : "In these times Yuz Asaf proclaimed his prophethood". On the other stone of the stairs he inscribed that Yuz Asaf was Yusu, Prophet of the Children of Israel.

   Mulla Nadiri further mentions that he saw "in a book of Hindus that this prophet (Yuz Asaf) was really Hazrat Isa (Jesus), Ruh-Allah (the Spirit of God)." He "had also assumed the name of Yuz Asaf". Nadiri adds : "He spent his life in this (valley). After his departure (death) he was laid to rest in mohalla Anzmarah (in Khaniyar)" (*Tarikh-i- Kashmir*, f. 69). For the text of the inscriptions see(Ibid., f. 35.)

2. These two inscriptions of the Koh-i-Sulaiman are still visible though in a mutilated condition :–

   (i) *Dar een waqt Yuz Asaf da'wa-i-paighambari mikunad, Sal panjah wa chahar*. (At this time Yuz Asaf proclaimed his prophethood, Year fifty and four).

   (ii) *Aishan Yusu paighambar-i-Bani Israel ast.*

(He is Jesus, Prophet of the children of Israel).

3. These inscriptions were intact and had not obliterated when Khwaja Haidar Malik Chadura wrote his *Tarikh-i-Kashmir* during the reign of Jahangir (*Tarikh-i- Kashmir*, f. 11, 12, 56; Also see Peerzada Ghulam Hasan, *Tarikh-i-Kashmir*, III, f. 25 (b).]

4. In a Sanskrit book, *Bhavishya Maha Purana* ascribed to Vyas, said to have been written in 3191 Laukika era (115 A.D.), it is reported from Suta (*Suta uwach*) that once (about A.D. 78) Raja Shalewahin "went on a peak of the Himalayas. There in the middle of the Hun country that mighty king saw sitting in the mountains a dignified person of white complexion and wearing white clothes". Shalewahin asked him who he was. He replied with pleasure : "Know me the son of God and born of a virgin. I am the preacher of *Mlachha* religion and follower of true principles". On hearing this the king said: "What is your religion?" He replied : "O Maharaj!on the disappearance of truth and the destruction of traditions (*maryada*) in the *Mlachha* country I appeared there as *Masih*. Through my work the guilty and the wicked suffered, and I also suffered at their hands". When asked to further explain his religion, he said: "It is love, truth and purity of heart and for this I am called Masih". Shalewahin returned after making his obeisance to him (*Bhvishya Maha Purana*, Bombay, 1959, pp. 465, 466, verses 17-32).

It is also contended by some that Jesus was resurrected in his spiritual body. If so, what happened to his mortal body? To this it is said: "We know nothing about what became of it (the body of Jesus), except that it did not decay or corrupt. Whether it was dissolved into gases or whether still *preserved* (Italics mine) somewhere as a grand memorial of God's love" (*Studies in the Scriptures, Series 2, p. 129- Bible and Tract Society, London)*.

Yes, the chosen one of God chose the choicest place on earth for the repose of his earthly remains. Surely, Kashmir is the grand memorial of God's love.

# 2

# LAND OF PROMISE

Prophet Moses migrated from Egypt. He was followed by a section of the Hebrews who settled in Palestine, the Holy Land (Deut., I : 8). He nominated Joshua as his successor to lead the next generation (Ibid., XXXI : 14). Moses himself was denied entry into Palestine (Ibid., I : 37; III : 26; IV : 21). He was directed to take journey in the opposite direction beyond the Jordan, i.e., beyond the eastern border of the Holy Land (Nu, XXVII : 12). This was the land promised by God to Moses and the Children of Israel.

There are five places mentioned in connection with this Land of Promise, viz., *Bethpeor* (Deut., IV : 46), *Heshbon* (Ibid.,), *Pisgah* (Ibid., IV : 49), *Mount Nebo* (Ibid., XXXIV : I), and the valley or plains of *Moab* (Ibid., XXXIV : 5, 6, 8).

All Biblical commentators have admitted that the sites of these places were unidentified. Peake says that "the sites are unknown" (Peake, *Commentary on the Bible*, p. 235).

Obviously, Palestine was not, and could not be, the Land of Promise. Moreover, the Land of Promise was exclusively meant for the *Children of Israel*, and not for the entire Hebrew nation (Nu, XXVII ; 12-13). It was beyond the river Jordan, the eastern border of Holy Land. Undoubtedly, the location of the above-mentioned five places would enable us to ascertain the Land of promise.

1. *Beth-peor* means the house (or place) of gaping or opening (Cruden's Concordance, p. 578). The river Jhelum is called *Behat* in Persian and Vehath in Kashmiri language (*Tarikh-i-Hasan*, I,150ff). Bandipur (or Bandipoor) in Kashmir was known as *Behatpoor*. (cf. *Rajatarangini*, viii,

2431). Bandipur is the place of opening or gaping in the sense that from this place the valley of Kashmir opens out. Also, the river Jhelum passes through a gap into the Wular Lake. So *Bethpeor* (*Behatpoor*), in all likelihood, appears to be Bandipur in Tehsil Sopore, Kashmir.

2. *Heshbon* is referred to in connection with pools. Tristran believes that it refers to the pools or stream in the valley of the Land of Promise (cf. Cant., VII ; 4). We have *Hashba* (Hazbal) in Kashmir, a small village, famous for its pools of fish, about twelve miles north-east of Bandipur (cf. *Survey of India*, Topo Sheet No. 43 —J/10).
3. *Pisgah* Spring (Pishnag) is about a mile north-east of Aham Sharif. Its water is famous for medicinal properties (cf. Vreese, *Nilamata*, p. 75, v. 889).
4. Plains or Valley of *Moab* (Mowu) is four miles north-east of Mount Nebo (cf. *Survey of India*, Topo Sheet No. 43-J/15).
5. *Mount Nebo*. The Mount Abarim and Mount Nebo have been considered identical (Dummelow, *Commentary on the Holy Bible*, p. 115). But facts are otherwise.
   (i) The Mount Nebo is a single peak of the Mount Abarim (Ibid.).
   (ii) The Mount Nebo has been mentioned in conjunction with *Beth- peor* (Deut., XXXIV : 6).
   (iii) If the identitiy of *Beth-peor* is established, Mount Nebo is to be searched within its vicinity. It cannot be treated in isolation.
   (iv) The identity of *Beth-peor, Heshbon, Moab* and *Pisgah a*re fairly well established. These names are not found anywhere else except Kashmir.
   (v) All these places are located within a range of few miles.

In Kashmir there is *Baal Nebu* (Niltoop), a peak of a range about eight miles north-east of Bandipur (Newall, *The Highlands of India*, II, 78, 79, 84, 86, 87, 90). Newall calls it "Naboo Hill".

From it Bandipur and the entire Kashmir valley is visible (cf. *Survey of India*, Topo Sheet No. 43- J/11).

The only tangible proof which is advanced in favour of Palestine being the land of Promise, is the verse :—

"And the Lord said unto Moses, Get thee unto the *Mount Abarim*, See the land which I have given unto the Children of Israel". (Nu, XXVII : 12, 13).

And the Mount Abarim is in Palestine. But we have Mount Ablu in Kashmir just above Mount Nebo. There are other facts which rebut this thesis.

1. In Palestine, only the Children of Israel did not reside. It meant for the entire Hebrew nation.
2. Moses could very well climb on the top of Mount Abarim (in Palestine) and cast his eyes eastward to catch a glimpse, if possible, of the peaks of the distant land assigned to him and the Children of Israel. It is perfectly natural and human though the attempt might be in vain.
3. The Mount Ablu commands beautiful view of the Kashmir Valley.
4. Moses from the Mount Abarim is not surveying the land and its surroundings, as he should have done out of curiosity and excitement as he does from *Pisgah* :

"Get thee up unto the top of *Pisgah* and lift up thine eyes, westward and northward and southward and eastward and behold it with thine eyes, for thou shalt not go over this Jordan" (Deut., III: 27).

5. "A place of broad rivers and streams wherein shall go no galley with oars, neither shall a gallant ship pass thereby" (Isa., XXXIII : 21). Palestine is on the sea-shore.
6. The Land of Promise was to contain, a *sea of the plain*, a huge lake of fresh water, Kashmir has its Wular Lake. Bandipur is situated on its banks. (Deut., IV : 49).

Moreover, the characteristic features of the Land of Promise have been clearly mentioned :

1. It was a "heaven on earth" (Deut., XI : 21).

2. It was towards the sunrising (Ibid., IV : 41).
3. It was "a land of hills and valleys that drinketh water of the rain of heaven" (Ibid., XI : 11).
4. It was a land of "Fat pastures and good, and the land was wide and quite and peaceable" (I Chron., IV : 40).

Palestine does not answer to these features (cf. Masterman, *The Holy Land,* pp. 7-12). But Kashmir does! Of course, no other country, east of the Jordan or the Euphrates, except Kashmir could boast of its springs, streams, rivers, abundance of fruits and flowers, and the charms of its meadows and the valleys. Quite appropriately Kashmir has been called *Jannat- ud-duniya* (the Paradise of the World) and *Bagh-i-Jannat* (the Garden of Paradise). It was for Kashmir when Sa'di of Shiraz said :

*Agar Firdaus bar ru-i-zamin ast,*
*Hamin asto, hamin asto, hamin ast.*

And that is why Emperor Jahangir, when asked on his death-bed about his last wish, whispered : "Kashmir and nothing else".

# 3

# TOMB OF MOSES

The Jewish legend surrounds the death of Moses with mystery. According to the printed tradition he was surrounded by a cloud and disappeared. God had taken him alive into heaven on account of his piety (*Jewish Ency.*, Art. Moses, IX : 53; Josephus, *Antiquities*, IV : 8, 48). But the original texts say that Moses disappeared and went to the Land of Promise (Nu, XIV : 12). Further we are told:

> "So Moses the Servant of the Lord died there in the land of Moab .... buried him in a valley in the land of Moab, over against Bethpeor: but no man knoweth of his sepulchre unto this day" (Deut., XXXIV : 5, 6).

According to the Christian belief, God not only buried him but buried his sepulchre also.

St. John Chrysostom was the first to point out in the correct direction :

> "But tell me, do not the bones of Moses himself lie in a far off land in the East" (Homily 26, Epistle to the Hebrews, Ch. III).

It is certain that Moses went over to the Land of Promise and no other country except Kashmir could be the Land of Promise. It is also obvious the Moses died a natural death and was buried. It logically follows that he must have died in Kashmir and buried somewhere in the valley.

1. On the top of Mount Nebu (*Baal Nebu*) there is a tomb.
2. The tomb is in a quadrangular enclosure and there are three other covered tombs. One of them is that of Sang Bibi, the hermitess, and the other two are of her disciples.

3. All these three tombs, like Muslim graves, are in the north-south direction. The fourth one, like Jewish graves, is in the east- west direction.
4. The tomb is centrally situated. From this place *Beth-peor* (Bandipur) is visible. Hazbal (*Heshbon*), *Moab* and *Pisgah* are close at hand. The area is full of places known as *Muqam-i-Musa,* the places of Moses.

And this tomb is known as the Tomb of Moses since time immemorial. The Kashmiri traditions, both written and oral, assert and identify this tomb as the tomb of Moses.

> "Moses came to Kashmir and people believed in him. Subsequently they continued to believe in him, others did not. He died and was buried here. The people of Kashmir call his tomb the Shrine of the Prophet of the Book" (Abdul Qadir, *Hashmat- i-Kashmir*, f. 7, Asiatic Society of Bengal MS. No. 192).

Moreover, Prophet Muhammad has said : "When Moses' death approached he prayed to God to be permitted to see the Promised land". His prayer was granted. Hazrat Abu Hurairah reports that the Holy Prophet added :"He (Moses) died there. If I were there I could have pointed out to you his tomb on the path of a rugged hill" (*Bokhari,* Vol. II, 16).

# 4

# TOMB OF MARY

When Jesus migrated from Jerusalem, Mary, his mother, accompanied him.

1. "Jesus was like unto the Holy Prophet (Muhammad). He and his mother, Mary (as a result of Jewish persecutions) had to migrate from Palestine and leave for a far off country and he went from country to country" (*At-Tabari*, III : 197).
2. "And We made the son of Mary and his mother a sign, and We gave them shelter on lofty meadows and spring" (The Holy Quran, XXIII : 50).
3. Since the Jews falsified the Prophet, they turned him out of the city, Jesus and Mary set out and went to Syria" (*Rauzat- us-Safa*, I : 134).

Mary died on the way and lies buried in Murree at Pindi Point.

1. The town Murree derives its name from Mari (Mary). The place was called Mari till 1875 (Kashmir Postal Rules, *Punjab Gazette* No. 673, A.D. 1869; Drew, *Jummoo and Kashmir Territories*, p. 527).
2. The Tomb of Mary adjoining the Defence Tower, is even today called *Mai Mari ka Asthan*, the resting place of Mother Mary (Ubi. Sup., p. 353).
3. The tomb is according to Jewish direction, East to West.

# 5

# OTHER MYSTERIES

**I.** *Asa-i-Isa* (Rod or stick of Jesus).

Made of olive wood, dark-brown in colour, 8-1/4 ft. long, 1-1/2 inch in diameter on the average, having a ferrule of steel and spear-head top blade, is the description of the *Asa-i- sharif* ascribed to Jesus Christ.

We read in *Rauzat-us-Safa* (Vol. 1, 135), *Jami-ut- Tawarikh* (Rashiduddin Fazlullah, Vol. II, 81) and *Wajeez- ut-Tawarikh* (Mufti Ghulam Mohammad Nabi Khaniyari, Vol. II, f. 286) that Jesus on his journeys carried a rod or stick (*Asa*) in his hand and used to walk on foot.

The rod is sacred and of great antiquity is established by the fact that it was formerly in the possession of Amir-i-kabir Hazrat Mir Sayyid Ali Hamdani of Kashmir. It is now deposited at the shrin of Hazrat Zain-ud-din Wali at Aish Muqam, some forty seven miles from Srinagar.

The rod is taken out and shown only in cases of acute distress with miraculous effect and that is why it is also called *Balagir* (the Catcher of Evils).

**II.** *Ka Ka Pal* or *Sang-i-Musa* (the Stone of Moses).

At Bijbehara in Kashmir there is a stone called *Sang-i- Musa.* It also finds mention in Kalhana's *Rajatarangini.* It is locally known as *Ka Ka Pal. Pal*, in Kashmiri, means stone.

The stone weighs about 110 lbs. There is a tradition about this stone that if eleven people sit round it and put one finger each beneath it and call out *Ka Ka, Ka Ka,* the stone would ordinarily lift itself from the ground to a height of about four feet. But it will not move at all with ten, twelve or twenty people. The stone keeps rising when eleven persons put their fingers (one each) below it and keep on shouting *Ka Ka, Ka Ka.* The figure eleven is symbolic and represents eleven out of the twelve tribes of Israel. Indeed, it is an invitation and a challenge!

**III.** *Muqam-i-Musa* (the Place of Moses).

There are places in Kashmir Known as *Muqam-i-Musa.* One is near *Auth Wattu*, the eight ways, in Handwara Tehsil.

The second place is at the conjunction of the rivers Jhelum and Sindh (not the Indus) near Shadipur. Sir Aurel Stein mentions it by the name of *Kohna-i-Musa* the corner-stone of Moses (*Rajatarangini*, I : 70). It is believed that Moses rested on this rock (The Holy Quran, XVIII : 63).

*Ayat-i-Maula.* (Aitmul), the Sign of God, two miles north of Bandipur, is also the place where Moses is said to have rested. It has Jewish grave.

**IV.** *Jewish Graves.*

The Hindus and Buddhists cremate their dead. The Muslims bury their dead in the North-South direction. But Kashmir abounds in graves, unlike Muslims ones, in the direction East-West.

The direction of Jewish graves is East to West with their head towards the East. Such graves in Kashmir are found at Ziarat-i-Balad-i-Rumi and Kulipura in Srinagar, Qavil in Palwama Tehsil, in the village Maqqam between Tangmarg and Srinagar, and Bijbehara. Vigne records that there were Jewish graves on or near Takht-i-Sulaiman (Vigne, *Travels in Kashmir, Ladak, Iskardo*, I : 395).

# 6

# EPILOGUE

Prophets are the link between material and transcendental, between heaven and earth, and between man and God. They appear among men as human beings to convey the divine message. After the fulfilment of the assigned mission, they cast aside their bodily garb and return to God.

If Jesus Christ, the Prophet of God (Peace be on him)' did not ascend to heaven *physically*, heaven would not fall on earth. The circumstances under which he bade good-bye to Jerusalem, were exceptionally miserable. It is clear that Jesus himself neither told anybody about his resurrection and subsequent ascension nor claimed it as one of his miracles. When the disciples of Jesus did not find him in Jerusalem, the natural and obvious conclusion for the simple folks was that God has called back his chosen one. Perhaps they were made to believe it.

The earthly remains of Jesus Christ lie buried in Srinagar, Kashmir. Truth has revealed itself. It will be the greatest injustice to Jesus to forsake him only because that it has been so far believed that he was in heaven *physically*. He is in heaven, no doubt, but *spiritually*.

Truth is ultimate and eternal. Truth is God. When we believed and disbelieved that earth was flat, and when we held and gave up that Sun moved round the earth, where is the harm in believing and disbelieving the resurrection and *physical* ascension of Christ. Of course, it is a challenge to the courage and integrity of the Church!

Coincidence is a normal feature of human life. But the coincidence of facts, establishes a reality. And the reality is that Kashmir is the land blessed by God and graced by the feet of his prophets.

**Plate 1 : The Decree-sheet issued by the Grand Mufti of Kashmir**

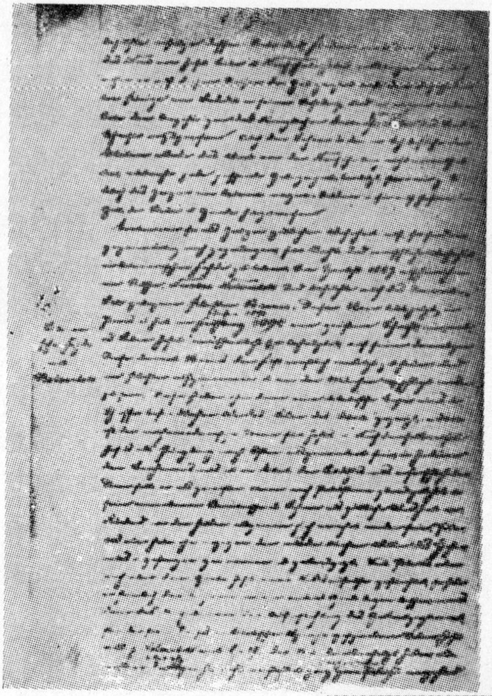

Plate 2 :
The German Diary of Drs. Marx and Francke, page 118

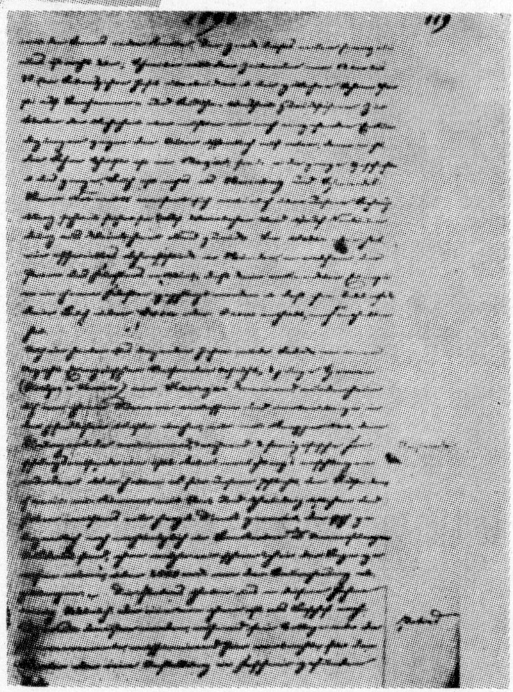

Plate 3 :
The German Diary of Drs. Marx and Francke, page 119

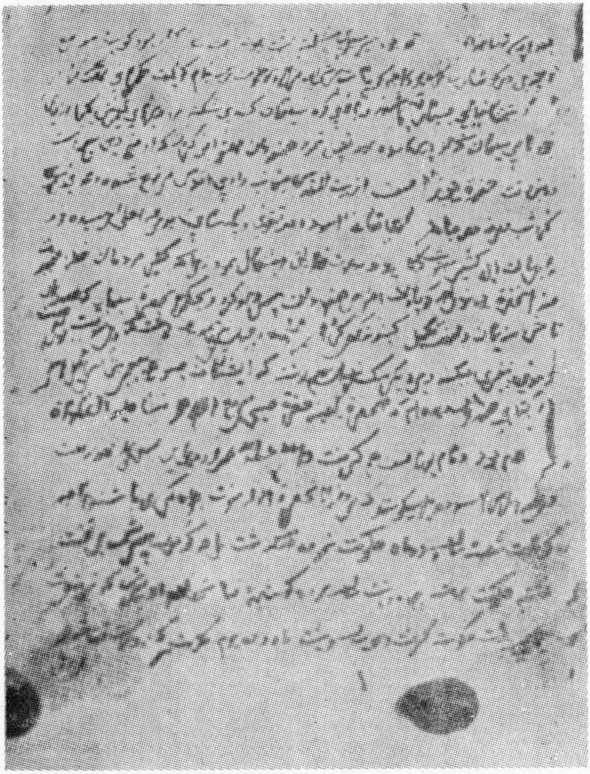

Plate 4 : Tarikh-i-Kashmir of Mulla Nadiri, f. 69

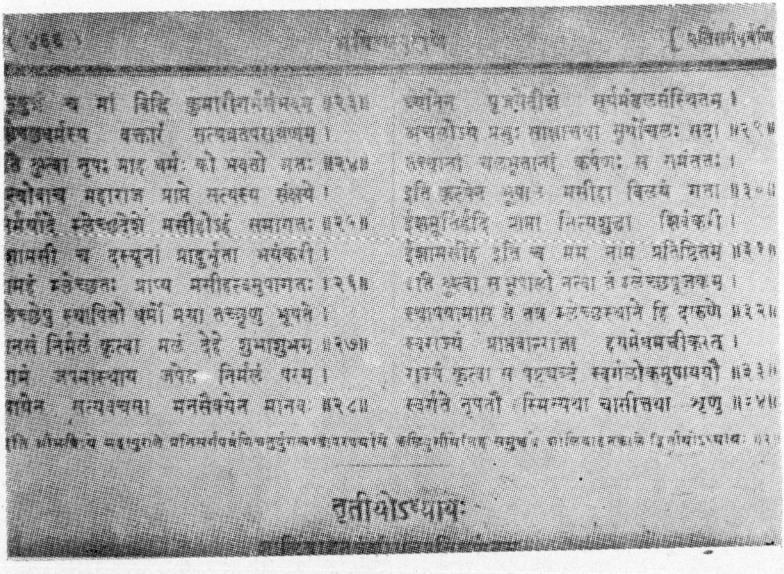

Plate 5 : Bhavishya Maha Purana, page 466

Plate 6 : Rauzabal

**Plate 7 : Cenotaph of Rauzabal with citation plate**

Plate 8 Behatpoor (Bandipur), Kashmir

Plate 9 Mount Nebo, Kashmir

Plate 10 : Tomb of Moses being pointed out by Wali Rishi, its care-taker

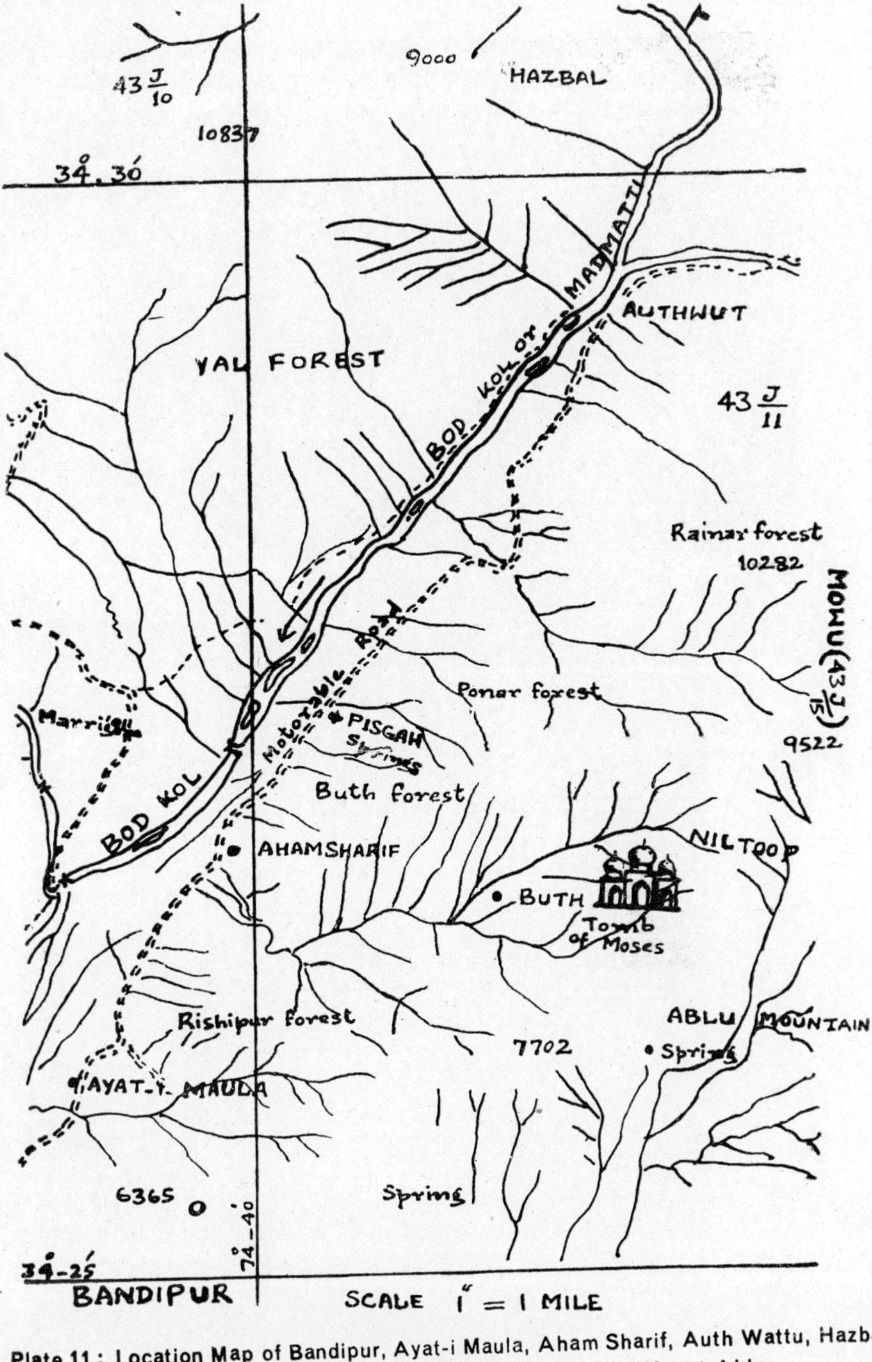


Plate 11 : Location Map of Bandipur, Ayat-i Maula, Aham Sharif, Auth Wattu, Hazbal, Moab, Mount Nebo, Tomb of Moses, Pisgah and Mount Ablu.

Plate 12 : Tomb of Mary

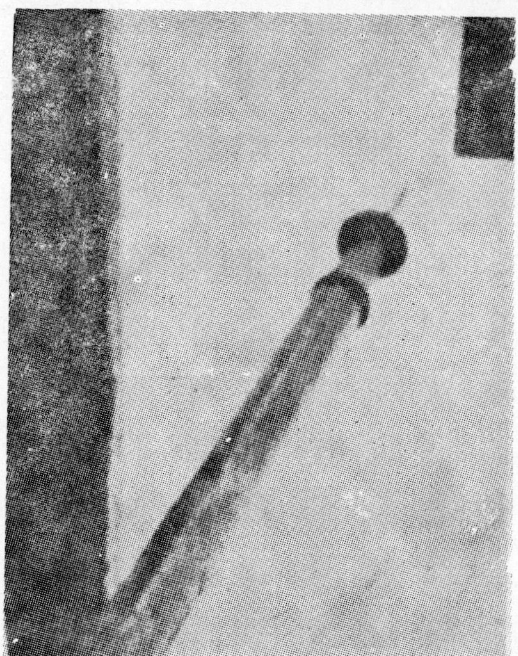

Plate 13 : The Rod of Jesus

Plate 14 : Ka Ka Pal or Sang-i-Musa at Bijbehara

Plate 15 :
Aham Sharif at the foot of Mount Nebo leading to the Tomb of Moses

Plate 16 Takht-i-Sulaiman

# SELECT BIBLIOGRAPHY


1. Abdul Qadir bin Qazi-ul-Quzzat Wasil Ali Khan, *Hashmat-i- Kashmir*, MS. No. 42, *Asiatic Society of Bengal*, Calcutta. Microfilm copy available in Research Library, Srinagar.
2. Andrews, A., *Apocryphal Books of the Old and New Testaments*, London, 1906.
3. At-Tabir, *Tafsir Ibn-i-Jarir at-Tabri* (Jami-ul-Bayan fi Tafsir-ul-Quran) of Imam Abu Ja'far Muhammad bin Jarir at-Tabri, 30 vols., 1299 A.H., Kubr-ul-Mar'a Press, Cairo.
4. Avicenna, *Canon of Avicenna* (Quanun-i-Bu Ali Sina), 5 vols., Urdu Trans. Sayyid Ghulam Husain, Newal Kishore Press, Lucknow.
5. *Bhavishya Maha Purana*, Bombay, 1959.
6. Buhl, F., *Canon and Text of the Old Testament*, tr. W.J.M. Macherson, Edinburgh, 1908.
7. Chadurah, Khwaja Haidar Malik, *Waqiat-i-Kashmir* or *Tarikh-i-Kashmir*, MS. Research Library, Srinagar. Also printed at Muhammadi Press, Lahore.
8. Cook, Edward, *The Holy Bible with Commentary*, 10 vols. London, 1899.
9. *Crucifixion by an Eye-Witness, The* Chicago, 1907; Urdu Trans. by Mian Mirajuddin, *Waqia Salib-i- Masih ki Chashmdid Shahadat*, 2nd ed., Lahore.
10. Dummelow, Rev. J.R., *Commentary on the Holy Bible*, London, 1917.

11. Edersheim, Dr. Alfred, *The Life and Times of Jesus, the Messiah,* London, 1906.
12. *Encyclopaedia Biblica,* 4 vols., London, 1903.
13. Fazlullah, Rashiduddin, *Jami-ut-Tawarikh.*
14. Farrar, Dean, F.W., *The Life of Christ*, London, 1874.
15. Ghulam Ahmad, Mirza, *Masih Hindustan Mein*, Qadian, 1908.
16. Ghulam Hasan, Pirzada, bin Abdur Rashid Shewa, *Tarikh-i-Kashmir*, 3 vols, MS. Research Library, Srinagar.
17. Gregory, A., *The Cannon and Text of the New Testament*, New York, 1907.
18. Hanna, William, *The Life of Christ,* New York, 1928.
19. Hastings, J., (i) *Dictionary of Apostolic Church,* Edinburgh, 1918.
    (ii) *Dictionary of the Bible,* 5 vols., Edinburgh, 1904.
    (iii) *Dictionary of Christ & the Gospels*, Edinburgh, 1908.
20. *Jewish Encyclopaedia*, 12 vols., Funk & Wagnalls, London & New York, 1905.
21. Josephus, Flavins, *Jewish Antiquities*, tr. W.H. Whiston, London, 1820.
22. Kamal-ud-din, Al-Haj Khwaja, *The Sources of Christianity*, Working, 1922.
23. *Kanz-ul-Ummal fi Sunanti al-Aqwal wal Afa'l* of Shaikh Alauddin Ali al-Muttaqi, 1214 A.H., Hyderabad.
24. Khaniyari, Mufti Ghulam Mohammad Nabi, *Wajeez-ut-Tawarikh*, Ms. Nos. 532 and 1048, Research Library, Srinagar.
25. Marx and A.H. Francke, Morovian Mission doctors *Diary* (in German), MS. in Leh (Ladakh).
26. Masterman, Dr. E.W.G., *The Holy Land.*
27. Merrick, Lady Henrietta S., *In the World's Attic,* London, 1931.

28. Meyer, Dr. Arnold, *Jesus or Paul*, tr. F.A. Wilkinson, London, 1909.

29. Mulla Nadiri, *Tarikh-i-Kashmir*, MS. with Ghulam Mohiuddin Wanchoo of Srinagar (now in West Pakistan).

30. Nazir Ahmad, Al-Haj Khwaja, *Jesus in Heaven on Earth*, 2nd ed., Lahore, 1952.

30. Nehru, Jawaharlal, *Glimpses of World History*, 2nd ed., Bombay, 1962.

32. Newall, Major-General D.J.F., *The Highlands of India*, 2 vols., London, Vol. I. 1882, Vol. II, 1887.

33. Notovitch, Nicholas, *The Life of Saint Issa,*, New York, 1890.

34. Peake, Rev. A.S.J., *Commentary on the Bible*, London, 1920.

35. *Quran, The Holy*, tr. Maulvi Muhammad Ali, Lahore, 1917.

36. *Rauzat-us-Safa fi Sirat-ul-Ambia wal Muluk wal Khulafa* (The Garden of Purity concerning the Biography of the Prophets and Kings and Caliphs) of Mir Muhammad bin Khawand Shah, 7 vols., Bombay, 1852.

37. Renan, Ernest, *The History of the Origin of Christianity*, tr. J. K., Allen, London, 1895.

38. Scofield, Rev. C. J., *The New Testaments and Psalms*, New York, 1920.

39. Stein, Sir Aurel, *Rajatarangini*, London, 1900.

40. Stroud, William, *On the Physical Cause of Death of Christ*, London, 1905.

41. *Studies in Scriptures*, series 2, Bible and Tract Society, London.

42. *Survey of India*, Topo Sheets.

43. Swete, H.B., *Gospel of Peter*, London, 1893.

44. Vigne, G.T., *Travels of Kashmir, Ladak, Iskardu*, 2 vols., London, 1842.

45. Vreese, K. De., *Nilamata or Teachings of Nila*, Leiden, 1936.
46. Wace, H. E., *A Dictionary of Christian Biography and Literature,* London, 1895.
47. Wallis Budge, Sir E. A., *Baralam and Yewasef*, Being the Ethiopic Version of a Christianized recension of Buddhist legend of the Buddha and the Bodhisattva, an English Translation with Introduction, University Press, Cambridge, 1923.

# Part I
# (B)

# 7

# SITE OF THE FOURTH BUDDHIST COUNCIL

Emperor Ashoka raised Buddhism to the status of a world religion. The bands of foreign invaders that appeared on the Indian soil were attracted by its catholicity and were converted to it in large numbers. But, by far the greatest name among the foreign patrons of Buddhism is that of Kanishka. His name in the Buddhist world is only second to that of Ashoka.

Kanishka (C.78-123 A.D.), the most illustrious of the Kushan kings, was originally a follower of some non-Buddhist tradition, but like Ashoka became a convert to the Gospel. Kanishka's vast empire extended all over North-Western India including Kashmir and Chinese Turkistan over which he ruled from his capital at Peshawar or Purushapura.

The reign of Kanishka is specially important in the history of the Buddhist Church, for we learn that, being perplexed in his theological studies, he convened with the permission of his teacher, Parshvika or Parshva, a Council (*Mahasaṁgha*) to settle the disputed doctrines. The representatives of no less than eighteen Buddhist sects were in attendance. Though Louis De La Valle Poussin (*The way to Nirvana*, Cambridge, 1917, p. 184) has questioned the authenticity of the reports, as this great Buddhist Council was held according to some reports at Jullundur in the Punjab, according to others at Kundalvana near Srinagar in the delightful *vale* of Kashmir.

According to Hieun Tsang, Kanishka wanted the Council to meet and deliberate somewhere in Gandhara but the place was objected to on account of its "heat and dampness". Then he Suggested Rajagriha where a similar Council was held previously. But the place was rejected on the advice of the principal monks for it was contended that the presence of a large number of heretical teachers there it was likely to lead to unnecessary controversy and futile discussion. Finally, on the suggestion of Parshva and with the approval of the other assembled monks it was decided to hold the Council in Kashmir where it was pointed out "the land is guarded on every side by mountains, the soil is rich and productive and it is well provided with food". Kanishka himself accompanied the selected monks to the Happy Valley where he founded a monastry for them.

The Council was attended by five hundred *arhats*, five hundred *bodhisattvas* and five hundred *pandits.* It sat for six months. The deliberations of the Council were guided by Vasumitra and in his absence Ashvaghosh acted as President. Their labours resulted in the compilation of the Vibhasa Shashtra and other comprehensive commentaries on the Canon, which after being engraved on "sheets of red copper" were sealed in stone chests and deposited in a stupa built specially for the purpose. Kanishka appointed persons to guard the deposit against possible heretical inroads and plunder. A historian of Ancient India expresses his hope: "who knows these invaluable documents may still lie buried there and lucky spade may one day bring them to light?"

So far the site of this great and epoch-making Council remains unidentified and undiscovered. Between Jullundur (the Punjab) and Kundalvana (Kashmir), the latter appears more probable for such a gathering---- a cool, refreshing and peaceful place for serious thinking and sound deliberations. Jullundur would obviously not have been selected when Gandhara was rejected on account of its "heat and dampness". Secondly, Jullundur being in plains and exposed to onslaughts of invading hordes could not have been selected as a safe site to deposit the precious documents for the use of posterity. Moreover, enormous construction work has taken place in the Punjab, and still no one has stumbled on these deposits.

Therefore, the attention must be concentrated on Kundalvana. If this Council was at all held, it was most possibly held in Kashmir at Kundalvana.

Kashmir is not only heaven on earth but it also abounds in heavenly mysteries. It has been blessed by the feet of prophets. Kashmir was a part of Kanishka's empire; hence no better place than Kashmir could be thought of for such a gathering. It was ideally, and to some extent, centrally situated.

In Kashmir, various efforts have been made excavations carried on to dig out the place and the deposits. But people have concentrated their attention towards north-west of Srinagar whereas the considerations for which Kashmir was chosen as the venue for the Council negatives the choice of a place on the busy highway and in the vicinity of the capital. On the other hand, the place should have been away from the hubbub of the city-life.

With this hypothesis that Kashmir was the venue, we may proceed to identify and locate Kundalvana. Kundalvana is the composite of *Kundal* and *vana.* Kundal means "a large ring worn on the ears", "a coil", "a circle", "a pendant", "halo of light", "a noose of rope" and *vana* means "a wood", "a jungle", "a grove", "a forest". As the name signifies, the place must be surrounded by forest circular in shape.

Kundalvana is no other than Kongwatan (also called Kangwattan, Kungwatan, Kongawatan — lat. 33° 36' long. 74° 49', *Gazetteer of Kashmir and Ladak,* compiled, under the direction of the Quarter Master General in India in the intelligence branch, Delhi, 1974), 67 km. from Srinagar in the South; Srinagar to Shupiyan 50 km.; Shupiyan to Ahrabal waterfall 11 km. Here the river Vishov falls some 50 feet over a precipice and is a wonderful sight, especially in the morning or at noon when the rays of the sun breaking on the spray form rainbows. The fall is seen best from the right bank. From Ahrabal, Kongwatan is only 6 km., the path is through forests on the right bank of the river Vishov. There is another way to reach Kongwatan—Srinagar to Kulgam (61 km.), Kulgam to Avil (16 km.) on the right bank of the river Vishov and Avil to Kongwatan (16km.), steep ascent through the forest, then descent to Chittapani (Chitti Nadi) and steep ascent again and down to Kongwatan.

From Kongwatan one goes to Kausarnag (14 km.), a climb or 5000 feet, good path along the right bank to Mahinag and some way beyond. Kausarnag is the largest mountain lake (3 km. long) in Kashmir at an elevation of 12,000 feet (3,646 meters) surrounded by the picturesque peaks of the Pir Panjal. In June, icebergs float on its surface and in September they melt to form a great expanse of sapphire blue water.

Kongwatan is a small grassy valley, very lovely, surrounded by pines and firs (circular in shape). It has all the amenities necessary for a prolonged camp of about two thousand people. Kongwatan is now inhabited by Gujars and there is a forest rest-house. The area in and around Kongwatan shows visible signs of rocks and ruins—possibly the remains of the monastry and stupa.

We have done nothing except to point out a possible site where the Fourth Buddhist Council met. Now it is for the archaeologists and the Archaeological Survey of India, if interested, to undertake exploration and excavation of the site. The other Buddhist countries might readily co-operate. It is not obligatory that every effort must be crowned with success. But we, think, it is worth-while as, in the case of success, it will be a great landmark and a revolution in the history of Buddhism and Kashmir will acquire the status of a place of Buddhist pilgrimage.

# 8

# KASHMIR'S CONTRIBUTION TO HISTORICAL LITERATURE (UPTO 19TH CENTURY A.D.)

Western Orientalists, almost all of them, have found three—fold fault with Indian history and historiography. In the first place, they say that the people in the East do not change; they are the same today and tomorrow meaning thereby that there is no change, no progress, no evolution and consequently no history. In the second place, they hold that Indians had no history. That is, there is no written record available of the Indian people in the past. It is argued and proved that the ancient period of Indian history is deficient in matters of historical writings but medieval India did produce abundant crop of historical literature. Lastly, it is alleged that whatever historical material is available, it concerns, almost exclusively, with the kings and his nobles, with battles, sieges and the royal paraphernalia. They do not portray the conditions of the people — their doings and actions, their thoughts and aspirations. Such a history could not be true or complete which does not treat of the contemporary religious, social and economic currents and cross-currents. A careful study of the historical literature produced in Kashmir negatives these charges.

Kashmir, in olden times, was as much part of India as Sindh, Bengal and Kerala — very loosely connected politically but basic ethnological and cultural unity and affinity was there. The beginning of the 18th century A.D., saw the end of the Indian Empire. The East India Company cast its ominous shadow on the Indian sub-continent. The servants of East India Company became interested in the historical past of their new subjects. They wanted to understand the Indians better in true historical perspective to be able to govern them well and to perpetuate their hold by exploiting their weak points. They studied, edited and translated Indian historical writings which were easily accessible to them. But, during all this process, Kashmir, its traditions and heritage, did not receive the attention it deserved. The most unfortunate position is that even today Kashmir's contribution in various fields, has not been properly highlighted. Kashmir may well claim to be the torch-bearer in the field of history writing. In every period of human history, even in the remotest past, we have historical records which compare well and surpass the productions of recent past.

In ancient period, Kashmir produced *Nilamata Purana*. It narrates the legends about the origin of the country. It gives the details of religious rites to be performed by the people. It describes in detail the *tirthas* (the places of pilgrimage). On the whole, the *Nilamata Purana* is a very interesting study. It faithfully depicts the religious, social and economic life of the time. It gives graphic account of the means of recreation such as music, dancing, theatrical performances and sports. Arts and crafts, dresses and ornaments, cosmetics, foods and drinks, domesticated animals, culture and trade, political thought and organisation, army and war, religious cults, festivals, philosophy and language, find detailed mention in the book. The *Nilamata Purana* is more a history of the people than of the kings.

The poly-historian Kshemendra (11th century A.D.) is a very helpful and useful author. He is rightly regarded as the doyen among the Kashmiri poets and chroniclers. In *Samayamatrika*, one of this best poems, he beautifully portrays the socio-economic life of the people. Sir Aurel Stein remarks:

> "His works, composed in the second and third quarter of the eleventh century, form important landmarks in several fields of Indian literature. Kshemendra seems to have had a genuine

interest, rare enough among Indian scholars, for the realities of his country and the life around him." (Stein, *Rajatarangini*, II, 375).

The *Lokaprakasha* is a very useful dictionary (*Kosh*) compiled through the efforts of many scholars including kshemendra. it is very important for the study of social life and administrative structure. It contains details about bills of exchange, bonds, commercial contracts, official orders and so forth. Stein praises its secular character and is grateful for the topographical details which it gives (Ibid., II, 376).

The *Rajatarangini*, the "River of Kings", written in 1148–49 A.D., is a history of kings, royal families and nobility. It is so well-known that it hardly needs any description. Suffice it would to say that the *Rajatarangini* is a class by itself in Indian literature. It has a striking resemblance in character to the chronicles of medieval Europe and of the Islamic East. Kalhana in writing *Rajatarangini* set a tradition for history writing. The mission of a historian, according to Kalhana , is to make vivid before one's eyes pictures of a bygone age. History has a unique gift of immortalising personages and events, and in this it even surpasses the mythical ambrosia, while the latter immortalizes only the man who drinks it, the former all those whom it touches. Kalhana was aware that his work would not only achieve permanence, but would enliven all the actors as well as himself. He had another object also in view. He says, "This saga, which is properly made up, should be useful for kings as a stimulent or a sedative, like a physic, according to time and place". Kalhana expected that both good and bad kings would derive profit from his work. He is a staunch advocate of historical impartiality. History, according to Kalhana:

> "was not something to learn but something to make people live and understand life. He gives both sides of all questions and points out the faults as well as the virtues of the kings and other characters whom he describes. Further, his observations show that the achievements of the great are merely answers to certain big needs in society and that success was only possible because the time was ripe". (R.S. Pandis, *The River of Kings*, p. xxvii).

Jonaraja, two hundred years after Kalhana, took up the thread and continued the narrative down to the reign of Sultan Zain-ul-

Abidin. He also called his book *Rajatarangini.* He gives a brief but useful account of the social and political condition of Kashmir from 1150 A.D. to the accession of Shah Mir.

After the death of Jonaraja in 1459 A.D, his pupil Srivara continued the narrative. He called his work *Jaina* (possibly *Zaina*) — *Rajatarangini* and gives a detailed account of the remaining years of Zain-ul-'Abidin's reign from 1459 to 1470 and of the reigns of his successors till the accession of Fateh Shah in 1486 A.D.

Prajyabhatta composed his *Rajavalipataka* and describes the history of the period from 1486 to 1512 A.D. Suka Pandit, a pupil of Prajyabhatta, wrote his chronicle covering the period from 1517 to 1596. He named his work *Rajatarangini.*

Notwithstanding the inferiority of the last four chronicles when compared with Kalhana's monumental work, it may be noted with satisfaction that their authors considerably improved the historical methodology. They are clear and crisp and events are narrated in a continuous flow. They throw ample light on the contemporary society.

The Mughals gave a booster to historical writings in India. But before the Mughal invasion of Kashmir Sayyid Ali Mutawalli, Khanqah-i-Mu'alla, Srinagar, wrote his *Tarikh-i-Kashmir* covering the period up to Yusuf Shah Chak's first reign. Sayyid Ali describes the part played by Sayyid Ali Hamadani and his son Sayyid Muhammad in spreading Islam in the Valley. The work is thus valuable for the religious history of the period. For the political history it is also very important because it is the earliest extant Persian chronicle of Kashmir.

The *Baharistan-i-Shahi* by an unknown author is a history of Kashmir from the accession of Rinchana to 1614, the pre-Islamic period is scantly treated. The author exhaustively deals with the Mughal conquest of Kashmir and is a useful source to check upon the Mughal accounts. It also relates in detail the life of Yusuf Shah and Yaqub Shah in exile and the manner of their death. The style is ornate and verbose but the work is in no way inferior in standard to other histories produced during the same period in other parts of India.

The most well-known Persian history of Kashmir is that of Rais-ul-Mulk Haider Malik Chadura. He began writing his *Tarikh-i-Kashmir* in 1618 and completed it in 1620-21 A.D. He was a Shia but he writes objectively and freely criticises Yaqub Shah for his anti-Sunni Policy.

Narayan Kaul 'Ajiz was a distinguished poet and litterateur. His *Tawarikh-i-Kashmir* written in 1710 A.D. gives an assessment of the reigns of the Sultans of Kashmir from purely historical point of view. His work may well compare with his Mughal counter-part Sujan Rai Bhandari of Batala's *Khulasat- ut-Tawarikh*.

The tradition of writing history was continued by Khwaja Muhammad Azam Didamari. His history entitled *Waqiat-i- Kashmir* or *Tarikh-i-'Azmi* was commenced in 1735 and completed in 1746. It is a short history of Kashmir in Persian and besides political history, gives a brief account of Muslim mystics and poets of Kashmir. It is a popular source of information for authors living in other parts of India.

On the models of Firdausi's *Shahnama*, Raja Sukh Jiwan Mal, Governor of Kashmir under Ahamd Shah Durrani, desired to have a Shahnama-i-Kashmir, and entrusted the work to Mulla Lal Muhammad *Taufiq*, Mulla Jan *Shami* and five others. Though the project fell through due to the death of Raja Sukh Jiwan, the extant portion testifies to the genius of those involved in compiling it.

Pandit Birbal Kachru wrote his *Majmuah-i-Tawarikh* in 1835 A.D. when Kashmir was under the rule of Maharaja Ranjit Singh. The work is of immense value in assessing the economic condition of the various classes of people during the later Mughal and Afghan periods.

The *Gulzar-i-Kashmir* by Diwan Kripa Ram, Prime Minister of Jammu and Kashmir in the days of Maharajah Ranbir Singh, is a history of Kashmir in Persian from the earliest times to 1857 A.D. It contains very useful appendices on products, arts and crafts and various trades carried on in the Valley.

The *Gulabnama* by the same author is the court history of Maharajah Gulab Singh (1846-57). The author, it seems, was inspired by Abul Fazl's *Akbarnama* and shares its virtues and vices.

Towards the close of the nineteenth century Pir Ghulam Hassan Shah Khuihami, gave us in three volumes his *Tarikh-i- Kashmir* popularly known as *Tarikh-i-Hassan.* It is a first-rate work and has all the virtues of a great history book. It deals with geography, political history and social and economic conditions of the people.

This is *Mushte namunah kharware* (A handful specimen from the granary). I have only picked up the landmarks in the field of historical writing in Kashmir. The survey makes three things clear. Firstly, Kashmir has a tradition in history writing and enormous historical literature was produced in the Valley. Secondly, Kashmir chronicles and histories distinguish themselves by taking into account the social and economic conditions of the people. And lastly, the authors are, to a great extent objective and impartial. Their greatest achievement is that they rise above parochialism and narrow communalism. Their tone and treatment, by and large, are secular.

# 9

# JAHANGIR IN KASHMIR : AN ACCOUNT OF ACCOUNTS

Salim, the child of many prayers, was brought up at a court which extended a splendid patronage to art, and in a city which was in itself a marvel of art. His aesthetic faculties were trained to a remarkable degree. His education made him fairly conversant with history and geography. He is fond of biographical details. His interest in botany and zoology would have done credit to any professional scientist. His delight in beautiful stones and artistic swords or hilts, was exquisite. Equally remarkable is his intense passion for beauties of nature. He loved stories and acquired the knack of graphic narration. He developed a somewhat poetic disposition paraded his skill in versification, and sowed his talk with poetic quotations.

When Salim in 1605, at the age of thirty-six, became Jahangir, the poet in him did not die. When late in life, in keeping with the traditions of some earlier kings, he wrote his diary, his early training and education proved a great asset. Henry Beveridge, the editor of Jahangir's Memoirs, says:

> "The Royal authors of the East had more blood in them than those kings whose works have been catalogued by Horace Walpole. To find a parallel to them we must go back to Julius Caesar, and even then the advantage is not upon the side of Europe. After all, the commentaries of the famous Roman are a little disappointing,

> and certainly the Memoirs of Babar and Jahangir are far more human and fuller of matter than the story of the Gallic Wars."

Jahangir was a most faulty human being, and his own account of himself often excites our disgust and contempt. But his account of himself has also its charm, for it reveals the real man, and so he lives for us in his Memoirs just as James VI lives in the 'Fortunes of Nigel' or Cladius in 'Suetonius and Tacitus.'

Jahangir is a true Indian. He dwells delightedly on the charms of Indian flowers, particularises the *palash*, the *bokul*, and the *champa*, and avows that no fruit of Afghanistan or Central Asia is equal to the mango.

The poet in Jahangir becomes ecstatic when he enters into the "Paradise on Earth". The beauties of Kashmir and the beauty of Jahangir's mind and heart, make his narrative simply enchanting. He describes the flowers and springs with poetic fervour. He would gaze, rapt with wonder and admiration, at beautiful rose or tulip, hill or rivulet. Of course, all this was taken to celestial heights by the presence of his heart's solace Nur Jahan by his side. What Khayyam wrote in verse, Jahangir recorded in poetic prose in his *Tuzk-i-Jahangiri.*

Jahangir visited Kashmir several times along with his father Emperor Akbar. When he became king, to avoid the heat and dust of the plains, Jahangir, almost every year, ran to Kashmir to repose in the lap of the nature.

Jahangir was married to Nur Jahan Begam in 1611. She had a fancy for the happy valley ; henceforth, the royal couple was the regular visitor.

In the second year of his reign, when Jahangir reached Kashmir and pitched on the bank of the Jhelum, he records "In the night a very strong wind blew, dark clouds obscured the sky, and it rained so heavily that even the oldest persons had never seen such rain within their memory. The rain ended with showers of hail-stones, which were as large as hens' eggs".

Jahangir dwells upon the source of Jhelum previously called Behat :

"The source of the river Behat is a fountain in Kashmir, called Virnag. The spring rises in a basin, of an octangular form. Its water is so clear that although its depth is said to be beyond estimation, yet if a poppy-seed be thrown in, it will be visible till it reaches the bottom", But the researcher in Jahangir was not satisfied with popular verdict:

"As I was told that the fountain was unfathomably deep, I ordered a stone to be tied to the end of a rope and thrown into it, and thus it was found that its depth did not exceed the height of a man and a half".

From Verinag, Jahangir reaches Pampur, the land of saffron. He mentions: "All the saffron of Kashmir is the product of this village. Perhaps there is no other place in the world where saffron is so abundantly produced". When he visited the saffron fields in the blossoming season, he noted: "In all other trees we see they first get the branches then the leaves, and after all the flower. But it is otherwise with this plant. It blossoms when it is only about two inches high from the ground. Its flower is of a bluish colour, having four leaves and four threads of orange colour, in length equal to one joint of the finger. This is saffron". Jahangir further mentions :

"In the season when it is collected, it has such a strong scent that people get headache from it".

Speaking about the Jhelum, Jahangir says :

"It passes through the heart of the city. No one drinks its water, because of its heaviness and indigestibility. All the people of Kashmir drink the water of a lake that is near the city, and is called Dal".

"In Kashmir there is plenty of water from streams and springs", says Jahangir. He notices the cluster of graceful *chanars* "together on one plot of ground, pleasant and green, join each other so as to shade the whole plot and the whole surface of the ground is grass and trefoil; so much so that to lay a carpet on it would be superfluous and in bad taste".

"Autumn and Spring in Kashmir are things worthy to be seen", recommends Jahangir. "I witnessed the autumn season," he states, "and it appeared to me to be better than what I had heard of it". The youthful exuberance of Spring was exhilarating.

Jahangir throws ample light on the economic life of the Kashmiri people. In Srinagar, Jahangir found only "four bridges made of wood and stone". The boat was the only means of transport. There were 5,700 boats and 7,400 boatmen.

Jahangir describes the weights and measures current in this part of the country. He treats of the routes to Kashmir and suggests the Pakhli route as the best if a person wished to enjoy the scenic beauty on the way.

The houses in Kashmir were constructed all of wood and went up to four storeys. The housetop was filled with earth over which flowers were grown which looked very pleasing.

The variety and taste of Kashmiri fruits find detailed mention in Jahangir's memoirs. Wine and vinegar were available in abundance. The vinegar was also used in making pickles. Rice (*bhatta*) was the main food of the Kashmiris which was cooked without salt. Generally, vegetables were boiled in water and a little of salt was added for taste. Oil and butter were used by people who were comparatively well off. Wheat was of inferior quality and was produced very little. Kashmiris did not take bread. Various kinds of meat and fish were easily available.

Men and women wore woollen cloth called *Pattoo*. They believed that without wearing *Pattoo* they caught cold and it was not possible to digest food without it.

Men of Kashmir shaved their head and wore turban. Kashmiri women wore long *kurtas* which covered them from head to foot.

Kashmiri shawls, says Jahangir, need no introduction. He mentions various varieties of shawls and compares them with those manufactured in Tibet.

The labourers in Kashmir usually used to get salt in return of their wages. Jahangir makes a particular reference of the shortage of salt in Kashmir which was imported from Hindustan "for salt is not produced in Kashmir". Jahangir continues: "Even in the beauty of the inhabitants there is but very little".

After writing such a comprehensive commentary on Kashmir, Jahangir admits his shortcomings. "It will require books", he says, "to detail the beauties and niceties of Kashmir". He sums up :

> "Kashmir is the ever-green garden. It is the pleasure resort for the kings and for saints and seers an ideal abode for seclusion and meditation".

That is why, while on death-bed, when asked about his last wish, Jahangir said : "*Kashmir and nothing else*".

# 10

# THE ARTS AND CRAFTS OF KASHMIR

The arts and crafts of Kashmir have been justly renowned, for centuries, all over the world. They consist mainly of handicrafts like woolen textiles of fleecy soft texture and infinite fineness in weaving, delicate embroidery work in silk and wool, handwoven carpets of finest warp and woof, lovely painting in wonderful designs on *papier mache* goods or on wood, fine traceries in wood-carving, deft weaving in willow- wicker, and superb metal-work, Of the cottage industries the most flourishing is that of wood-carving—which is not only beautiful but also of great utility, and which finds a ready and expanding market throughout the world, especially for work suited to modern requirements (such as screens, drawing and dining room sets, smoking cabinets, and other articles for personal use) which are exquisitely manufactured in well-seasoned walnut-wood. An entirely indigenous form of wood-work (known as *Khatam bundi* ) is used for the decoration of ceilings, which is done in panels of pinewood in a various geometrical designs, fitted together in grooves. Another important cottage industry is the making of numerous useful and pretty articles of wickerwork.

The surroundings of Srinagar are so beautiful that it is not at all surprising that the city has long since evolved unique artistic craftsmanship. There is scarcely a cleverer artisan than the Kashmiri, who with primitive tools, turns out highly artistic and beautiful articles. The fame of Kashmiri shawls, the whole of one of which will pass through a signet ring, has for centuries past spread to the farthest ends of the earth; its finest ambroideries rival those of the best French seamstresses, its carpets compete succcssfully with the Chinese, Iranian, Turkish ones, its silver-ware compares favourably with that turned out by the most fashionable shops in London, furs that delight the fair sex and might have come from Paris, and countless other articles of use and adornment, which are made to perfection. It is but natural that a state which attracts so large an influx of visitors annually, as does Kashmir, should also turn its attention to the manufacture of such articles as tourists chiefly require. Even the common workers of Srinagar are versatile craftsmen, and the visitor will rejoice to behold carpet and silk weavers, embroidery-makers, leather-workers and gold, silver and copper-smiths busily engaged in plying their trades under the very gaze of the visitor — working with a quickness and concentration, which would astonish him.

That Kashmir was well known, from ancient times, as much for the beauty of Nature as for its arts and crafts, is evidenced by what Ree's Encyclopaedia (1819) has to say about the ancient glory of the craftsmanship of Kashmir :

> "There seems no reason to doubt that the Romans were well acquainted with the shawls of Kashmir, which are fabrics of a brilliant and beautiful texture. The history of their manufacture is proof of a very high degree of perfection to which the fabrication of woollen cloth had been carried on in former times, for shawl is only woollen cloth woven without a twill and unmilled; but it is spun to so great a degree of fineness, from wool peculiarly soft, that it has never been rivalled by European nations".

And the British were so enamoured of the beautiful shawls of Kashmir, with curious designs embroidered with the deft fingers of Kashmiri artisans, that in the Treaty of 1846 (between the Kashmir Darbar and East India Company), it was one of the items that every year Rs. 8,000/- worth of shawls and *rumals* the Darbar would have to send to the British Sovereign of India.

But this fascinating Kashmir craft received a severe blow, when the taste of the rich people in India became diverted, and the cheap and fragile imitation goods produced by foreign exploiters began to be dumped on the Indian shores. As a result of lack of patronage, the prosperous craftsman of old Kashmir had to abandon his hereditary trade and became an ordinary labourer where his artistic talents could no longer be utilised. Thus came about the decline and fall of that astonishing ancient craftsmanship of Kashmir. But thanks to the independence of the country, now concerted efforts at all levels are being made to revive and nourish the arts and crafts of Kashmir.

To give more details, the most beautiful of the renowned Kashmiri shawls are produced by three methods: by embroidering upon a plain foundation cloth; by weaving the pattern alongwith the foundation cloth; and by weaving a pattern as an integral part of the foundation cloth subsequently embellishing it with embroidery. The first is the most expensive method, but does not necessarily produce the most artistic results.

The following account of the Kashmir shawl industry (from the *Magazine of Art* for 1901, Vol. XXV, p. 452) gives an idea of the decline of this once great industry:

> "The magnificence of the celebrated hand-worked shawl of Kashmir received its first and fatal check through the outbreak of the Franco- German war. Previous to that the demand for those fabrics was so great, in France, that a special agent from Paris resided at Srinagar for the sole purpose of superintending their purchase and export. Before the commencement of the war a special class of workmen (the *shal-baf*, or the shawl-worker) was accustomed to spend years on the out-turn of single first-rate specimen. The material was the main item of cost, the fine *Pashmina* wool selling in Kashmir for its weight in silver".

The country people of Kashmir clothe themselves chiefly in a heavy woollen fabric named *pattoo*, and, in addition, require heavy woollen blanket, *loie*. These fabrics are largely made from hand-spun, coarse wool yarns.

The carpet industry, which is one of the largest in the state, the annual production of which is valued at in millions, thrives exclusively on export trade with America and Europe. But the yarns employed by the carpet factories is mainly imported from Europe as the local wool is not of sufficient good quality. It was Sultan

Zain-ul-Abidin Budshah (1423-1474) who for the first time introduced carpet-making in Kashmir. And the Kashmiri craftsman, whose imitative instinct was developed to a marvellous degree, was quick to reproduce in works of art Nature's beautiful sceneries with which he was surrounded.

The speed of making the average carpet varies from four feet per day to two inches a month, depending upon the intricacy of the work and design. The expert in this picture can only do one inch per month, and there are 2,400 knots per square inch. Such a carpet of fairly large size, when completed, costs well over Rs. 10,000/-.

Carpets with as many as 400 knots to the square inch are now made at Srinagar factories; silk and pashmina wool are sometimes used to bring out the more delicate shadings in the design, and the stitch with which the Iranian weavers used to give their carpets density, has been successfully adopted. Herati and Kerman carpets have also been extremely well produced, and the Yarkandi patterns very ingeniously imitated. The hand-made carpet industry of Kashmir is now the single largest industry in the State.

Another allied industry — which is located almost entirely at Anantnag, and the only one outside Srinagar — is that of making *gabbas*. These are woollen fabrics made of *Pattoos*— to be used as floor-coverings, bed spreads and table- cloths. The background is of diverse colours and is covered — in whole or in part — by highly ingenious geometrical and other designs either by means of embroidery or stitching. If lined with some suitable and durable cotton material (like ticking) they last four years. More expensive than the felt *namdahs*, they are very much cheaper than the hand-made carpets.

In addition to the manufacture of carpets, there is, in Kashmir, a most interesting "carpet-rug" industry, based upon milling up or felting partly woven fabrics, and then figuring them with embroideries in most beautiful manner. These "*namdahs*", as they are called in common parlance, are very warn, if used as bed-mattresses, and make excellent coverings, which have steadily held their own even in these machine-ridden times.

Papier mâchè was long synonymous with the very name of Kashmir, and numerous articles — from dressing-tables to toilet sets, finger bowls, candle-sticks, and boxes for various purposes — used to be manufactured of paper-pulp and laquer. It is even now of great interest to watch a skilled artisan at work in painting wooden articles, instead of those made of paper- pulp. The making of papier mache articles in Kashmir is one of the leading arts that has come down from generation to generation, since time immemorial. God created Kashmir when He was a bit free; Kashmiris further beautified what they got from Nature. That is why, today, all roads lead to Srinagar, not Rome.

# 11

# ZIARATGAHS IN JAMMU

Few persons know that Jammu, the famous city of temples, the winter capital of the State of Jammu and Kashmir, abounds in Ziarats of Rishis, Makhdums, Shahids and Sayyids. It is true that the lofty and gilded *Shikharas* of temples give an obvious impression at the first sight. But beneath the shady trees, in the groves, and in the remote corners of the city, are the unpretentious graves, respectfully called Ziarats, of Muslim saints and sufis. This may explain the riddle of the cultural synthesis and essential unity and oneness of the people of Jammu and Kashmir. It is incorrect to hold that "Islam came in on a strong wave, on which rode a fanatical king and a missionary saint, and history records that the Kashmiris became Musalmans." (Cf. Imperial Gazetteer of India, Vol. XV, 1908, p. 102). The history of the people of Jammu and Kashmir is not to be interpreted in terms of religion. The key is to be found in the role and influence which saintly souls, — far removed from religious dogmas, fanaticism, orthodoxy, communalism and sectarian consideration —, exercised over the minds of the masses, both Hindu and Muslims. As in the field of politics and administration, so in socio-religious evolution, this cultural fusion, liberalism and enlightenment, are the characteristic features of the people of the State.

Near the Satwari Police Station, at the back of the aerodrome and just by the side of runway, there is the Dargah of Piran-i-Pir Fard-i-Wahid Imad-ul-Mulk Hayrat Baba Buddhan Shah. His real name was Shamsuddin. It is narrated that formerly the grave was unknown and when the runway for the aerodrome was constructed, it passed through the grave. After the completion of the runway, when planes tried to take off, they failed to do so and some of the planes were destroyed in the attempt. No one was able to know the reasons for this unusual phenomena. So, one night, the saint revealed himself to the authorities in their dream and asked them not to disturb him in his sleep and change the road and the runway. The authorities finding no way out acted on the advice of the saint. The Government itself reconstructed a *pakka* grave with enclosures all around. After that the planes experienced no difficulty and there were no accidents. They now take off after saluting the tomb. The wreckage of some of the planes are still to be seen on the western side of the Dargah.

This made the Ziarat the centre of attraction for the people of all beliefs and shades. On every Thursday, a sort of fair (*mela*) is held and an unbroken chain of thousands of people, — men, women, and children, Hindus, Muslims, Sikhs and Christians, poor women and ultra modern girls, beggers in rags and gentlemen in their imported clothes, naked *sadhus, jogis* and *faqirs* —, kneel down and prostrate before the grave. Non-Muslim military personnel appear prominent among the devotees. They burn incense, place wreathes, pour mustard oil in the lamps burning here in the niche all the twentyfour hours and make offerings of money, flowers and sweets, they rub the *rakh* or *bhashm* on their forehead. They fan the grave with *morchhal* (fan made of the feathers of peacock) and press cenotaph as if they were pressing the body of the saint who lies buried below. They pray, they beg, they shout, they cry and make promises of lavish offerings in case their wishes were fulfilled. Some flowers and sweets as offered to the saint are taken home, sweets are eaten with respect as *Prasad* or *Tabarruk* and flowers preserved as holy relic. Red and green flags are hoisted all round the Ziarat by the devotees. Just opposite the Dargah Sharif, there is a temple of the Creater where the priest prays in solitude while the multitude flocks to the grave of a saint, the created one.

On the slopes of Gumat, there is the Ziarat of the Arabian Saint Jalaluddin Jamal Noorani Makki Madani popularly known as Baba Roshan Shah Wali. He was the eldest of the five brothers. It is said that long before the advent of Islam into Kashmir, the Pir graced this place , and delivered the message of the brotherhood of Islam. Every year on December 18, the *urs* (nuptial) ceremony is organised on behalf of the *Majlis-i-Auqaf-i- Islamia,* Jammu which works under the Jammu and Kashmir Muslim Wakafs Act 1959 (Act No. X of 1959). Even today it is considered auspicious for wrestlers and for that matter any other person to touch the grave and descend the steps down below. It is disrespectful, hence inauspicious, to walk up the steps to the Ziarat which is taken as an affront by the saint. The grave is unusually very long meaning thereby that he was a very tall man.

In Gandhi Nagar lies buried the Gujar saint Baba Ibrahim Shah who died some sixty years back. He was a lean and thin person with dark-brown complexion. He lived in a small hut. He talked in sufistic strain. He had many wounds on his body but never cared to get them cured. He used to take very simple food consisting of barley bread. People used to take very rich and sumptuous dishes to him but he never touched them.

Behind the Science College there is a Ziarat of great fame of the saint known as Zahir Wali who is very popular with the non-Muslim population. It is said that when construction work for building the college started, the Parsi Principal of the College Dadina saw in the dream that the saint was telling him that he was lying there and he should not be disturbed. Instead a *pakka* grave with a separate enclosure and boundry wall should be constucted. A gorkha chowkidar also narrated a similar story rather he was slapped by the saint for disturbing him in his sleep. The Principal apprised the state government about it. Maharaja Partap Singh was ruling the State. The Maharaja, it is told, had a great regard and respect for Pirs and Faqirs. He himself visited the site alongwith the Principal and ordered for the construction of the Khanqah. The Ziarat became very famous because of the visit and personal interest of the Maharaja.

Pir Meetha (the sweat-tongued) belonged to the family of Sayyids and is primarily the saint of water-carriers. It is narrated that the Raja of Jammu suffered from leprosy. In those days the water was supplied to the people including the royal house-hold by water-carriers who used to fetch it from the River Tawi and the wells round about it. One day, a water-carrier (*Jiwar*) was carrying water for the royal household, Pir Meetha who was sitting on the road, touched it. The water-carrier became very angry as the water was polluted by the touch of a Musalman. He went back, cleansed the utensils and again carried water. The Pir again touched it. The water-carrier again went back and brought fresh water after cleansing the utensils. The Pir again touched the utensil. The water-carrier became desperate and carried the polluted water for the Raja. The water-carrier used to carry the water as touched by Pir Meetha and the Raja used to drink that. This happened for about a fortnight. Surprisingly, the Raja was cured of his chronic disease. He became curious. At along last the water-carrier narrated the whole story. The Raja rushed to Pir Meetha and enrolled himself as one of his *murids*. The water-carriers *en masse* became his disciples. Before partition, the water- carriers from the undivided Punjab used to flock to Jammu on the occasion of his *urs* which falls on the 1st of December every year. It is said that the tomb of Pir Meetha (in the mohalla of the same name) was built by the Raja. The tomb is the reflex of the composite Indian culture. Along the Quranic inscriptions, the peacock also finds a place.

As we enter the mausoleum of Qutb Zaman Baba Jiwan Shah, on the main gate it is inscribed :

*Nam Faqir tanawa Jiwan Shah,*
*Qabr banadi Jiway.*

Translation : The name of this Faqir is Jiwan Shah,
He is alive though outwardly dead.

Jiwan Shah was of local origin. His father was a dyer. He was a *mast qalandar* and had renounced the world. He led a celebate life. He used to answer questions allegorically and his answers were mostly correct and appropriate. That is why, he had a large following hailing from the various parts of the country including learned and influential people, e.g., Principal Sharga of Prince of Wales College. It is said that Maharaja Partap Singh and Maharaja Amar Singh also used to visit him. Sometimes, Maharaja Pratap Singh used to take the saint to his palace. He had fixed a *Wazifah* (subsidy, endowment), both in cash and kind for the saint but he knew nothing about it nor cared for it. Baba Jiwan Shah died on Thursday, February 22, 1919 and this is the date on which his *urs* ceremony is observed. His Ziaratgah is in a spacious quadrangle. In front of the tomb, there is a room in which hangs the photograph of the saint. Here people burn lamps and offer flowers.

In Karbala, we have the mazar or grave of considerable antiquity of Pir Deedar Ali Shah. On the 10th of Muharram, Yuljinah procession is taken out from Pir Meetha and the token burial ceremony is performed here.

In Ustad Mohalla, there is the tomb of Baghwale Baba in the Municipal Committee garden. The *urs* ceremony is performed in the month of *Jeth*. The grave is visited both by Muslims and Hindus on every Thursday. People have great regard for Baba Jalla (Jalauddin) and Baba Shahna (Shan Bakhsh). They were *mast qalandars*. They belonged to Jammu and died in thirtees of the present century.

Facing the Palace, on the B.C. Road in Ram Nagar above the river Tawi, there is the memorial of Panch Pir, who rested here on this spot for some time. He is not buried here; he is buried somewhere in Pakistan. People burn lamps and offer flowers on the platform. Flags are hoisted all round. By the side of it there is the *Lingam*. The worshippers worship both the Muslim Pir and Hindu god.

# 12

# KASHMIR THROUGH THE AGES–The Gujars of Kashmir

Denzil Ibbetson and J.C. Nesfield endorse the view that caste is mainly occupational in origin, i.e., occupations which were organised into guilds slowly became exclusive and stratified into castes. The origin of caste, as a matter of fact, is a subject which has given rise to a great deal of speculation, some of it wild, some of it ingenious, and all of it inconclusive. A new school of theorists has now arisen. They postdate the origin of caste to comparatively modern times, and secondly, they look for its origin in the nature of the elements composing early Indian society, and for its development in the working of social forces on those elements. The period between 300 B.C. to 300 A.D. is an important period of Indian history from the point of view of social development. It was the period during which several great invasions of India occurred of the Sakas, the Yavanas, the Pahlavas, and the Kushans. Unfortunately, we know little or nothing of the effect that they produced in social field, though these must have left their mark on society. But, luckily, we do know something of the results of a later invasion, that of Huns.

In 465 A.D., there occurred an inroad of 'white' Huns or Ephthalites. These were savages from the Central Asian steppes, and closely akin to the Huns who invaded Europe under Attila. By 500 A.D. the hordes of these white Huns had overrun northern India, and a Hun kingdom been set up with its capital at the present Sialkot. Mihiragula (Mihirakula), their last king, a bloodthirsty tyrant, was defeated and slained about 528 A.D. by a coalition of Indian princes, and with his death the power of the Huns came to an end. Mihiragula, the King "cruel as death", also ruled over Kashmir. The people still point to a ridge on the Pir Panjal range, Hastivanj, where the king, to amuse himself, drove one hundred elephants over the precipice. enjoying their cries of agony.

Of late, due to the researchers of A.M.T. Jackson, evidence has been discovered which connects some of the modern Indian castes with these Huns. The Gujar caste takes its name from Gujara, a tribe which is frequently found coupled in inscriptions with the Huns, and was obviously related to them. Hun is still the name of a Gujar sect or subcaste, which makes the connection more clear. The Gujara carved out a couple of kingdoms in Rajputana; the capital of one of these was at Bhinmal or Bhilmal.

The Gujars are found all over Russian Turkistan, Persia, Afghanistan, Pakistan and India. They profess different religions like Islam, Hinduism, Sikhism, Jainism, etc. The total Gujar population in India, according to the Census Report of 1931, was 2430669 – Men : 1323538, Women:1107131. In the State of Jammu Kashmir the Gujars numbered 402781 in 1931. Barring Ladakh, the Gujars are to be found in every district of the State but they predominate in Poonch and Rajouri. So numerically the Gujars are a factor to be reckoned with and they form the third important group after Kashmiri Muslims and Hindus and Sikhs taken together.

The Gujars in the State of Jammu may be divided into three broad divisions : Local or Residents, those who permanently live in villages; semi-local or non-residents, those who live in villages for some time and migrate to various places and pastures; and the Nomads or Gypsies, who wander from place to place. These nomads are further sub-divided into two: Dudhi Gujars, the herdsmen who mainly keep buffaloes and earn their living by selling milk; and Gujar Bakarwal, who keep rams and goats and earn their livelihood from wool, milk and selling he-goats. The Bakarwal Gujars are again divided into two: the Kahnaris and the Ilais. All these nomadic people, in summer months, move up to the splendid grazing-grounds above the forests and in the winters they migrate to Jammu, Reasi, Udhampur, Kathua and even to Pathankot and Gurdaspur in Punjab.

In Kashmir, though all the Gujars are Muslims, they have nothing in common with other Muslims in matters of dress, food, habits, customs and manners. Their mother-tongue Gujari, resembles more with other Indian dialects including Braj Bhasha. The Gujars, like the Muslim Rajputs generally preserve their rule of hypergamy in the shape of refusing to give daughters to families from which they have taken wives. Shalwar and Kurta are the common dress for both men and women. For head-dress, men generally wear turbans and women, caps, dupta and kasaba. They are very religious and men generally keep beards following the example of the Prophet of Islam. The Gujar women usually wear ornaments of silver and they part their hair in numberless plaits.

The menfolk are generally tall with long nose and large prominent teeth. They have long head and broad fore-head. They are dark-brown to wheatish in colour. The women are well-built, slim and smart, very agile, wiry and cute with wheatish complexion. Jahangir would not have complained about the lack of salt in the beauty of Kashmir had he seen these beauties. The Gujars on the whole are a hardy people. Both men and women work together.

Simplicity, honesty, truthfulness and sympathy for others, are the basic traits of their character. They keep their promise and are known for hospitality. They are sincere, devoted to duty and loyal to their masters. They are brave and courageous. Above all, they are great patriots, and nationalists. They made India their home and sought against all the invaders including the invasion of Mohammad bin Qasim. They did not allow Sultan Mahmud of Ghazni and Maharaja Ranjit Singh to enter the valley of Kashmir. During the Indo-Pak Wars of 1965 and 1971, the Kashmiri Gujars fought bravely against the Pakistanis. Some of them were honoured with Padm Shri and Asoka Chakra for the heroism they displayed during those difficult times.

The marriages among Gujar Bakarwals are mainly performed in the summer and the marriage processions go from one pasture to another. The party usually rides on horses and the bride is also brought to bridegroom's residence seated on a horse. On such occasions horse-races are organized as fun and past-time.

In the village of Wangat—district Srinagar, there is a famous mausoleum of Baba Larvi, a Ziarat, which is much revered by the Gujars. Though the Gujars are Muslims by religion, they regard Goga Chauhan or Goga Pir as their spiritual Guru. This is another example of their eclecticism in matters of religion and the secular traditions they imbibe. The Gujari folk literature is very rich which includes folk songs both for the occasions of joy and sorrow and folk tales with special reference to one Raja Dhara.

The Gujars are a backward community in the State of Jammu and Kashmir but due to their efforts and encouragement from the State Government they are catching up. They are a people with great potentials. Given to education and civilization they are bound to prove themselves an asset for the State of Jammu and Kashmir in particular and for the country as a whole.

# 13

# UNDERSTANDING SHEIKH MOHAMMAD ABDULLAH

The real solution of the political problem of the Indian subcontinent was a federation. It is absolutely impossible to forcibly unite under one yoke the diverse human urges and aspirations, cultural patterns and ways of life. Such an attempt might be practically desirable, but it is certainly unsound, historically speaking. To bring the whole of the Indian sub-continent under an imperial sway, without giving the various units a respectable amount of free hand to manage their internal affairs and a full scope to develop their personality, has proved futile. History testifies to this. When the strong hand of a ruler was absent, the provinces and the states brought under control by force of arms, declared independence, and managed their own affairs in their own ways. A Government at the centre brands such attempts by smaller units and the states as 'rebellion', while the people of those states considered it a liberation movement, a way of independence. Chand Sultana, Baz Bahadur, Maharana Pratap, and Shivaji, are worshipped as heroes in their own areas though labelled as rebels by the rulers at the centre. If this basic fact would have been understood by our leaders, there would have been no partition of the country, and again Bangla Desh would not have come into existence, but for the follies of the administrators of the Western wing of Pakistan. The solution which the Founding Fathers of the United States of America found for their very acute bewildering situation, should have served as the beacon for the Indian politicians. Today, America is the mightiest country on earth.

There is no use to weep over the spilled milk. But even India of today has the same dimensions. We are all Indians. Yet, every region and every area has some special characteristics. The sum total of all these traits and trends, is the great *Indian Culture.* The unity in diversity is the hallmark of the Indian life. No one culture of a particular area or of a particular people or group, represents or means by any stretch of imagination 'The Indian Culture'. Hence it is a folly to think that any state which does not conform to the pattern of some one at the centre, is disobedient or rebellious. You cannot build flat and open houses in Shimla or Srinagar as you do in Madras or Delhi.

If you want to understand Sheikh Abdullah, understand the people of the Jammu and Kashmir State; if you want to understand the people of the state, understand the climatic conditions prevalent in this part of the country; if you want to understand the weather and the climate of the area, understand the geographical situation of the region; if you want to understand the geography of the State, understand the Pir Panjal range. Sheikh Abdullah and the Pir Panjal range are identical. The Pir Panjal has a precious jewel, a heaven in miniature, in its bosom; the bosom of Sheikh Abdullah burns for the wellbeing, dignity, honour and self-respect of the people of Jammu and Kashmir.

History tells us that Kashmir has always fought for a life free from domination and political coercion. Kashmir is the paradise on earth, so all possible efforts were made by rulers and conquerors in the past to pocket it. But Kashmir has consistently defied such an attempt. This does not mean that Kashmir wanted to live in isolation. No, Kashmir wanted to live in peace, at peace with all the races, religions and communities. This is the key to the understanding of the political situation in Kashmir. Kashmir looked to other outside powers and forced only to safeguard its own institutions and freedom. Kashmir welcomes rulers as saviours, but when they tried to grab the land, the people of the State threw them away, may be with the help of another power.

Kashmir invited India and joined hands with it primarily to safeguard its identity and way of life. Kashmir rejected Pakistan when she found that joining hands with Pakistan meant assimilation and domination. Kashmir is a part of India though it enjoys a special position under the Constitution of India. Kashmir is secular, Kashmir is socialist in the real sense. You can see real democracy and brotherhood in Kashmir. Kashmir declared secularism, socialism and democracy as its goal long before 1947. The *Naya Kashmir* testifies to this. Kashmir is already in the mainstream of national life but mainstream might not be confused with complete political merger or assimilation. And in all this no one can deny the proud place which Sheikh Mohammad Abdullah occupies. He is the champion and true spirit which is Kashmir. It is a folly to suppose that Sheikh Abdullah is an individual. He is an institution. He is the conscience of Kashmir and Kashmir toes his line no matter whether he is alive or dead.

The Americans Henry Clay, John Quincy Adams, Daniel Webster, Andrew Jackson, Stephen A. Douglas, Thomas Hart Benton, Abraham Lincoln—all had love for the Union, all had love for their states and regions, all saw no conflict, rather a mutually nourishing connection, between these two loves. These famous men and the millions of followers for whom they spoke were *patriots* who had met every test set by Rousseau—inclination, passion, necessity—and had attached their ultimate patriotism to a nation so huge and loose-jointed that the sight of it would have sent Rousseau, not to forget Montesquieu, into a state of shock.

Sheikh Abdullah loves Kashmir, also loves India. The two loves are not contradictory or mutually exclusive. He loves his children; he loves his parents. He fights his own parents to give due share to his own children. Politically speaking, there is a generation gap. Sheikh Abdullah is the link, the bridge. Stronger the bridge, the younger Kashmiri generation might be induced to come out of their nests to play their role and enjoy the spacious courtyard of their grand-parents. So the bridge, the spirit behind it, and what it symbolises, need not be disturbed in the interest of the greatest good of the greatest democracy of the world to which every one of us belong, including the Lion of Kashmir.

# Part II

# 14

# KASHMIR'S CONTRIBUTION TO CHINESE BUDDHISM

Kashmir played a key role in the history of Buddhism.[1] Buddha is said to have observed : "The kingdom of Kashmir is where it will be easiest to lead the religious life. For contemplation and meditation, will that be the best place".[2]

In due course of time, the first schism in original Buddhism occurred at the Council of Vaśāli, held in c. 383 B.C. At this Council two rival groups representing the original and liberal elements came into existence. The dissident group called itself Mahāsānghika, or Māhāyān, i.e., the Great Vehicle. The former doctrine was destined to have a far- reaching influence on the history of Buddhism as a world-religion.[3] It was the main spirit and source of cultural activity of the Buddhists of India during 7th and 8th centuries A.D.[4] Its main contribution to Buddhist doctrine was its concept of a transcendental Buddha who is omnipresent and omnipotent, who manifests himself in an earthly form to conform to the needs of the people.[5] Therāvāda school got further fragmented into Sarvāstivāda (the doctrine that all exists) school.

Sarvāstivāda school flourished in Kashmir. It was from Kashmir that this school was introduced into China. This helps to explain that the translators of Sarvāstivādin canon in China were mainly Kashmiris. Sarvāstivāda school is considered to be Hinayan, as it is an offshoot of the Theravāda school. It has a complete canon of its own written in Sanskrit.[6] One of the results of the fourth Buddhist Council convened by Kanishka, the Kushan Emperor, was the rise of Sanskrit Buddhism.[7] Henceforth Sanskrit became the language of Buddhist thought and discussions all over the North.

**Kashmiri Missionaries in China**

In China like many other countries Buddhism entered through various roads. The geographical situation of Kashmir touching the boundaries of Afghanistan, Persia and Central Asia conferred upon it the role of the preceptor of Buddhism in Tibet, Ladakh, Khotan and China. Kashmir did it with honour. A continuous stream of erudite Kashmiri monks, proficient in linguistics and exegetics, gifted with the audacity of explorers contributed immensely to the spread of Buddhist learning in Central Asia and China through the translations. It was the first Indian province which not only started the tradition of translating the Buddhist lore since the fourth century, but also contributed to their formation.[8]

Jean Naudou is of the opinion that the Vinaya of the Mūlasarvāstivadin was not only edited but was also composed in Kashmir.[9] Later on missionaries carried its copies to China and translated it into Chinese.[10] The Mahāvibhāśa, the great Exegesis. "is a compilation established by teachers in Kashmir". Its Sanskrit version is no more available. But its Chinese translation by Sanghabhadra, a Kashmiri, is still available.[11]

Sanghabhuti was the first Kashmir monk to go to China. He reached the Chinese capital in 381 A.D. and remained there till his death. He translated a number of Buddhist texts into Chinese. The most important of his works was the commentary on Vinaya Pitaka of Sarvāstivāda School.[12] His translation of *Arya-Vasumitra-Bodhi-Dattvasangiti-śāstra* completed in 384 A.D., is available in Chinese.[13]

Doyen among the Kashmiri missionaries is Kumārajiva, who first gained mastery on the canon of the Sarvāstiavāda school, but afterwards concentrated on the Mahāyān Sutras. Having been converted to the great vehicle he won over his teacher Bandhudatta to his new faith.[14] In 379, A.D. the fame of Kumārajiva reached China. The ruler of China laboured almost for two decades to adorn his capital, Ch'ang-an, with this brightest jewel among the scholars. Kumārajiva was kept as a prisoner by king's general Lū Kuang, a non-Buddhist, who kept him under rigorous imprisonment in western China for seventeen years.[15] Different dates are given of Kumārajiva's arrival in China ranging between 401 A.D. to 408 A.D.[16]

Ch'ang-an was the centre of Buddhist learning. The Hsiao-yao Garden was placed at the disposal of Kumārajiva and his fellow monks. He immediately started his cyclopean task of translation,[17] with a thousand monks sitting in daily sessions, as he had already attained proficiency in Chinese language during his captivity at Liang Chou. Sometimes, the ruler, Yao Hsing, personally participated in those proceedings by holding the old translations which were used by Kumārajiva as the basis for comparison. He was honoured with the title *Kuo-Shih*, the national preceptor. From 402 A.D. he and his colleagues poured forth a steady stream of translations, which included some of the most important items in the Chinese canon. The *Amitābhasutra*, basic text of the Pure Land School in China, was translated in 204 A.D. Next year Kumārajiva started on the *Perfection of Wisdom* in 25,000 lines and completed it in 404 A.D. In this year, the *Treatise in One Hundred Verses* was also completed, this work, together with the *Treatise on the Middle* and the *Treatise on the Twelve Gates* finished in 409 A.D. constituted the basic *texts* of the San-Lun School in China. In 405 A.D. he completed a massive work, 100 Chūan, *Treatise on the Great Perfection of Wisdom.* In the following year, he finished two important Mahāyāna *Sutras*, the Lotus of the Good Law and the Sutra spoken by Vimalakirti. In 410 A.D., appeared the translation of the Sutras on the ten stages, and in 412 A.D. the treatise on the Completion of Truth. Another work translated into Chinese between 402 A.D.—412 A.D. by him was the *Mahāmāyuri- Vidyāranjanu, Tāntrikadhārni,* translated into Chinese by Kumarajiva between 402-412 A.D.[18]

Through his translations, Kumārajiva was responsible for the establishment of an important Mahāyāna School in China, the San-Lun or School of the Three Treatises. The three treatises, all translated by Kumārajiva, which form the basis of this school are *Chung-lun* (Treatise on the Middle), the *Po-lun* (Treatise in One Hundred Verses), and the *Shiherh-men Lun* (Treatise on the Twelve Gates).[19]

Buddhasena was a scholar in Buddhist learning. His specialisation was yoga, a discipline in which the Chinese were very much interested. The Chinese monk, Tche-yen, who was in Kashmir at that time, persuaded Buddhasena to accompany him to China so as to get the latter's manual precisely entitled as Yogācārabhumi to be translated into Chinese. Buddhasena did not return to India.[20]

Buddhabhadra, a clansman of the Buddha, met the Chinese monk Chih-yen in Kashmir while the latter was studying under Buddhasena. he was persuaded to go to China. He first arrived Ch'ang-an in c 408, A.D.,when Kumarajiva was still the arbiter of Buddhist learning. Disagreements apparently arose between the two over some aspects of discipline, Kumārajiva had been provided with royal quarters, and also with the pleasures of the inner apartments, which to a strict disciplinarian monk like Buddhabhadra were undesirable. It appears that doctrinal differences also were responsible for the lack of rapport between the two. Kumārajiva belonged to Mahāyān school, whereas Buddhabhadra was a Sarvāstivāda adherent. Buddhabhadra first went to Lu-shan, where he was warmly welcomed by Hui-yuan, who had already heard of his reputation as a *dhyāna* master. Through the translation activity of Buddhabhadra, the teachings of one of the most famous masters of Dhyāna, Buddhasena, were introduced to the Chinese.[21] He also translated into Chinese Avatamsāka of Mahāyān literature in the beginning of the 5th century A.D. Its text Buddhavataṁisāka Mahāvaipulva Sutra consists of sixty chapters.[22]

Gautam Sanghadeva or in the Chinese Kiu-tan Seng-kia-thpo, meaning community God, was a Kashmiri Buddhist monk, who went to China in 384 A.D. He remained in North China until 391 A.D., and afterwards went to South China.[23] He was in China when Sangabhuti was also there. In collaboration with Fo-mien, he translated into Chinese the first of the Seven Sarvāstivāda Abhidharma texts in 380 A.D. His other translations were Madhyamāgama sūtra similar to Majjhima Nikāya of Hināyāna school named in Chinese transliteration kun-o-han- king, the Abhidarma Hridayaśāstra in 391 A.D., and Tridharmaka sāstra in 397-398 A.D. In all, he translated eight works into Chinese. One of them was lost in 730 A.D.[24]

Buddhayaśas, another Kashmiri, and a friend of Kumārajiva arrived in Ch'ang-an in 408 A.D. Between 410-413 A.D., he translated four works into Chinese. Notable among them were Dirghagama and Dharamaguptaka-Vinaya. Besides these he translated Abhidharama-prakaranapāda Śāstra of Vasumitra, with the help of Gunabhadra.[25] Vimalaksha was also an associate of Kumārajiva, who worked with him in the translation work in China. Ater Kumārajiva's death, in 413 A.D., he went to South China and worked there for the rest of his life. One of his two works is not traceable since 730 A.D. The surviving work is Daśadhāya-Vinaya-Nidana or preface to Daśadhya Vinaya. The Kashmiri missionaries had also worked in South China. Buddhajiva, a collaborator and companion of Fa-hsien, reached South China by sea in 423 A.D. He was a follower of Mahiśāska school and taught Vinaya in Kashmir.[26]

Fa-hsien, during his travels in Central Asia and India, had collected a large number of Sanskrit manuscripts. Buddhajiva translated some of them into the Chinese. Out of three Vinaya translations one is lost and two Mahiśaska Vinaya and Pratimoksha of Mahiśaska are available. He seems to have remained in China until his death.[27]

There were a host of Kashmiri monks in China engaged in the translation work. Some of them were Punyatrata, Suraj Gupta, Dharamayaśas, Dharma Mitra, Prajna, (Tien-si-Tsi-in Chinese transliteration) Buddhavarman, and Guṇabhadra. Dharma Mitra translated Ākāśagarbha Bodhisattvadharni Sutra. Buddhavarman, a specialist in Vibhāsa, translated Mahavibhāsa śāstra in sixty chapters. Gunabhadra translated Saṁyaktāgama.[28]

Guṇavarman, unparalleled among the missionaries in proselytisation, was a scion of the royal family of Kashmir.[29] He spurned the crown to kiss the cross, with unflinching devotion and dedication, he converted the whole of Java and the neighbouring islands to the Buddhist faith.[30] He was a laureate, having committed thousands of *sutras* to memory. He belonged to Sarvāstivad School. Guṇavarman's fame spread far and wide and the emissaries from neighbouring islands came in large numbers inviting him to visit their homeland. The Buddhist theologians in China requested their Emperor to invite Guṇavarman. The Emperor sent emissaries to Guṇavarman with an invitation to visit China. He agreed and reached Nanking in 431 A.D. after converting nearly all the islands on the way.[31] The Emperor personally received him at Nanking, and built a magnificent monastery for him—Jetavanvihara—after the name of the famous monastery in India. Guṇavarman was not destined to live long and died a year after, in 432 A.D. But the last year of his life was full of intense activity. He translated eleven Sanskrit works into Chinese. He expounded and preached Sadharma Pundarika at Nanking and did much to advance the spiritual welfare of the people. He organised a Sangha of Chinese nuns for the first time. His one year stay at Nanking matches with Kumārajiva's lifelong labours at Ch'ang-an.[32]

In the 7th century A.D., three scholars from Kashmir, viz., Buddhapala, Ratnācinta and Arjun proceeded to China and translated a number of Buddhist books into Chinese.[33] Ratnācinta was a specialist in Vinaya. He reached O-yang in China in 693 A.D., and founded a monastery, named Tien-Chu-sse, i.e., 'The Monastery of India' and translated seven works from Sanskrit between 693 to 706 A.D. He died in 721 A.D.[34]

During the 10th century A.D., the Chinese annals mention the name of Tien-si-tsai, a native of Kashmir, who came to the capital of China, Nanking, and the Chinese Emperor made him the in-charge of the Board of Translators. As a result of his efforts that the Board was able to enrich the Chinese Buddhist literature by more than two hundred works.[35]

In 1005, another Kashmiri monk, Mu-lo-she-ki (name in the Chinese transliteration) went to China and carried on the missionary work in collaboration with many more Indian monks.[36]

## Chinese Pilgrim Students In Kashmir

The activities of the Kashmir missionaries in China had a great effect upon the Chinese. It aroused greater interest than before among the Chinese for Buddhism and Indian culture. The Chinese scholars inspired and intoxicated with their adopted religion, visited Kashmir and India so as to know Buddhism at its source and came in direct contact with Buddhist culture.

Fa-yong, accompanied by a party of 25 monks visited India in 420 A.D. They stayed in Kashmir for one year to study Sanskrit language and the Buddhist lore.[37]

Hiuen Tsang, the illustrious Chinese pilgrim, travelled for 16 years (629-645 A.D.) through Central Asia and India. On his arrival in Kashmir, he was given a royal welcome. He remained in Kashmir for two years studying select *Sutras and śāstras* and visited sacred Buddhist places.[38]

Wukong came to India in 751 A.D. during the Tang period in China. He spent several years in Kashmir, studying the Buddhist texts.[39]

Oukong known also as Dharmadhatu came to Kashmir in 759 A.D. through the Kabul valley and Gandhara. He lived in Kashmir for four years, and took the vows of a Buddhist monk. He studied Sanskrit and learnt Vinaya in seven sections from three teachers. In the convent of Mong-te or Mundi Vihara, he learnt the Śilas and studied Vinaya of the Mūlasārvāstivād.[40]

## Contribution of Kashmir To Chinese Buddhism

"Kashmir" says P.C. Bagchi, "takes the leading part in the transmission of Buddhist traditions directly to China. The number of Buddhist scholars who went to China from Kashmir is longer than that of those who went from other parts of India. Kashmir was the most flourishing centre of Buddhist learning in this period. It was the centre of the most powerful Buddhist sect of Northern India, the Sarvastivada".[41]

According to a Buddhist tradition, Buddha is said to have made a forecast to Vajrapani and Madhyandina that a disciple of Ananda would propagate his religion in Kashmir a land of blue forests 'Nilanilam vanarajim'.[42]

His forecast proved true. Kashmir not only taught to China Sarvāstivāda, and Mahāyān doctrine, but also was an important academic centre for the study of Abhidharama texts. Vasubandhu condensed the texts into one book called *Abhidharma mokśsakarika*, the book being terse, he wrote a commentary on it. Commentary of Vasubandhu was a classic work. The Kashmiri scholars translated it into Chinese, which is still widely studied in all Buddhist monasteries in China.[43]

The period between 380-385 A.D. was characterised by the influx of foreign missionaries in China and the translation of several important scriptures into Chinese. Some of these foreigners came directly from Kashmir, the stronghold of Sarvāstivāda school of Hinayān Buddhism. The vast scholastic systematisations in the field of Abhidarma for which this school was famous were still unknown in China. Among the missionaries who opened this literature to the Chinese, the pioneers were the Kashmiri specialists Sanghadeva and Sanghabhadra. They reached Ch'ang-an in China around 381 A.D.[44]

Among the prominent Kashmiri missionaries on yoga, was Dharambhiksu, the master of yoga, who became very popular among the Chinese students.[45] Many of them came to Kashmir to study, "What they were calling the *dhyāna,* that is to say a Buddhistic form of yoga, purified and spiritualised, which was being cultivated in that country with predilection."[46]

Kumarajiva is traditionally regarded as the first teacher of Madhayāmika doctrines in China, and an expounder of Ch'eng-Shih Tsung[47] and Nieh-p'an-tsung.[48] He is a symbol of the spirit of cultural cooperation between India and Central Asia and of the efforts made by Buddhist scholars to spread Indian culture in China.[49]

Through the efforts and indefatigable labours of these selfless missionaries in the earliest of the 4th century, the Chinese people began to adopt Buddhist monastic rituals.[50] During this period a number of monasteries were established in northern China.

Ratnācinta, a Kashmiri monk, founded 'Tien-chu sse' monastery.[51] The many-storeyed towers called pagodas in China are in their origin *stupas* erected over relics in India and Kashmir.[52] These Kashmiri and Indian monks gave Sino Buddhism, Buddhist literature, Indian sculpture and painting, and endowed it with "component parts of Indian civilization and culture."[53] The Kashmiri scholars also established with the help of the Chinese different schools Buddhism which were products of the Chinese response to Buddhism, and indicated how the Chinese mind took over certain basic Buddhistic principles and reshaped them to suit the Chinese temperament, so that the schools were no longer Indian systems introduced into China, but were really schools of Chinese Buddhism. Such were the T'ien-t' ai, Hua-yen, Pure land, and Ch'an.[54]

The Kashmiri missionaries influenced the Chinese in the concentration of mind, mindfulness, meditation, and equanimity.[55] Another impact of the translation made by the Kashmiri Buddhists, was inculcating in the Chinese a desire to translate the scriptures themselves. Thus they attained proficiency in Sanskrit language. The new terms coined by the Buddhists gradually found their way into the Chinese vocabulary, and in the course of time they have been fully accepted by them, who never suspected that they originated from some foreign language.[56] The introduction of Sanskrit alphabet into China influenced phonological studies in a number of ways. The first is the introduction of *fan-ch' ieh* system. Heretofore, the Chineses had attempted to indicate the pronunciation of a character by the use of homonyms, but in the *fan-ch' ieh* system the initial sound of the first character is combined with the final sound of the second to give the pronunciation. This method was undoubtedly influenced by the Chinese experience, with the Sanskrit alphabet. Close acquaintance with the Sanskrit alphabet led to another innovation of great importance in phonology, namely, the formulation of the thirty *tzu-mu* or phonetic radicals by the monk Shou-wen during the latter half of the T'ang dynasty. There is still another phonological contribution for which Buddhism is responsible, namely, the reconstruction of Chinese pronunciations of the past.[57]

Worship of Buddha by repeating his names, offering prayers to him, and singing his praise were popular both in India, (Kashmir) and China.[58] The Chinese religious life became more meaningful by assimilating the teachings of Buddhism in terms of human sympathy, love and compassion for all living creatures. Its doctrines of *Karma*, immortality of the souls, and ultimately salvation brought spiritual consolation to countless numbers. One by-product of the compassionate concern for all living beings was the establishment of charitable institutions.[59] Buddhist philosophy especially its conception of reality which permeated everything in nature and the notion of universal impermanence, had an abiding influence on the poets and artists, and influenced their aesthetic outlook. Buddhism also brought to the Chinese a deep religious feeling and a profound faith, which inspired great works of art in China, such as in Yun-Kang, Hung-men, Tunhuang and other places.[60]

The translation work of the Kashmiri monks in China is creditable. Their labours gave to Buddhism in China, its own identity, which is known as the Chinese Buddhism. For carrying out the translation work and to maintain Buddhist contacts between India and China, the Sung Emperor established the Imperial Institute for Transmission of Buddhism.[61] The establishment of the Institute synchronised with the arrival of the Indian and Kashmiri monks to the Sung Court.[62]

The Kashmiri monk Dharmabhadra and his cousin Danapala, after their arrival in China 980 A.D., took up the charge of the Institute and translated most of the canons. As a result of their indefatigable labour ninety works were produced.[63] The missionary and literary activities of Fahsien, Buddhabhadra, and Kumārajiva greatly contributed towards the growth and diffusion of Buddhist literature.[64]

The hospitality extended to the Chinese pilgrim students in Kashmir was proverbial. Hiuen-Tsang was treated as a royal guest, and was given all sorts of amenities.[65] The king kanishkā, appointed some scores of monks headed by *Bhatanta Yas'a* to help Hiuen-Tsang. The Queen Amritaprabha, the wife of King

Meghavahana, according to Kalhana, built a *vihara* for the foreign monks.[66] The efforts of the Kashmiri missionaries conquered the hearts of the Chinese Emperors. They began inviting Buddhist scholars to China. The increased intercourse with the Indians naturally led to a further advancement of Buddhism in China, and ushered in what may be called its most glorious period in that country.[67]

## References

1. *Encyclopaedia of Religion and Ethics*, ed. James Hastings, 1940, p. 201. The Buddhism, founded towards the end of the 6th century B.C. "is one of the three great world religions. Its original and essential doctrine is that all earthly existence is suffering, which could be overcome through renuncination and ultimately *nirvan* or eternal death."
2. L' introduction du bouddhism dons le Kashmir, *Journal Asiatique*, Paris, Dec. 1865, pp. 486-487; *Kashmir, Buddha Jayanti Number*, July 1956, An article by Nalinaksha Dutt, *Buddhism in Kashmir*, p.158.
3. James Hastings, *op.cit*.
4. *Mahavastu,* I, pp. 124-150.
5. K.S. Kenneth Ch'en, *Buddhism in China*, New York, 1957, Princeton 1964, pp. 12, 80.
6. *Ibid*., Like the Pali canon, it consits of three parts: the *Vinaya* or Rules of Discipline, *Sutras* or discourses of Buddha, *Abhidharma*, the Higher Discourses.
7. Sir Charles Eliot, *Hinduism and Buddhism*, London, 1921, Reprint, New York: Barnes & Noble, 1971, I, p. XXVI. It came first by land from Central Asia. The official date for its introduction by this route is 62 A.D. But it was probably known within the Chinese frontier, before that time, though not recognised by the State. After the fourth century many of these religious journeys were made by sea and it was thus that Bodhidharma landed at Canton in 520 A.D. A third stream of Buddhism, namely Lamaisam, came into China under the Mongol dynasty in 1280 A.D.
8. Jean Naudou, *Buddhists of Kashmir*, Delhi, 1980, p.3.
9. *Ibid*., p. 2.

10. *Ibid.*; S. Lévi, *Journal Asiatique*, Paris, Jan. Feb. 1915, p. 60.
11. Jean Naudou, *op.cit.*, p. 2. A summary of that Vibhāsā, translated into Chinese in 383 by a Kashmiri named Sanghabhadra, may be also the work of a monk of Kashmir, whose Sanskrit name is concealed in the Chinese transcription Che-t'o-p'an-ni; P. Demie'ville, *Les Sources Chinoises, L' Inde Classique*, Calcutta, 1938, Tome II, pp. 398-437.
12. P.C. Bagchi, *India and China*, Bombay, 1950 p. 35.
13. B. Nanjio, *A Catalogue of the Chinese Translation of the Buddhist Tripitaka, The sacred canon of the Budhhists in China and Japan*, Oxford, 1833, No. 1289.
14. K.S. Kenneth Ch'en, *op.cit.*, pp. 82-84.
15. P.N. Bose, *Indian Teachers in China,* Madras, 1923 p. 61; K.M. Panikkar, *India and China*, Asia Publishing House, 1957, p. 28; P.N. Bagchi, *op.cit.*, pp. 47-48; Rahul Saṁnkritayan, *Yatra Ke Panne* (Hindi), p. 191; Radhakrishnan, *India and China*, Bombay, 1944, p. 27.
16. P.N. Bose, *op.cit.*, p. 61; S. Kuroda, *Outline of Mahayan*, p. 23, Kumārajiva reached China in 491 A.D., whereas S.C. Dass, in *Indian Pandits in the Land of Snow*, Indian Reprint, Delhi, 1978, says that he reached China in 408 A.D.
17. Sir Charles Eliot, *op.cit.*, Vol. ii, pp. 41, 55, 84, 85; Vol. III 203 sq., pp. 210, 247, 251, 294, 313, 321, 373.
18. *Journal of U.P. Historical Society*, Vol. XV, p. 26f.; *Kashmir, Budha Jayanti Number*, op.cit., A paper by P. Dattatreya, p. 174. The most influential of the many works translated by Kumarajiva and his collaborators was the *Saddarmapundarika* "Lotus Flower Scripture of Mysterious Law". There had been three or four translations of it before, but not apparently with great success......It is an amazing work, a drama of time and eternity.
19. Kenneth Ch'en, *op.cit.*, pp. 82-85.; Bagchi, *Le Canon Bouddhique on Chine,* Paris, 1927, Tome 1, p. 183.
20. Jean Naudou, *op.cit.*, p. 4.
21. *Ibid.*; Eliot, *op.cit.*, ii, p. 85; Kenneth Ch'en, *op.cit.*, pp. 107, 109.
22. P.C. Bagchi, *India and China op.cit.*, p. 140; Sarla Khosla, *History of Buddhism in Kashmir*, Delhi, 1972, p. 148.
23. P.C. Bagchi, *op.cit.*, pp. 211-212; P.N. Bose, *op.cit.*, p. 54; *Nanjio catalogue*, No. 1288.; *Kashmir Budh Jayanti Number op.cit.*, p.

175. Being a master of Abhidharma he wrote several books on this branch of Buddhism and also revised many previous translations of the texts. He had acquired a great proficiency in the Chinese language. Later on he came to know that a powerful school of Buddhist learning had been established at Lu-Shan in the South of China by a Sogdian monk, Huiyuan, who by the way played a great part in the co-ordination of Buddhist learning in China. Gautamasangha therefore decided to go to Lu-Shan and reaching there in 391 A.D., he gave hismelf up heart and soul to the propagation of the Buddhist doctrine.

24. *Ibid.*
25. P.N. Bagchi, *op.cit.*, pp. 133, 206; *Nanjio catalogue, op.cit.*, No. 1292.
26. P.N. Bose, *op.cit.*, p. 69.
27. *Ibid.*, p. 73; P.C. Bagchi, *op.cit.*, p. 39.
28. P.N. Bose, *op.cit.*, p.73; P.C. Bagchi, *op.cit.*, pp. 133, 140, 206.
29. Ganhar, *Buddhism in Kashmir and Ladakh*, Srinagar, n.d., p. 77.
30. Nanjio Cat., *op.cit.*, Nos. 137, 138; Eliot, *op.cit.*, iii, pp. 176-177.
31. PNK Bamzai, *A History of Kashmir*, Delhi, 1962 p. 103.
32. P.C. Bagchi, *op.cit.*, pp. 39, 40, 212; P.N. Bose, *op.cit.*, pp. 75, 79-80, 81.
33. Jan Yuan Hua, "Kashmir's contribution to the expansion of Buddhism in the Far East", *Indian Historical Quarterly*, Vol. XXVII, 1961, p. 98.
34. *Kashmir Budh Jayanti Number*, *op.cit.*, p. 176.
35. *Ibid.*
36. *Ibid.*
37. P.C. Bagchi, *op.cit.*, p. 65.
38. *Kashmir Budh Jayanti Number, op.cit.*, "Yuan Chwang on Kashmir," an article by Radha Kumud Mookerjee, p. 162; P.C. Bagchi, *op.cit.*, pp. 65, 70-71; P.N. Bose, *op.cit.*, p. 113; Thomas Watters, *On Yuan Chwang Travels in India*, Indian Reprint, Delhi, 1961, *vol. I, p. 259;* Samuel Beal, *Si-Yuki*, London, 1889, ii, p. 72.
39. P.C. Bagchi, *op.cit.*, p. 78.
40. Thomas Watters, *op.cit.*, pp. 258-59.
41. P.C. Bagchi, *op.cit.*

42. *Kashmir Budh Jayanti Number, op.cit.*, An article by Nalinaksha Dutt, p. 158. Buddha Said, "He would further subdue the malevolent Huluta Naga, and extend the seat on which he would sit cross-legged miraculously to cover the whole of Kashmir and thereby ousting the Nagas from their habitation, and making the vast country of 60,000 villages an abode of meditating monks."
43. *Ibid.*, p. 159.
44. E. Zürcher, *The Buddhist Conquest of China*, Leiden, 1959, i, p. 202.
45. Jean Naudou, *op.cit.*, p. 4.
46. P. Demieville, *op.cit.*, Tome II, pp. 398-437.
47. The Satyasidüdhi School.
48. The Nirvan School.
49. P.V. Bapat, ed., *2500 Years of Buddhism,* 2nd ed., 1964, pp. 239-241.; Sir Charles Eliot, *op.cit.*, p. 204.; S. Lévi, *Journal Asiatique*, 1913, II, p. 344.
50. P.V. Bapat, ed., *op.cit.*, An Article by G.H. Sasaki, "Principal Schools and Sects of Buddhism," p. 124.
51. *Kashmir Budh Jayanti Number*, p. 176.
52. Eliot, iii, *op.cit.*, p. 325.
53. P.N. Bose, *op.cit.*, p. 145.
54. Kenneth Ch'en, *op.cit.*, p. 297.
55. *Ibid.*, p. 472.
56. Thus Prajn̄āparamitā became pan-jo po-lo-mi-to, *nibbana* became nieh-pan, *arhat* or *arahan* became a-lo-han, *dhyāna* became ch'an., vide, Kenneth Ch'en, *op.cit.*, p. 372.
57. *Ibid.*, p. 484.
58. Lalmani, *Studies in the Buddhistic Culture of India*, p. 75.
59. *Ibid.*
60. P.V. Bagat, ed., *op.cit.*, An article by P.C. Bagchi "Central Asia and China".
61. Buddha Prakash, ed., *Studies in Asian History and Culture*, 1970, An article by Jan-Yun-Hua, Ch'uan-Fa Yuan, The Imperial insitute for transmission of Buddha-Dharma in Sung China, pp. 71-72.

62. *Fo-tus T'ung-Chi, A General Record of Buddha and Patriarchs*, compiled by Monk Chih-p' an in 1258-1269 A.D.; *Taisho Shinshu daizokyo*, (Taisho editon of Tripitaka in Chinese), No. 2035, Tokyo, 1924-34.
63. Buddha Prakash, ed., *op.cit.*
64. Rahul Saṁkritayan, *Buddha Saṁskriti,* Calcutta, 1952; P.K. Mukherjee, *Indian Literature in China and Far East*.
65. Thomas Watters , *op.cit.*, Vol i, p. 69.
66. Kalhana's *Rajatarangini*, i. Third Book, Stanza 9, commentary by Raghunath Singh, Varanasi, 1976.

    भोगाय देश्यभिक्षणां वल्लभाऽस्याऽमृत प्रभा ।
    विहार मुच्चैरमृत भवनाख्यमकारयत् ॥

67. P.C. Bagchi, *Sino-Indian Studies*, vol. 1, pp. 1-17, 65-84.

# 15

# SOURCES OF THE HISTORY OF KASHMIR

The Indians, before the advent of the Muslims into India, did not maintain historical records almost as a rule. There was no system of maintaining archives and repositories. This scarcity in historical literature is aptly expressed by Dr. R.C. Majumdar : "We have to admit that the literary genius of India, so active and fertile in almost all conceivable branches of study, was not applied to chronicling the records of kings and fall of states and nations"[1]. Again, "It is a well-known fact that with the single exception of *Rajatarangini* (History of Kashmir), there is no historical text in Sanskrit dealing with the whole or even parts of India."[2] But it should never mean that the sources for the study of the history and culture of Kashmir are very few and far between, though it is very unfortunate the scholars do not take the trouble of going beyond *Rajatarangini.*

The Greek, Chinese and indigenous records and accounts form a very important source of information for the period preceding tenth century A.D. For the period between tenth century to twelfth century, the sources may be divided into two broad categories : Muslim chronicles or Arabic literature and Kashmir chronicles.

### Muslim Chronicles

Among the Muslim sources Al-Beruni's India is a mine of information. It is trustworthy and most reliable on topography, routes, sacred places and customs and manners of the people. Stein is all praise for Al-Beruni's critical acumen and laborious research and says that "he could look through the mountains".[3] Al-Beruni utilized his long stay at Ghazna and in the Punjab (1017-30 A.D.) to collect information on Kashmir. In the first chapter of his book, *Kitab-ul-Hind*, he writes that Mahmud of Ghazna "utterly ruined the prosperity of the country (of India), and performed those wonderful exploits by which the Hindus became like atoms of dust scattered in all directions".[4] That was the reason, according to Al-Beruni, that Hindu sciences fled to places like Kashmir and Benares.[5] He refers to Kashmir as the high school of Hindu learning and repeatedly mentions Kashmiri authors. It appears that among his informants, if not among his actual teachers, there were Kashmiri scholars.[6] He makes a particular mention of his Kashmiri informants with whom he conversed regarding the miracles of Kudaishahr, i.e., the Kaptesvara Tirtha. The way in which pilgrimage to this place was described to Al-Beruni makes it quite certain that the narrators had personal experience of the Tirtha. The same holds good about his note on the pilgrimage to the temple of Sarada.[7] The details regarding a local Kashmiri festival and the anecdote about the propagation of the Sisyahitavritti in Kashmir could not have reached him but by verbal communications.[8] Al-Beruni also refers to Kashmiri almanac, which in the opinion of Stein, could only be secured through Kashmiri Pandits.[9]

Abu Raihan Muhammad Ibn Ahmad Al-Beruni composed certain Sanskrit treatises and circulated them among the people of Kashmir. This speaks of special relations which he had with Kashmir. He graphically narrates the rigid isolation of the Valley. Such a statement could only be possible when he had direct contacts with the people of the Valley.[10] There is much strength in Mark Aurel Stein's opinion that Al-Beruni accompanied Mahmud of Ghazna in his unsuccessful invasion of Kashmir, which probably took place in 1021 A.D. It afforded him ample opportunities to acquaint himself with the topography of the region with local assistance.[11]

Al-Beruni's account of Kashmir is mainly contained in chapter XVIII, which gives "various notes on the countries of the Hindus, their rivers and ocean"[12]. Fortunately, it is more detailed with regard to Kashmir. Al-Beruni gives in broad outlines the political division of the mountain region which lies between the great Central Asian watershed and the Punjab plain. He refers to the pedestrian habits of the people and the use of palkis by the nobles. The description is very precise and is corroborated by Kalhana. He further observes :

> "They are particularly anxious about the natural strength of their country, and therefore take always much care to keep a strong hold upon the entrances and roads leading into it. In consequence it is very difficult to have any commerce with them. In former times they used to allow one or two foreigners to enter their country, particularly Jews, but at present they do not allow any Hindu whom they do not know personally to enter, much less other people."[13]

Al-Beruni gives a vivid picture of the Kashmir Valley. The capital is correctly described as "being built along both banks of the river Jhelam, which are connected with each other by bridges and ferry-boats". The climate of Kashmir, as described by Al-Beruni, is far more exact than any other account available to us previous to the second quarter of the nineteenth century.[14]

Al-Beruni's account is not only scientific but the only detailed account available in regard to Kashmir for the first quarter of the eleventh century A.D. His historical perspective, penetrating insight and deep understanding could not be overestimated.

> "He does not blindly accept", says Professor Sachau, "the traditions of former ages; he wants to understand and criticise them. He wants to sift the wheat from the chaff, and he will discard everything that militates against the laws of nature and of reason."[15]

*Muru' Fu-L Zaheb* of Al-Masudi is another Arabic work on India with a passing reference about Kashmir. He was a great traveller and an acute observer. He deservedly continues to be one of the most admired writers in Arabic. His book, which was translated into English by Sprenger with the name *Meadows of Gold*,[16] gives only that Kashmir is a kingdom with many towns and villages enclosed by very high and inaccessible mountains, through which leads a single passage closed by a gate. The number of towns and villages is estimated at from sixty to seventy thousand.[17] This scanty detail by this well travelled observer is due to habitual and physical seclusion of the people and the country in those days. He died in Egypt in 345 A.H. (956 A.D.).

*Muzhatu-L Mushtak* of Al-Idrisi gives a brief reference about Kashmir. He was born at Centa, in Morocco, towards the close of the eleventh century.[18]

**Kashmir Chronicles**

The Kashmir Śaiva philosopher, literary critic and intellectual giant, Abhinavagupta, was born between 950 and 960 A.D. in a Brahmin family, which had migrated from Kanauj to Kashmir during the reign of King Lalitaditya. He was a prolific writer whose works cover a wide range of subjects —Dramaturgy, Rhetoric, Philosophy and Philosophy of Poetry. His main contribution is to Śaiva philosophy and his expositions are simply superb.[19] His attitude to life and its chief actor—man—is summed up in this couplet:

> यस्त च पादौ च मनुश्चौ च सुसयतम ।
> विधा तपश्च शील च स तीर्थफसमश्नुते ॥

> "He Whose hands, feet, mind, learning, religious austerity and conduct are well balanced (restrained), enjoys the fruits of pligrimage (even without going there)."[20]

Kshemaraja, who flourished in the reign of Samgramaraja (1003-1028 A.D.), wrote many treatises, such as *Shiva-Sutra-Vritti*, *Spandasandoha* and many commentaries on Tantras. *Shiva-Sutra-Vritti* is important with regard to Saivism in Kashmir.

Kashemendra, rightly regarded as the doyen among the Sanskrit poets of Kashmir and among the Kashmir chroniclers, is the most useful authority. He was born on the Dal in the locality where the Nishat Bagh now stands in the days of Ananta. Kshemendra's father, Prakashachandra, was a rich man but very learned and of generous temperament. The exact date of Kshemendra's birth is unknown but his literary career runs from 1037 to 1066 A.D. Kshemendra studied at the feet of several teachers but notable among them is Gangaka. His studies covered Hindu Law, Sanskrit grammar, politics, medicine, music and painting. He is said to be the author of many books, of which thirty-four are believed to be available.

Kalhana has criticised his *Nripavali* for many errors and accuses him of "consistent carelessness".[34] Keith in his *History of Sanskrit Literature*, has discussed Kshemendra's *Brihatkatha Manjari* and other works at some length.

In *Samayamatrika*, one of Kshemendra's best poems, an attempt has been made to describe the snares of courtesans. It is a collection of stories, in which there is an interesting account of the wanderings of his heroine Kankali through the length and breadth of the Valley. Numerous places of her wandering are traceable on the map. These places have been described with local variations and colour, which make the rendering extremely interesting. In this poem we, for the first time, find mention of the Pir Panjal Pass (Pancaladhara) and its hospice (matha). We also get a glimpse of the ancient salt trade routes. It also mentions a Buddhist convent, the Krityasrama Vihar, where Kankali's conduct as a nun is the cause of no small scandal. His portrayals have a social content. Unlike the chroniclers of his time, he has not neglected the ordinary people.[22]

Stein remarks:

> "His works, composed in the second and third quarter of the eleventh century, form important landmarks in several fields of Indian literature. Kshemendra seems to have had a genuine interest, rare enough among Indian scholars, for the realities of his country and the life around him".[23]

Mankha, the fourth son of Veshovrata and grandson of Pandit Mammata, was a great poet of independent mind. Ruyyaka, the celebrated author of *Alankarasarvasva*, was the teacher of Mankha. Mankha rose to the post of the Director of Dharmarth and also became the Foreign Minister. Raja Sussala looked upon him as a great philosopher. Mankha was the contemporary of Kalhana. He wrote his first book *Shrikanthacarita* at the age of twenty-five, probably in 1039 A.D.[24] The book, though brief, is similar in character to Bilhana's *Vikramankadevacharita* in its description of Kashmir and Pravarapura. Jonaraja has written a commentary on this book which is very useful in explaining the points of local interest.[25]

Bilhana, the poet, was senior to Kalhana in age. He was born in Khonamoosha or Khonmuh, six miles from Srinagar. His father, Jyeshtha Kalasha, was a learned Brahmin and an authority in Sanskrit grammar.[26] Finding no scope for his talents, he bade good-bye to his native land at the tender age of sixteen in the reign of King Kalasha (1063-1089 A.D.).[27] He visited important places in Northern India and travelled to the Deccan. He became famous as the court-poet of the Chalukya King Tribhuvanmalla Parmardi of the South. He is the author of *Vikramankadevacharita, Karna-Sundari Mala* and *Chaurapanchasika.*

In the last Canto of his historical poem, the *Vikraman kadevacharita*, Bilhana vividly describes the beauties of the Kashmir Valley and its capital. The main importance of the poem consists of the exactitude of the topography. Professor Buhler, during his tour of Kashmir in 1875, had the satisfaction of visiting the poet's birth place, the present village of Khonmuh, and verifying on the spot every point of the description which Bilhana gives of that "coquettish embellishment of the bosom of Mount Himalaya".[35] As a poet his style and language is very lucid and enchanting.

The *Lokaprakasha* is a very useful dictionary (*kosh*) compiled through the efforts of many scholars including Kshemendra. It is particularly useful for the study of the social life and administrative structure. In Book II the name of Shahjahan finds mention, which suggests that some portion of the work was compiled as late as the seventeenth century A.D. The work represents a strange mixture of the usual dictionary and a practical handbook dealing with the various topics of administration and private life in Kashmir.[29] Stein praises its secular character and is grateful for the topographical details which it gives.[30]

The *Lokaprakasha* consists of four parts. The first part deals with the four principal castes and sixty sub-castes. It also gives the titles of the ministers and officers of the state. The second part, which seems to have been written during the Muslim period in

Kashmir and upto the seventeenth century A.D., gives details about bills of exchange, bonds, commercial contracts, official orders and so forth. This part is the biggest and most important of all. The third part supplies us with a list of synonyms of different varieties of fish, birds and mice, and of salt, gold ornaments and gold coins. The fourth part begins with a satire on the Kayasthas (i.e., writers and physicians) and on Brahmins who had become Muslims. It also gives a list of the districts of Kashmir. The *Lokaprakasha* supplies the earliest list of Kashmir parganas. The pargana list contains local names of ancient date, side by side with comparatively modern ones. The only drawback of the work is that it is difficult to know exactly when the different sections were compiled.

**Mammata and Other Poets of the Period**

The beginning of the twelfth century A.D. saw three celebrated scholars decorating the literary firmament of Kashmir. They are Mammata and his two brothers. Mammata was the second son of the scholar Jaiyata Bhatta, the eldest was Jaiyata and Uvvata was the youngest. All the three brothers were noted litterateurs, but Mammata was the most distinguished of them all. His book *Kavya-Prakasha* on prosody is very valuable and is prescribed for higher examinations in Sanskrit language. Eighty seven commentaries are known to have been written on the *Kavya Prakasha* of which twenty five are available. Mammata is said to be the maternal uncle of Harsha, the great poet king of Kanauj. The *Shabda Vyapar Vichara* is another well-known work of Mammata on grammar in which the usage of words has been discussed.

The period under review has the rare distinction of having Kalhana's *Rajatarangini*, "The River of Kings"— the most important source of the history of Kashmir. But the whole ancestry and the life of the author is hidden in oblivion. Kalhana shares the common fate of the Indian authors of note whose memory lives solely in their works. The introductory note attached to the end of each book of the *Rajatarangini*, gives the name of the author as 'Kalhana', the son of the great Kashmiri minister, "the illustrious Lord Caṅpaka". Historical deductions reveal that he was a Brahmin by caste. The Sanskrit style of *Rajatarangini* is similar to that of the accepted style of the Pandits of Brahmin descent. The introduction to each book of his chronicle is begun by prayers to Shiva in his form of *Ardhanarishwar* representing the God in union with Parvati. Besides, Jonaraja, the continuator author of *Rajatarangini*, has referred to Kalhana with the epithet "dvija". A study of his chronicle displays his friendly attitude towards Buddhism. His faith may be epitomised in one word "eclecticism". The name Kalhana was derived through the Prakrit "Kalha" from the Sanskrit word "Kalyana", meaning "blessed".

Kalhana wrote his work during the years 1148-1149 A.D. The style and the spirit of the work shows that the author must have attained a mature age. The elaborate description of the sunsteady conditions of Sussal's reign (A.D. 1112-20) makes it clear that he must have been of age at that time. Hence, his probable date of birth might have been the beginning of the twelfth century.

The century of the birth of Kalhana was marked, in the history of Kashmir, by a dynastic upheaval resulting in many important political changes. King Harsha (1089-1101 A.D.) seemed at first to give Kashmir a period of good government but he fell victim to his own lavishness and extravagance. After his murder, Kashmir, for seven years more, witnessed civil wars which brought death and destruction in their train.

Kalhana was gifted with a scientific approach and a critical temperament. His portrayal of the various classes of Kashmiri people is very graphic and true to life. The reaction of the common folk to the disturbed political conditions of the time is full of realistic touches. He says that the people were "callously prepared to welcome any change". His description of the idle and indifferent city crowds and their feelings shows that he thoroughly understood the nature of his countrymen.

The unsettled political conditions of the time negatived all chances of patronage to the creative works of art; hence *Rajatarangini* was not written under the patronage of any king. Kalhana had a high sense of responsibilities. He considers only historians "worthy of praise, whose word, like that of a judge, keeps free from love or hatred in relating the facts of the past . . . . . "and surpasses even the stream of nectar,.... and can place the past times before the eyes of men."

It is interesting to note that Kalhana prepared himself for the role of a poet. The Sanskrit classical poetry cultivated by Kalhana reveals that he had an intensive training in the Indian rhetoric, the Alamkarshastra, and had equal mastery of Sanskrit grammatical lore. His literary studies were deep and comprehensive. All the known literature of his time, beginning from Epics to Kalidas's work *Raghuvansha and Meghaduta* and Bilhana's *Vikramankadevacharita* and *Harshacharita*, were read by him. Stein says : "His literary training, indeed, had been of the strictly traditional type and manner in which he employed it shows no conscious departure from the conventional norm. Yet it is clear that Kalhana was not a man of schools, absorbed in his Shastras".

Kalhana scrupulously studied the original sources including inscriptions of various kinds before the started writing, the *Rajatarangini*. He also studied coins and inspected buildings.

Kalhana found all possible avenues to his hereditary career closed on account of the unsettled political conditions of the country. So the best way to employ his talents, he thought, was to write down the history of his country from the ancient down to his own time. He was also inspired by regional patriotism. By painting a glorious picture of the past he wished that his countrymen should shed the inferiority complex, feel proud and try to emulate their past traditions. Therefore, the Great Asoka, he says, was the kind of the King whose examples were to be followed. It is Kalhana's sheer patriotism when he says :

> "Kashmir may be conquered by the force of spiritual merits, but not by the force of soldiers."

Kalhana has honestly and impartially related the events. While recording the contemporary happenings Kalhana has presented the principal figures in their individual characters and not as types. Here he represents a contrast to Bana and Bilhana in treating historical personages, who have painted their heroes all white and enemies all black.

The *Rajatarangini* is a class by itself in Indian literature. it is very much different from Charitas, which were composed under royal patronage. The scholar-poets of Charitas had the rare gift of inventing fables and myths and applying their talent in glorifying the achievements of their patrons. Their works are masterpieces of literature dabbling in subtle poetic art, rhetorical embellishment and Alaṁkarshastra. The *Rajatarangini* on the other hand, is the work of a detached and impartial mind, viewing the past and present with historical acumen and not in a spirit of hero worship or pleasing the patron. The *Rajatarangini* not only forms a class by itself in Sanskrit compositions but has a striking resemblance in character to the chronicles of medieval Europe and of the Islạmic East.

While writing the first three books (chapters) of the *Rajatarangini*, Kalhana made full use of tradition whether written or oral, and the chronicles which were evidently based on such traditions. In writing down these traditions, at times, the critic in Kalhana comes out. For instance, he mentions three traditions of the death of King Lalitaditya, without stating what is true, and comments : "When the great meet their end there arise stories indicative of their uncommon grandeur". King Meghavahan's exploits have been described in such a fancifiul manner that Kalhana himself is apprehensive that they might not be accepted as true but he tries to justify them by comparing them with the cruelties of Harsha, which, in their time might not be believed, but for them were eyewitness accounts.

For the last two chapters of his book the main sources were his contemporaries, his father, fellow-countrymen and his own memory. Thus many incidents of the treachery of Bhikasacara's troops, he categorically writes, were witnessed by him. It is no surprise that much of the history of the previous two generations, he got from his father and father's friends, who held keyposts in the royal court.

To give the details, *Rajatarangini* consist of eight books (chapters) of unequal size, written in Sanskrit in nearly 8,000 verses of rare literary merit. The text may roughly be divided into three sections:

1. Books I-III, are based on traditions.
2. In Books IV-VI, dealing with Karakota and Utpala dynasties, he has made use of the works of earlier

chroniclers who were contemporaries or near contemporaries of the events they described.

3. For Books VII-VIII, dealing with the two Lohara dynasties, he made use of personal knowledge and eyewitness accounts, the latter often perhaps received at second or third hand.

The style of *Rajatarangini* is not crude or difficult. These are scattered verses adorned in flowery language, or donned in fanciful imagery, in country Sanskrit. It goes to Kalhan's credit that, unlike *mahakavis* who create scope for a particular *rasa* in a poem, Kalhan simply 'uncovers' a particular rasa in a situation and appropriately, manifests it in creative treatment, without getting bogged down in conventional technicalities. Kalhana's idea was that even a historical text must be a work of art and he tried to make his work attractive to readers. His accounts are graphic and vivid except in his last two books, where so many characters are introduced without proper introduction. Kalhana who had maintained strict adherence to chronology from the beginning of the books had in the second and third sections not followed it to the letter. Evidently he was writing his book for those, who were familiar with the events of the period.

Kalhana in writing the *Rajatarangini* sets a tradition for history writing. His book, after him, was continued by four successive historians from the point where he left, to some years after Kashmir's annexation by the Mughal Emperor, Akbar.

The mission of a historian, according to Kalhana, is to make vivid before one's eyes pictures of a bygone age. History has a unique gift of immortalizing personages and events, and in this it even surpasses the mythical ambrosia, 'while the latter immortalizes only the man who drinks it, the former all those whom it touches'. Kalhana was aware that his work would not only achieve permanence, but would enliven all the actors as well as himself. He had another object also in view. He says : "This saga, which is properly made up, should be useful for Kings as a stimulant or a sedative, like a physic, according to time and place". Kalhana expected that both good and bad kings would derive profit from his work. He was a staunch advocate of historical impartiality.

Kalhana's assessment of more recent happenings is fair. He paints no character wholly black or white. He had the courage of conviction to criticise even the reigning king Jaisiṁha's reign[31], when political murders and diplomatic reprisals were order of the day. He gives a graphic account of sycophants, parasites and flatterers, holding high position in Jaisiṁha's government. He had deep insight into man's nature and his psychology. He says :

> "As in heaven the little clouds change shape, and take on the form of elephants, leopards, monsters, serpents, horses and other beasts —so do the waves of feeling change in the hearts of mortals, from kindness to harshness as the moments vary."

The didactic feature of *Rajatarangini* may be traced to the selection of *śanta rasa* in a sentiment of resignation. Here Kalhana's avowed motive is to show that material prosperity and royal possessions are objects of transitory glory. The evil acts of man recoil on him by the strange hands of destiny. About the exploitation of the subjects by the king, Kalhan says : 'The riches which the king amass by tormenting people go to the rivals or enemies or are consumed by fire."[32] Ill gotten wealth does not last long. In the same way, acts of policy, statecraft and individual conduct are again and again praised and analysed in the light of *Dharma* or *Nitishastra*.

The *Rajatarangini* appears to wage a war in favour of benevolent despotism and deprecates feudalism. Believing in orthodox *rajniti* (statecraft), Kalhana had his own conception of good government. Explicitly or implicitly the *Rajatarangini* carries the idea that a strong king is the ideal king, who has firm control over unruly elements, but is benevolent towards his people and sympathetic to their wishes. He chooses his ministers with discretion, and listens to their counsel with respect. Kalhana has shown his unflinching disapproval of the Damars, the petty feudal chiefs, who were the cause of anarchy and confusion in Kashmir since the death of Harsha. Another motive, perhaps, in writing the *Rajatarangini* was that of inspiring the kings of Kashmir with their ancient glory and prowess, and to curb the unruly elements, who aimed at making the king weak. He says :

> "The crab kill its father, and the white ant destroys its mother, but the ungrateful Kayasthas, when they become powerful, destroy everything."

At times Kalhan becomes pessimistic. The words put in the mouth of Harsha symbolises it :

"This land, after having been a virtuous women, has fallen like a prostitute into the arms of the insolent. Henceforth, whoever knows how to succeed by mere intrigue will aspire to that kingdom, whose power has gone". Here the historian shows his prophetic vision. He is no more simply a poet or a scholar.

The *Rajatarangini* is a saga showing the force of *karma.* Whatever good or bad a man does in this life, Kalhana believes, he reaps the harvest for that in the life to come. Often the force of karma shapes events and provides the basic moral sanction. Fate, according to Kalhana, is the second force influencing the human destiny. The Kashmiris were under the spell of fate, which made Kalhan to remark 'fate is the mine of all miracles'.[33] Fate is sometimes used as a synonym for God. God or the Gods often influence human affairs. Sometimes adverse fate is overcome by those who trust in their arms. Here also the *Rajatarangini* gives another hopeful message to his countrymen that whatever fate or the Creator might have in store for them, only a strong king confident of his powers could save Kashmir. The *Rajatarangini* interlinks *karma* of the kings with that of their subjects. Good kings arise through the merits of their subjects. A king and his subjects could mould the orders of nature.

This great work has also some shortcomings. The sources used by Kalhana were not critically analysed and discussed. His narrative becomes more legendary and anecdotal in the middle of the ninth century, when one seems to reach contemporary records.

> "Of the defects of the records and the conflicting opinions which according to Kalhana's introduction rendered his task difficult, we nowhere receive a distinct indication."

Fabulous stories, manifest impossibilities, exaggerations and supertitious beliefs have been described as historical truths, which betray his credulity. He has not separated historical legends from history. Similarly, Kalhana's chronology is also not based on scientific data. Of course, one cannot expect critical judgement in matters of chronology from an author who had started dating history from a legendary date of the coronation of Yudhisthira from the epics, and attributes three hundred years to a single ruler, Ranaditya. Kalhana could not and should not be blamed for this, as it was a general trend among Indians, so precisely described by Al-Beruni:

> "Unfortunately the Hindus do not pay much attention to the historical order of things, they are very careless in relating to chronological succession of their kings, and when they are pressed for information, and are at a loss, not knowing what to say they invariably take to tale- telling."

The *Rajatarangini* also presents a contrast within itself–its earlier part is more of a fiction, and the later part, that is early medieval part, is real history. It vividly described the falling glory of Kashmir,—palace intrigues, murders, seditions, civil wars and treachery. The life of the ordinary common folk has not been touched. It is the history of kings, royal families and nobility, justifying the title "River of the Kings".

Kalhana's work was continued by Jonaraja, Srivara, Prajabatta and Suka. The *Rajatarangini* has made Kalhana immortal but Kalhana himself was sure about the worth of his work.

Even the gods must die ;
But sovereign poetry remains,
Stronger than death.

## References

1. R. C. Majumdar, ed. *The Vedic Age*, Bombay, 1965, p.47.
2. C. H. Philips, ed., *Historians of India, Pakistan and Ceylon*, Great Britain, 1961, Reprinted 1962, 1967, p. 13.
3. M.A Stein, *Rajatarangini* , edited and translated, Delhi, 1961, II, p. 359.
4. Edward Sachau, *Al-Beruni's India*, London, 1888, Delhi Reprint, 1964, i. p. 22.
5. *Ibid.*, i, p. 173.

6. *Ibid.*, ii, p. 181.
7. *Ibid.*, see note B, i. p. 37.13.
8. *Ibid.*, i, p. 135.
9. *Ibid.*, i, p. 391.
10. *Ibid.*, Preface, p. xxiv; Professor Sachau's Introduction, p. xx.
11. Stein, p. 360 (II).
12. Vide *Al-Beruni's India*.
13. *Ibid.*, p. 206.
14. *Ibid.*, p. 211.
15. *Ibid.*, Preface, p. xxv.
16. The first part of the *Meadows of Gold* was translated into English by Dr. Sprenger, London, 1814. Also see the French trans. by MM. Barbier de Meynard and Pavet de Courteille, Paris, 1851.
17. Sprenger, I, 382.
18. A full translation of the whole work into French was published at Paris in 1836 and 1840 by M. Jaubert and from this Elliot translated some extracts into English.
19. *Glimpses of Kashmiri Culture*, ed. Prof. K.N. Dhar, Series III, Srinagar, Kashmir, 1977., An article by P.N. Pushp, Sanskrit kaavya of Kashmir, p.11, Abhinavagupta's reflective hymns, despite their mystic content, are characterised by a robust outlook on life :

    मा किञ्चित् त्यज मा गृहाण विरम स्वस्थो यथावस्थित:

    Renounce naught, cling to nothing, enjoy yourself
    unruffled, howsoever circumscribed you be.
20. Ibid., Series I, 1975, An Article by K.N. Dhar, Abhinavagupta—the Philosopher.
21. U. N. Ghoshal, 'The Dynastic Chronicles of Kashmir', *The Indian Historical Quarterly,* September 1942, p. 198.
22. *Glimpses of Kashmiri Culture*, op.cit., 1975. K.N.Dhar says : Ksemendra did not err in his duty towards his brothren and though being a rebel did initiate a very healthy trend...... He made heroes and heroins of ordinary mortals in flesh and blood—the courtesan, the clerk, the miser and many others called from ordinary life.
23. Stein, *op.cit.*, II, 375.

24. *Glimpses of Kashmiri Culture*, op.cit., 1977. He seems to have led to tirade against sycophancy in court poetry, and explains with pride that he has not flattered anybody except Shreekantha. Equally significant in his reaction against the growing tendency of the age to overburden verse with decorative artifices, and also his strong plea for a sympathetic and unbiased study of all genuine poetry :

    यातास्ते रससार संग्रहविधि निष्पीड्य ये
    वाकतत्वेक्षुलतां पुरा कतिपये तत्वस्पृशश्चक्रिरे

25. Jonaraja, *Commentary on Mankha's Srikanthacharita*, edited by Durga Prasad and Kashinath Pandurang Parb, Bombay 1900.

26. Professor Buhler, to whom we owe the discovery of Bilhana's chief work, has given in his Introduction an admirable analysis of the *Sarga* XVIII, as illustrating the poet's biography. For his description of contemporary Srinagar see Report of a Tour in search of Sanskrit Manuscripts made in kashmir, Rajputana and Central India, Journal of the Royal Asiatic Society, Bombay, Extra number (XII), 1877, pp. 7ff.

27. *Vikramaankadevachanita*, iv, 83, 85; *Hamdard*, Srinagar September, 14, 21, 1941., A.B. Keith, *History of Sanskrit Literature*, Oxford 1928, pp. 153-158.

28. Prof. Buhler : Kashmir Report, ff 4.

29. Professor A. Weber has published the extracts of the work in *Indische Studien*, pp. 289-412. Also see XVIII, 298, 300.

30. Stein, *op.cit.*, II, 376.

31. *Ibid.*, VIII, 1555 :

    सन्त्येवास्यापि विषमा स्वभावा दोषता जनः।
    येषां विपाकभव्यत्वमजाननाणयत्मयम् ॥

32. *Ibid.*, VIII, 1951, 1959 :

    सपत्नसादहितसाद्यपि वा वह्निसाद्भवेत्  ।
    द्रविण क्षोणिपालानां जनतोपद्रवाजितम्॥

33. *Ibid.*, II, 94.

    सवाश्चर्यः  विधिः ; Ibid., VII, 1455

    लक्ष्मी तडिक्रचापं कीर्तिबालाका शौर्यगर्जितम् ।
    प्रतापशक्रचापं च मागधेयाम्बुदानुगम ॥

# 16

# KOTA RANI - The Last Flicker of Hindu Kashmir

In India the law explicitely does not give the women to succeed their fathers as rulers, still in some cases the queens or regents have come up and ruled the country most efficiently and effectively. Kashmir had also a tradition of queens, who had made a mark in history. Kota Rani also comes in this category. She came at a time when Hindu Kashmir like rest of India was a prey to fissiparous tendencies of their rulers and the feudal lords known as Dāmars ate into the vitals of the kingdom. Personal gain was their only motive, sacrificing the national interests. Kashmir had lost contact with the outside world. The Hindu rule in Kashmir started on its downward course until its decline in about 1320 A.D. under Suhadeva. The Dāmars like the British barons had grown powerful and held the kings at bay. Their constant revolts plunged the country into confusion Life and property were not safe, agriculture had declined and there were periods when trade came to a standstill.[1]

This was the time when India was subjected to the inroads of Muslim invasion. Mahmud of Ghazni failed to conquer it due to its impregnable physical features[2], but Islam had penetrated into Kashmir through Muslim traders and soldiers of fortune. They were followed by missionaries and adventurers, and it is they who were responsible for introducing Islam into valley.[3]

### Dulacha's Invasion

Suhadeva (1301-1320), though a coward by nature, was determined to establish law and order and to make people happy. But like his predecessors he neglected the defences of the country by leaving the passes unguarded. As a result, adventures and spies entered the valley without any difficulty.[4] Socially and morally the court and country had sunk into the lowest ebb.[5] Falsehood, intrigue, deceit, discord and dishonesty were the order of the day.[6] Suhadeva appointed Ram Chand, the most powerful and influential feudal-lord (Kottaraja) of the Lar Valley, his chief minister. Under his able administration, Kashmir once again became prosperous, but the stars were against her, as the Mongol invader Dulacha burst upon Kashmir like a volcano, bringing death and destruction in 1320 A.D.[7]

Suhadeva and his government was paralysed by this deadly overblow. He tried to purchase Dulacha instead of giving a resistance. He imposed taxes on all castes including Brahmins. There were agitations against this cowardly conduct in some sections of the people and Brahmins protested against this policy by fasting. The bribe whetted the greed of Dulacha, who instead of retreating indulged into an orgy of violence unparalled in history. 'Kashmir became almost like a region before the creation, a vast field with a few men, without food and full of grass'.[8] Ram Chand during this upheavel carried out his duties faithfully and tried to conserve the slender resources of the kingdom and maintained a semblance of authority, as the king had fled to Kishtwar. In the absence of the sovereign the people looked upon Ram Chand for protection, who had moved to Andrakot from the hilly Gagangir. After the departure of Dulacha in the words of Jonaraja:

> "those people of Kashmira who had escaped capture, issued out of their strongholds, as mice do out of their holes. When the violence caused by the Rākshasa Dulacha ceased the son found not his father nor the father his son nor did the brothers meet their brothers."[9]

Ram Chand virtually ruled the country. He applied, healing touch to every afflicted soul. In the Herculean relief and rehabilitation task he was helped by his charming and comely daughter Kota. Gifted with intelligence she picked up the art of administration through her father. But the overbearing barons known as Kota (castle) rajas, entrenched in their castles and holding rich tracts of land, consistently flouted his authority.[10] Under these circumstances, the king always looked out for help. At this time two foreigners made their presence in Kashmir—one was Shahmir [11] and the other was Rinchan,[12] whose full name was Lha- chen-rgyal-bu-rin-chen (Lhachen rgyalbu Rinchana). Raja Suhadeva gave protection and employment to both of them.

**Revolt of Rinchan**

After Suhadeva's flight Rinchan came under the employment of Ramchand, who was wielding the royal authority in the absence of the king. Here he met Shahmir. Destiny or adversity united them to make history. Both had been eyewitnesses to the wholesale destruction and chaos caused by the Mongols. They found the king as well as people coward, spineless and timid. Such a fluid political condition whetted the ambition of Rinchan, who wanted to usurp the power from Ram Chand and become the Sovereign of Kashmir.[13] But he knew his limitations, he could not defy Ram Chand openly. Therefore he took recourse to a ruse. He sent his Ladakhi followers in the guise of merchants, selling wollen clothes to the town of Lar. They carried on their normal trade so as to allay suspicion.[14] One day, they entered the fort under the pretext of trade with their weapons concealed under their long robes, and attacked the fort. Rinchan also joined them and murdered Ram Chand treacherously. He took Ram Chand's son, Rawan Chand under custody and proclaimed himself the king of Kashmir in 1320 A.D.[15] The people of Kashmir were so much demoralised that they accepted anyone who proclaimed himself the ruler.[16]

Rinchan being shrewd and pragmatic understood well that the stability of his rule depended upon the goodwill of Kashmiris. He took recourse to the policy of appeasement. He befriended Rawan-Chand and his estranged family. After releasing him he conferred upon him the title of *Raina* (Lord or Master), made him his commander-in-chief, and gave him the pargana of Lār and the province of Ladākh as jagir.[17] He then persuaded Kota Rani to marry him, in this way Rinchan succeeded in gaining the loyalty of Rawan Chand.

Meanwhile Suhadeva returned from kishtwar to claim his kingdom, but found no support for his cause within Kashmir.[18] But this event made Rinchan to try something so as to identify himself with the country and people. He approached Devaswami, who was the head guru of the Śaiva Hindus, and entreated him to admit him to his faith. Devaswami spurned the petition.[19] Thereupon, Rinchan got converted to Islam through the benediction of Bulbul Shah, a Muslim fakir. So he became a Muslim and adopted the name Sultan Sadruddin.[20]

Rinchan after a short rule of over three years died of a head injury, which he suffered when an abortive attempt was made on his life.[21] Rinchana left behind a son named Haider who was under the custody of his trusted counsellor, Shahmir.[22]

## Udayāndeva—The New Ruler of Kashmir

Rinchan's death in 1323 let loose three political parties to scramble for power. They were the royalists, the agriculturists, and Rani's party. The royalists were led by Udayanadeva who had caused the death of Rinchan. The agriculturists led by their land lords (Kottarajas) were not keen to run the government themselves. They supported Shahmir. Kota Rani's party upheld the cause of the minor prince Haider. Her main support were the Lavanyas[23], who were vacillating and unreliable. Shahmir was cunning and diplomat. He had seen Kota Rani's administrative ability and *Savoir-faire* during the rehabilitation work after the departure of Dulacha from the valley. He knew that the time was not ripe for usurping power, and to checkmate Kota's growing power he brought a puppet in Udayan Dev, the brother of Suhadeva, as the ruler of Kashmir, who was living in Swat as an exile. Parmu says that Shahmir offered the throne to Udayanadeva in preference to Prince Haider or Kota Rani who had a stronger claim as Rinchan's legal heirs. To weaken the Rani's party further he negotiated marriage between Raja Udayandeva and Kota Rani. With these ullerior motives he restored the Hindu rule. It gained him popular applause and proved the basis of his political aggrandisement in future.[24] But M. L. Kapoor does not agree with Parmu. His contention is that the Muslim rule had already started with Rinchan. The rising against him was neither a national one nor directed against the Islamic rule in Kashmir:

> "It also passes beyond our comprehension how Kota Devi's marriage with Udyandeva weakened her position. When two rivals are united, do they become weaker or stronger? Was it easier for Shah Mir to control Udyandeva when married to shrewd Kota Devi or without this marriage? Is it not correct to say that Udyandeva's rule lasted so long because Kota Devi was by his side and without her his rule would have been short-lived?"[25]

Parmu's logic seems to be more correct, as Kota Rani as a regent of her minor son would have wielded real power and strengthened her roots as against Shah Mir. Haider, the son of Kota Rani , was in the hands of Shahmir and later events have shown that he used him as a trump card to browbeat Udayan Deva and Kota Rani.

Raja Udayan Deva was ultra - religious, weak minded and very conservative. He spent his time in bathing, penance and prayer. He dressed like an ascetic and while travelling tied bells to his horses to avoid injury or death to any living being.[26] He did not perform his royal obligations. By her charm and bewitching beauty Kota Rani quickly gained ascendance over the king, whom she, in a short time, relegated to the background. From now onwards she was the virtual ruler of the kingdom. Her impact over the king and kingdom is described by Jonaraja in the following words :

> "She was, as it were, the mind, and the king, the body, who carried out her orders."[27]

Meanwhile Shahmir, who had nursed an ambition to capture the throne since his entry into the valley, began consolidating his power after Rinchana's death. Many of the nobles (Kottarajas) were brought to his side by wise distribution of subsidy while many were coerced into neutrality. Lavanyas had also become turbulent taking advantage of a weak and impotent royal authority.[28]

Unlike Udayandeva Kota Rani had become apprehensive of the growing authority of Shahmir. To divide his strength she sent away his two sons, Jamshed and Alisher to administer the northern district of Kamraj.[29] Then she selected Bhatta Bhikashana[30], a Brahman of great sagacity, diplomacy and tact, as her adviser and commander of state forces.

**Second Mongol Invasion**

While Kota Rani was engaged in consolidating her position and prestige, a tornado in the form of the Mongol invader, Achala[31], swept over the valley, which rudely disrupted her plans. Like his brother Suhadeva, Udayandeva fled like a coward to Ladakh leaving behind his family and his subjects to their fate. Kota Rani decided to resist the invader. She rallied all her forces, with a determination not to allow the repeat of Dulacha' doom and devastation. Like a gallant, patriotic woman she enthused her subjects and also enlisted the help of Shahmir and his supporters. In consultation with Shahmir she made a fervent appeal to refractory (Kottarajas) feudal lords and chiefs to come under her banner to fight against this national crisis. In this appeal she recalled to their minds the deplorable conditions which prevailed in Kashmir after Dulacha's invasion. Her appeal enthused them to fight and repel the enemy. Knowing fully well that even her united forces were no match against Achala's forces, therefore she resorted to diplomacy. She sent a word to Achala that as the throne has fallen vacant due to the flight of the king, she and her ministers were ready to install him as the king, provided his army was sent back. Achala believed her, and keeping only a small detachment with him, sent the rest of his army to his home. After accomplishing her desired mission, she attacked Achala. His detachment was defeated. Achala was captured, and was beheaded under the orders of the Queen.[32] At once Kota Rani became the idol of the people. Shahmir had also played a dignified role during this crisis. In the words of Jonaraja :

> "Strange that this believer in Allah became the saviour of the people. As a dried up river allows men to cross it, and gives them shelter on its banks; even so this believer in Allah, calm and active, protected the terrified subjects."[33]

Undayandeva returned to the capital. Kota Rani :

> "respectfully received him with her head bent down, even as the eastern hill receives the gloom-dispelling full moon on its head."[34]

After Udayandev's return Shahmir became more assertive. He kept the king in constant fear by threatning to depose him and place

Rinchan's son Haider on the throne. Jonaraja graphically describes the torture:

> "He frightened the king day and night by holding up Haider before him, even as one frightens a bird by holding up his hawk."[35]

Shahmir made no secret of his plans. He fortified himself on the Chakdar hill.[36] While these intrigues and counter -ntrigues were going on ,Udyandeva died on Shivaratri night in 1338 A.D. He left behind a minor son, named Jatta. Kota Rani fearing an open revolt by Shahmir kept the death of her husband a secret for four days.[37] She knew that Shahmir would not tolerate her sovereignty, and would do his best to overthrow her. She decided to declare herself as the queen passing over the claims of both sons. She was helped by the Lavanyas in her enthronement.

**Kota Rani As a Ruler**

Kota Rani ruled Kashmir from 1338 A.D. to 1339 A.D. She held her court personally, dispensed justice, appointed and dismissed her ministers. To avoid Shahmir, she removed the court to the fort of Andrakot.[38] Her administration is praised by Jonaraja :

> "As the summer rain allays dust and heat, and nourishes plants, even so she brought back prosperity to the subjects."[39]

Again he says :

> "As the canal nourishes cultivated fields with water, so did the queen nourish the people by brestowing much wealth on them. She was to the kingdom what the moon is to the blue lotus; and to the enemy she was what that luminary is to white lotus."[40]

In other words she was a capable ruler, and during her short rule of five months, Kashmir prospered.

**TURN OF THE TIDE**

With all her abilities she could not stem the rot which had infected the body politic of the state, which was inching towards degeneration and decline. Moral values had disappeared, and disaffection was rife. Kota Rani pitted Bhatta Bhikashana against Shahmir, and showered favours upon him. He was a good selection. He was an eyesore to Shahmir, who resorted to a base stratagem.

Shahmir circulated the news that he was suffering from a deadly disease, and would be dead any moment. Kota Rani sent Bhatta Bhikashana to enquire about Shahmir's health. When he arrived at his residence followed by his bodyguards. They found Shahmir's palace overcast with gloom on account of impending death. Thus Bhikashana and Avātara went to see the patient leaving his bodyguards at the gate. When they came into the presence of the so called patient, the latter sprang up and killed unarmed Bhikashana and Avatār .[41] The incident provoked widespread condemnation. People were in her favour. This was the right moment to arrest Shahmir. But she got slipped her life's opportunity, in not arresting him on the advice of her ministers[42], who were in the pay of Shahmir, and were his informers.

Shahmir favoured by luck, besieged her in her fort at Andrakot. The Lavanyas stood by the queen and fought relentlessly. Shahmir would have been defeated, but his alliances with the powerful feudal lords rescued him from the precarious position. The forces of Lutsa, the Lord of the Marches and a relative of Shahmir, attacked the Lavanyas from the rear, and Shahmir launched a strong counter offensive from the front, and thus surrounded the Lavanyas.[43] Seeing victory in sight he rewarded his officers and allies preffusely, She resisted his advance fighting gallantly, but was overpowered, and capitulated. To avoid massacre of her supporters she accepted his conditions — to be his queen and to share the throne with him.[44]

Jonaraja says that the queen was won over by his assiduity and he took possession of Kotta (castle) as well as queen Kota. He spent one night with her in the same bed, and when he rose in the morning, he caused her to be captured by Tikṣhṇas.[45] Her two sons were also imprisoned. The historian's epilogue is :

> "the queen was dropped from her kingdom like a star from the sky."

She died in 1339 A.D.[46]

Her death is shrouded in mystery. The Persian chroniclers have given different versions of her death. One version is that Kota Rani rejected the marriage proposal of Shahmir, because she had been defeated by him. She committed suicide by driving a dagger into her belly.[47] Another authority says that Shahmir having overpowered the queen in her castle prevailed upon her to be his wife.[48] Hasan gives a very picturesque account. On his wedding night Shahmir, now Sultan Shams-ud-Din, was waiting for weded wife and his conquest. Bedecked in resplendent dress and scintillating jewels she stepped into his chamber. As each of her legs moved forward her anklets yielded melodious notes and a cascade of perfume was unleashed. No Emperor could have desired a more rapturous climax to his quest for love and power. When Shahmir advanced to receive Kota Rani in his arms, she drew out a dagger from under her garments and ripped open her bowels, and said to Shahmir, "This is my acceptance."[49] Thus the curtain was rungdown on the Hindu rule of Kashmir.

## AN ESTIMATE

The overthrow of Kota Rani was an epoch-making event in the history of Hindu Kashmir. It was a revolution. It exposed the Hindu rule with its feet of clay. There was no revolt or rising neither in favour of Kota Rani nor against Shahmir. This shows that the people were so sick of the weak and intriguing rulers of Kashmir that they willingly accepted a foreigner as their ruler. Jonaraja says that her downfall was the result of her *karma* or acts.[50] In reality she is to be blamed for her downfall.

One of the most important cause is that Kashmir lost its contact with the outside world .Thus, it became insular. It deprived itself of the changes, happenings and developments outside Kashmir.

Kota Rani appears to have been grossly selfish, ambitious and very foolish. Her interests were immediate and not remote.[51] She had a weakness for power. It was for power that she married Rinchan, the murderer of her father. For power she had remarried Udayan Dev. The best course for her would have been to install her son Haider on the throne, and herself as the regent. After the death of Udayan Dev again the opportunity came to her, she could have declared Udyan Dev's minor son Jatta, as the ruler and would have acted as a regent. But time and tide do not wait for anyone.

Again she got a very trusted minister in Bhatta Bhikashana. Her first and prime duty was his protection. She ought not to have sent him to enquire about the health of Shahmir. She could have sent some other minister. Shahmir had made a dent in her court, her ministers were in his pay, and Kota Rani was totally ignorant of the fact. If the survival of the fittest is the lesson of politics, then between Kota Rani and Shahmir, the latter was more fit than the former. She was checkmated by Shahmir. But Shahmir could not be absolved of the crimes he committed. He was unfaithful to the salt, and thus acted against the tenet of his own religion. Murder of Bhatta Bhikashana in such an inglorious way is an indeliable stain upon his character. His alleged ignominous marriage with the queen of Kashmir and widow of his two masters was a sin and a crime.

With all the shortcomings she was nevertheless a remarkable woman. She was a diplomat which is proved by Achala's annihilation. Her courage and ability to rule over insubordinate Kottarajas deserves admiration. Comparing her with Razia Sultan, Chand Bibi and Durgavati, the Indian queens during the Muslim rule in India, the gross selfishness of Kota Rani stares in the face. All the four lost their lives. Razia Sultan was put to death after her defeat, Chand Bibi by her own people while fighting against the Mughals and Durgavati fearing an outrage on her honour while fighting against Emperor Akbar's army drew her dagger plunged it into her breast and died as a martyr. Had Kota Rani Committed suicide before being captured by Shahmir, she would have earned the title of 'Martyr'. The history of the queens of Kashmir shows that though they were capable administrators, but were totally devoid of maternal instincts. Queen Didda got her grandsons murdered, so as to be able to rule Kashmir herself. Seeing this Kota Rani was no exception in discarding the claims of both of her sons. Nevertheless she is one of the romantic figures in the history of Kashmir.

## References

1. These feudal lords of Kashmir had usurped all power in their fortified castles (upavesana), Kalhana's *Rajtarangini*, English translation by Sir Aurel Stein, London, Westminister, 1900, VII, 1254; VIII, 648, 929, 1124 etc.; To modern Kashmiris they survive in the term *kottaraja* or feudal chiefs, Walter R. Lawrence, *The Valley of Kashmir*, London, 1895, p. 185.

2. Mahmud of Ghazni tried twice to invade but failed, M. Nazim, *The Life and Times of Sultan Mahmud of Ghazna*, Cambridge, 1931, pp. 104-5.
3. Mufti Muhammad Shah Shah Saādat, *Bulbul Shah Saheb*, (urdu), Lahore, 1360/1941, pp. 7, 23.
4. Haider Malik Chadura, *Tarikh-i-Kashmir*, Research Department Library, Srinagar, ff. 93b - 94b.
5. Stein, *op.cit.*, No. 195.
6. Haider Malik, *op.cit.*, ff. 93b - 94b., Jonaraja, *Rajtarangini* , II, Calcutta, 1897-98, pp. 4 - 17.
7. Jonaraja, *op.cit.*, p. 15, According to him Dulacha came after Laukika 4389 (Śaka 1235).; According to Parmu, taking into account the dates given by Jonaraja, Zulju's invasion comes to the year 1320 A.D., R.K. Parmu, *A History of Muslim Rule in Kashmir*, Delhi, 1969, p. 72.; Stein states that Dulacha entered the Kashmir valley from the Zoji-la-Pass, which route was also followed by Mirza Haider Dughlat in 1532, Stein, Notes on Ancient Geography of the Pir Pantsal Route, *Journal of Asiatic Society of Bengal*, 1896 (Part) I, para 58; Abul Fazal, *Ain-i-Akbarī* , English translation H.S. Jarrett, Vol. II, p. 381.
8. Jonaraja, *op.cit.*, edited by Peterson under the name *Dvitiya-Rāj-tarangini*, Bombay, 1896, pp. 152-155.
9. *Ibid.*, J.C. Dutt's translation, p. 17.
10. P. N. K. Bamzai, *A History of Kashmir*, New Delhi, second revised edition 1973, p. 168.
11. Nizamuddin, *Tabaqāt-i-Akbari*, ed. B. Dey and Hidayat Husain, Vol III, p. 424; Muhammad Qāsim Firishta, *Ta'rīk-i-Firishta*, Bo. ed. 1832, p. 647, Shahmir came to the valley in 1313 A.D. Suhadeva, who was then ruling Kashmir, employed him and gave him a village near Bāramūla as a Jagir.
12. Due to warfare between Baltis and Ladakis, in which his father was murdered by the Baltis. Though Rinchan was able to avenge his father's death, finding his life in great danger he entered Kashmir through Zoji-la-pass; Jonaraja, *op.cit.*, J.C. Dutt trans., p. 17; *Baharistan-i-Shahi* (anonymous), India Office library, f. 10a; A.H., Francke, *Antiquities of Indian Tibet*, Calcutta, 1926, vol. II, p. 98.

13. Hasan b. 'Alī Kashmirī, *Tarikh-i-Kashmir*, Bodleian 315, 82b; *Baharistan-i-Shahi, op.cit*, f. 12 b.
14. Haider Malik Chādura, *op.cit.*, Ms f. 30 a.; JonaRaja, R.C. Dutt's translation, stt. 167-69.
15. *Baharistan-i-Shahi*, *op.cit.*, 12a-b; Hasan, *op.cit.*, 95 b; Haider Malik Chādura, *op.cit.*, 99a. ; Mohibul Hasan, *Kashmir Under the Sultans*, Calcutta, 1959 , p. 38.
16. Parmu, *op.cit.*, p. 78.
17. *Baharistan-i-Shahi*, *op.cit.*, 12b; Hasan, *op.cit.*, 96a-b; Haider Malik Chadura, *op.cit.*, 99b.
18. *Baharistan-i-Shahi*, *op.cit.*, 13a; Hasan, *op.cit.*, 96b; Haider Malik Chadura, *op.cit.*, 100a.
19. Janaraja, J.C. Dutt's Translation, pp. 20-21.
20. Baharistan, f. 15a.
21. Jonaraja, J.C. Dutt's translation, p. 23; Anonymous, *Tarikh-i-Kashmir*, Munich Manuscript, K. Hof-Und Staatsbibliothek, Muenchen, 50a.
22. Baharistan-i-Shahi, *op.cit.*, f. 15b; Hasan, *op. cit.*, 101a; Haider Malik Chadura, *op.cit.*, 104a; Nizamuddin, *op.cit.*, vol. III, p. 425, Calls Haider as Chandra.
23. Janaraja, J.C. Dutt's translation, *op. cit.*, p. 27. Now they are known as 'lons', Rajatarangini, VII, stanza 1171 and Stein's note; Lawrence, *op.cit.*, p. 306
24. R.K. Parmu, *op.cit.*, p. 82.
25. M.L. Kapoor, *Studies in History and Culture of Kashmir*, Jammu, 1976, p. 86.
26. Janaraja, *op. cit.*, p. 24.
27. Ibid., *Baharistan-i-Shahi*, *op. cit.*, f. 16a; Hasan, *op.cit.*, 101b.
28. S.C. Ray, *Early History and Culture of Kashmir*, New Delhi, 1969, Second ed. 1970, p. 95.
29. Janaraja, *op. cit.*, p. 24, Kamraj is the ancient Kramaraja (Kamraz), now the northern territorial district of Baramulla; *Ain-i-Akbari*, (Jarett), vol. II, p. 368; Stein, *Ancient Geography*, para 85.
30. Jonaraja, *op.cit.*, p.25.
31. *Ibid.*; Shaikh Abdul Haqq, *Akhbar-ul-Akhyar*, Delhi, 1910, p. 97.
32. Jonaraja, *op.cit.*, p. 25.

33. *Ibid.*, p. 26.
34. *Ibid.*, p. 26.
35. *Ibid.*, p. 27. "As a tree in a marsh is overcome by lotus-covered water, so the king was overcome by Shahmera".
36. *Ibid.*, p. 27; *Rajtaranagini*, Stein's translation, II, pp. 461-62.
37. *Ibid.*, p. 28.
38. *Ibid.*, p. 31; Jonaraja names the place by its ancient name Jayapidapura. Under the Sultanate rule in Kashmir it was called as Indarkot or Undarkot.
39. *Ibid.*, p. 28.
40. *Ibid.*
41. *Ibid.*, p. 29.
42. *Ibid.*
43. PNK Bamzai, *op.cit.*, p. 173.
44. R. K. Parmu, *op.cit.*, pp. 84-85.
45. Jonaraja, *op.cit.*, pp. 31-32.
46. *Ibid.*
47. H. Malik Chadura, *op.cit.*, f. 106.
48. *Baharistan-i-Shahi*, *op.cit.*, f. 17a.
49. Hasan, *op.cit*, p. 169; Narain Kaul Aziz, *Tarikh-i-Kashmir*, Research Dept. library, Srinagar, Kashmir, states that she committed suicide, But Parmu accepts the version of Jonaraja; S.L. Sadhu, *Tales From the Rajtaranagini*, Srinagar, 1967, p. 126.
50. Jonaraja, *op.cit.*, p. 32; "The results of our acts manifest themselves in every direction, and generate wisdom or ignorance."
51. R. K. Parmu, *op.cit.*, p. 86.

# 17

# JONARAJA—THE CONTINUATOR-AUTHOR OF *RAJATARANGINI*

But for Kalhana and his *Rajatarangini*, Ancient India has little in the field of historical literature to present to the world. The *Rajatarangini* is not a single piece of work of one author. It is a connected and co-ordinated work of five chroniclers — Kalhana, Jonaraja, Srivara, Prajyabhatta and Suka.

Jonaraja, two hundred years after Kalhana, picked up the thread left by Kalhana, completed Jayasiṁha's reign and continued down to the rule of Sultan Zain-ul-Abidin. Like Kalhana, Jonaraja's life and ancestry are hidden into oblivion. His own writings as well as that of his pupil Srivara, furnish us with scant information about his ancestry and life. His commentary on the *Prithvīrājavijaya* of Rājānaka Jayanka and the *Srikanthacarita* of Mankha throws some light on his ancestry and lineage.

Jonaraja was the son of the Bhatta Nonaraja and grandson of Shri Lolaraja. At one place in the *Prithvīrājavijaya,* his name is given as Jyotsnākara, but he was better known as Jonaraja. He also gives his name as Jonaraja in his *Rajatarangini* and is mentioned as such by his pupil Srivara. Srivara had great respect and regard for his teacher and eulogizes him thus :

> "There was on this earth, my teacher, called Jyotsnākara, who was for ever a mine of nectar of speech, a devotee of Shiva, possessed of wealth and fame, of true promise, who had subdued

> anger, who was the leader of the circle of Brahmans, who honoured Brahmans, of noble conduct, who was always honoured by the King, tranquil, having countless merits, who had mastered the sense of the Vedas and the Codes of Law, who was engaged in the performance of daily ablutions and prayers, who was respected by the hosts of pupils intensely attached to him, who, when in royal court looked like Brahaspati and was accompanied by a large body of followers.[1]

Jonaraja was a great scholar of Sanskrit language and literature. He acquired fame in his own life time. He attracted the attention of the reigning King Zain-ul-Abidin, who gave him all patronage.[2] Jonaraja was entrusted with the charge of writing a history of Kashmir. He was in high esteem of the Sultan, who bestowed upon him the title of Rājānaka, which appears in his commentary on *Shrikanthcarita.* This is further testified by Vallabhadeva, the compiler of the *Suchāsitavali* who says that the three verses in the book were written by Rājānaka Jonaraja. As there is no Jonaraja famous as a poet, we may easily infer that the reigning Sultan honoured Jonaraja with the Rajanaka. Jonaraja was also a renowned teacher, which is confirmed by Srivara as he uses the epithet "*Brahaspati*" for him. He was not an eclectic in faith like Kalhana. He was a great devotee of Lord Shiva. His *Rajatarangini* opens with a prayer addressed to Shiva, *Ardhnarisvara,* The two, out of three, of his commentaries contain poems dealing with the theme of Shiva.

Jonaraja's probable date of birth is 1389 A.D., Srivara gives 1459 A.D., as his date of birth which is obviously incorrect.[3] Jonaraja was able to complete his *Rajatarangini* inspite of the exhaustions of old age. In the colophon of his commentary on *Prithvirajvijaya,* he complains of his mental tiredness to carry out intellectual pursuits, and perhaps he did not write after that.

Jonaraja's fame mainly rests on Rajatarangini which is a chronological history of Kashmir from Jaisiṁha to Zain-ud-Abidin; its shorter recension has 976 verses and longer recension contains 1334 verses. His Rajatarangini may be divided into two parts: the one, from 1128 to 1354 and the second from 1355 to its abrupt ending. The earlier portion of the book is rather sketchy. The second, beginning with the accession of Shihab-ud-din in 1354, is more detailed. We do not know when he stopped writing or whether he wrote upto the year of his death in 1459.

Besides, Rajatarangini, he wrote three other books : Commentary Mankha, on *Srikanthcharita* of Mankha, Commentary of the *Kiratarjuniya* of Bharavi written in 1449 A.D., and the Commentary on the historical poem, *Prithvirajavijaya* of Rajanaka Jayanak.[4]

Like Kalhana he calls his work a *Kavya*[5], and shows his proficiency in *Alankarasastra.* His approach is objective. The only defect which impairs the historical narrative, is the vagueness of diction. His phraseology, sometimes, does not communicate the precise information required for drawing correct conclusions. His compressed expressions are puzzling. The puns conceal historical facts. Words are susceptible to different interpretations. It may be noted that metaphorical language and stylistic dabblings belonged to the age and not to the man alone. Like Kalhana , his work is aimed to guide the kings.

He Mongol invasions of Dulacha and Achla, and Ladakhi Rinchan are dealt with briefly, and other invasions of the Mongols are not mentioned at all.[6] He does not clearly explain Dulacha antecedents. Thus the most important event which produced far-reaching consequences, suffers from brevity of expression.[7] Still the appellation Dulacha proves invader's Mongol origin, appears to be Indianised form of du-lu-hou-chi, the Chinese adaptation of the Mongol Darukachen. This explains that Dulacha was not the personal name of the invader, but the designation of his office in the Mongol administration. P.N. Pushup names Dulacha as Zulqadr Khan. Jonaraja graphically depicts the horrors caused by the desperadoes like Rinchan.

> "And when Dulaca left, the surviving citizen come out of their hideonts like frightened rats; but the Threat of Rinchan was still these, as if the sunset beak with its lofty cliff was obstructing movement of the moon after it had just escaped the Raahu's grip.[8]

His treatment of virtue (*Punya*), sin (*Pap*), and the impact of *Kaliyuga*, is in accordance with orthodox Hindu thinking. He considered fate supreme in determining the course of history[9]. Sometimes, he introduces supernatural agencies in his theme, which help in tight situations.[10]

Jonaraja's *Rajatarangini* is an important source in tracing the history[11] from Jaisiṁha to Zain-ul-Abidin. It describes the disintegration of the Hindu rule, the spread of Islam and the establishment of the Muslim Kingdom in Kashmir. The events contemporary to the reigns of Sultan Sikandar Ali Shah and Zain-ul-Abidin Budshah, find a more detailed mention. He graphically depicts the conditions of the people before the advent of Islam into the Valley. He makes it clear that Islam got a footing in Kashmir before the foundation of the Sultanate. Jonaraja was a Brahmin and while describing the anarchic situation in the beginning of the 14th century, appears to be a bit partial to the role of his own community. He has showered much praise on his patron Sultan Zain- ul-Abidin, is not undeserved.

The topography, as given by Jonaraja, is on the whole reliable. He is well-acquainted with the old nomenclature of the Valley. The later portion of jonaraja's work is very informative. Unfortunately he died in 1459 before he could complete his work.

Whereas Kalhan's Rajtarangini is classed under historical poetry in Sanskrit literature, no such honour has been bestowed upon Jonaraja's *Rajtarangini.* It is at places versified prose, to borrow the epithet from Buhler. Raghu Nath Singh has rightly remarked:

> "Jona Raja after recording an event proceeds further; he even skips over the chain of events at the slightest possible hint. He does not stay behind to explain it, but transfers this burden to the reader. -------- The *Raj Tarangini* of Jona Raja is history. It is neither a biography nor an eulogy."[11]

His historical methodology is inferior to that of Kalhan. He has not interpreted the facts, has only narrated them skelton bare. Many important events like Rinchan's advent of Sayyid Ali Hamdani in Kashmir, and Zain-ul-Abidin's coming to power twice, have not been mentioned.

## References


1. *Kathakautuka*, ed. R. Schmidt I, 41-45.
2. Srikanth Kaul, ed. *Rajatarangini of Jonaraja,* Hoshiarpur, 1967, p. 32.
3. Srivara, *Jain Rajtarangini*, text, ed. by Srikanth Kaul, Vishveshvaranand Institute, Hoshiarpur, 1966, pp.1-6.
4. श्री जैनोल्लाभदेनस्य साम्राज्ये जोनको द्विजः ।
   खर्षिविश्वमिते शाके यथामति यतिष्यते ॥

   M. S. No. 751, Research Dept., Srinagar.
5. *Janaraja's Rajtarangini* st. 8.

   दर्पग्लानिभवां राजपान्थानां तापसन्तितम ।
   हतुं संरोपितः काव्यद्रुमो भाविफलोदयः ॥
6. *Jonaraja's Rajtarangini*, stt., 142.

   दुलचाख्यः कर्मसेनचक्रवर्तिचभूपतिः ।
   कश्मीरान्स तदैवागात्सिंहो मृगगुहामिव ॥
7. Yuan-Chao-Pi-Shi (The Secret History of the Mongol Dynasty), english translation by Wei Kwei-Sun, Aligarth, 1957; Henry H. Howorth, *History of the Mongols*, London, 1876, 1888; III, p.153; E. Bretschneider, *Medieval Researches*, London, I, p. 138, n.368; Smkanth kaul, *op. cit.*, pp. 34-35.
8. Sanskrit Kaavya of Kashmir, by P.N. Pushpa in *Glimpses of Kashmiri Culture*, Series III, 1977, Published by Shri Paramananda Research Institute, Srinagar, Kashmir.
9. Jonaraja's *Rajatarangini*, *op. cit.*, St. 597.
10. Ibid. St. 388.
11. *Glimpses of Kashmiri Culture*, *op. cit.*, quoted in 'Sanskrit Chronicles and Sultans of Kashmir'.

# 18

# Zain-ul-Abidin's Sulah-i-kul - THE HALLMARK OF ISLAM IN KASHMIR

India being a sub-continent, the upheavals, convulsions or calamities felt in its one part failed to produce slightest effect on the other. The best example is illustrated by Islam in India. If on the north west side it entered the Indian frontiers with arms, in south India and Kashmir it came with the message of Quran, which teaches peace and toleration. The dominant feature of Islam, as its very name implies, is the making of peace. A Muslim is one who has made his peace with God and man. Peace with God implies the complete submission to his will, and obedience to the law of creation, while peace with mankind implies the doing of good to one's fellow creatures:

> "Yea, whoever submits himself to Allah and is the doer of good to others, he shall have his reward".

In Kashmir the first harbinger of this message of human love, fraternity, and equality, which in the modern terminology may be termed as 'spiritualised socialism' was Bilal Shah, popularly known as Bulbul Shah — a disciple of Shah Niamatullah Farsi of *Suhrawardi* order of the Sufis.[1] He started peaceful conversions of the Hindus in Kashmir.[2] Other Sufis Amir—i—Kabir, known as Sayyid Ali Hamdani, his son Mir Mohammed Hamdani and Sayyid Mohammad Hisari followed suit. In the spread of Islam in Kashmir, the local Muslim sufis, popularly known as *Rishis* or *Babas* played a significant role. The founder of the *Rishi* order was Shaikh Nur-ud-Din alias Nand *Rishi*. Some of the well known *Rishis*, who joined his order were Baba Nasr-ud-Din, Baba Bam-ud- Din, Baba Hanuf or Hanif-ud-Din and Sayyid Baba. It is due to their influence that Kashmir in all the ages has been free from fanaticism, bigotry, persecution and carnage.[3]

The teachings of these saints, Sufis and mystics are best reflected in the philosopher king Zain-ul-Abidin, affectionately known as *Badshah* or Great king[4]. Like a true follower of Islam, he obeyed the injunction of the holy Quran, "Surely the noblest among you in the eyes of God is one who is most mindful of his duty." Shahi Khan, the most illustrious of the five sons of Sultan Sikandar, ascended the throne of Kashmir in 1420 A.D., assuming the title Zain-ul-Abidin, which was conferred upon him by his brother Ali Shah.[5] Though Kashmir was free from religious persecution and inquisition, yet the last two rulers of this dynasty are *bete noire* in its history[6]. Zain-ul- Abidin began his rule with a healing touch, putting balm to every afflicted soul — in marked contrast with the previous regime[7]. Jonaraja, his court chronicler, says that with the accession of Zain-ul-Abidin a new sense of security and assurance pervaded the atmosphere.[8]

## A PRECURSOR OF AKBAR

Akbar, who is lauded with so much praises for his catholicity and *Sulah-i-kul* (peace with all), has a forerunner in Zain-ul-Abidin, who preceded him by one hundred and forty one years. He restored confidence in the terror stricken Hindus[9] by granting them complete religions freedom. He understood that a state could prosper only when all its subjects irrespective of caste and creed contribute to it[10]. Talent should be the criterion for the jobs. A welcome invitation was extended to all those *Brahmins*, who had fled in panic[11]. The government made proper arrangement for their rehabilitation by offering them jobs, stipends and rent-free lands[12]. He gave full freedom to Hindu converts to Islam to return to their original faith, if they so wished.[13] If they could not rejoin Hinduism, the fault lay with the short sighted and obscurantist Hindu society,[14] in spite of this according to Persian chroniclers many of them returned to their original faith.[15]

**Removal of Disabilities Against non-Muslims**

The disabilities against the Hindus imposed during the preceding reigns were removed. They were allowed to apply *tilak* on forehead, wear their dress and study scriptures[16]. The Hindus had to pay a tax on the plot of land used as cremation ground[17]. Srivara, his court historian, brought it to the notice of the Sultan, who immediately got it repealed and punished guilty officers[18]. The Sultan did not want to intervene in the social system of the Hindus, therefore the *sati* system for the Hindu widows, which was banned by Sultan Sikandar[19] was again revived.[20] The cow slaughter was banned,[21] and also killing of birds and fish in several *nagas* ie, springs sacred to Hindus. The Sultan reduced the amount of *jizya* imposed on non-believers under the Islamic law, from two *pals* (equivalent to eight tolas) to one *masha,*[22] to retain the Islamic nature of state in theory. In practice this paltry sum was not even realised.[23] He allowed temples to be repaired[24]. His name is also associated with the construction of Shiva and Sun temples in the newly founded cities of Zainagiri and Siddhapuri[25]. Besides, he is said to have built *mathas, vihars* and monasteries for his non-Muslim subjects.[26] He put an end to the destruction of temples and breaking of idols (*but-Shikni*). In Ladakh he protected the gold image of Buddha from desecration by the Muslim soldiers of some foreign country.[27] The Sultan allowed the Hindus to celebrate their social and religious festivals with the traditional gusto and fanfare.[28] To please his non-Muslim subjects, he also participated in *Nagyatra*[29], *Ganachakra*[30], *Vyath Truvah*[31], and *Chaitra f*estival.[32] On these occasions he gave sumptuous feasts, and distributed costly presents.[33] He also made pilgrimages to Amaranth[34], and famous shrines of Vijayesvara and Naubandhana hill.[35] While he was returning from the pilgrimage it snowed which was considered very auspicious.[36]

Viewed with objectivity his pilgrimages to the Hindu shrines and temples were made to understand the philosophy of Hindu religion, and as well to know the ethnology, geography, and location of different and distant parts of his country, so as to be on guard in case of any rebellion or invasion. His humanism and liberalism touched the Hindu hearts so much so that they honoured him with the appelation of *Narayanāvatara.*[37] The deification was the result of the effulgence of gratitude towards their benefactor.[38] Similar sentiments were expressed by a section of the Hindus in the times of Akbar and his son Jahangir and grandson Shahjahan, when they did not take even a drop of water until they saw the Emperor through the window (*jarokha darshan*).[39]

## HARNESSING THE TALENT

Human psychology since the dawn of civilization has been to get justice and recognition for the talent. Zain-ul-Abidin understood it, and thereupon merit was the corner-stone of the administrative appointments. In modern parlance 'rule of law' with its associates 'equality and justice' was established. His court was adorned with a galaxy of celebrities, Muslims as well as Hindus like the *Nav Ratna* (nine jewels) of Akbar. Thus, Many of his non-Muslim subjects rose to high positions in the state administration.[40] Shirya Bhatta was minister for justice and Hindu ecclesiastical affairs. Tilak and Simha were high officials. Karpur Bhatta was king's personal physician. Rupya Bhatta was the court astrologer. Rupyabhanda was an architect,[41] who constructed for the Sultan a number of buildings including the celebrated Zainalank.[42] Jaya Bhatta, was perhaps linked with *zakat*, through whom one core of rupees were distributed annually. Two of his military commanders, Malik Daulat Chand, and Malik Autar Chand were Hindus.[43] Tilakacharya, a Buddhist, was given a high position.[44] Besides, the top Hindu officials, they were also employed in the lower hierarchy.[45]

## PATRONAGE TO ART AND LETTERS

Islam is the first religion in the world to place the acquisition and cultivation of knowledge before the worship of God. In Islam, therefore religion and science are co-related. In the eyes of the Prophet to explore the realms of nature and the hidden corners of the universe is not merely a service in the cause of humanity, it is a service in the glorification of God, says he :

> "He, who leaves home in search of knowledge, walks in the path of God",

and again,

> "It is incumbent on every one, male or female to acquire knowledge. -------- The ink of the scholar in more holy than the blood of martyr."

Imbued with this spirit Zain-ul-Abidin, gave patronage to Sanskrit literature, so that his Muslim scholars were to be benefited by the rich treasure of Sanskrit through translation and vice versa. He extended invitations to the scholars, who had fled the valley.[46] He founded a seminary known as '*Dar-ul- Ulam*' at Nawshera.[47] Under his orders of Kalhan's *Rajtarangini*, '*Ramayana*' of Valmiki, Vyas's '*Mahabharat*', *Vrihat-kathasar*, *Hatakeshwar Samita*, and Puranas were translated into Persian,[48] Vice versa several Persian works were translated into Sanskrit. Notable among them is the classical romance of Mulla Jamis, '*Yusuf Zulekha*', which was rendered in Sanskrit by the court historian Srivar bearing the title 'kathakautaka'.[49] The notable Hindu Scholars of his time were Jonaraja, Srivara, pandit Notthasoma, Avtar Bhatta, Yodha Bhatt and Narhari.

The Sultan renewed the patronage to drama, dance and music.[50] The new form of music was called as *Sufiana Kalam*. He instituted a separate department of music under Srivara.[51] He gave patronage to arts and crafts. Wooden edifices were a common sight. Stone-polishing, stone-cutting, bottle-making, window-cutting, gold-beating etc. were introduced in his time.[52]

**Detractors**

Like Akbar's Badayuni, Sultan Zain-ul-Abidin had his own detractors. They could little understand caltholcity and farsightedness of the Sultan. While one historian accuses him of harming the cause of Isalm,[53] the other calls him a *bedin* (infidel).[54] Another authority says :

> "He (Zain-ul-Abidin) paid attention neither to infidelity nor Islam."[55]

In truth his policy of propagating Islam was based upon the tenet of Quran, which enjoins *La Ikraha Fila-i- din*, ie, there is no compulsion in Islam. The Sultan did not force proselytisation, but attracted the Hindus by his example of a true Muslim. Conversion did take place. A characteristic example of a Hindu convert to Islam is of Daryav Khan mentioned by Jonaraja.[56] The Sultan honoured the learned men of Islam as his preceptors.[57] He consulted Shaikh-ul-Islam on matters of theology and jurisprudence[58], and designated himself *Nabi- i-Amir-ul-Muminin*, the Deputy Commander of the Faithful.[59] He had a religious turn of mind and observed punctiliously the injunctions laid by Islam ie., prayers and Ramzan fasts.[60] The appraisal of the rulers does not come from eulogists but from the detractors.

Hence, Akbar was not the first preceptor of *Sulah-Kul*, but much before him it was preached and practised by a Sultan in Kashmir. Zain-ul-abidin's pragmatism makes his rule as 'The Age of Enlightement'. He stood for certain values and ideals, which till today are relevant to the Indian Secularism.

## References


1. Mohibbul Hasan, *Kashmir under the Sultans*, Srinagar, 1974, p. 207.
2. R.K. Parmu, *A History of the Muslim Rule in Kashmir*, Srinagar, 1977, p. 465; G.M.D. Sufi, *Kashir*, Vol. I, 1949, p. 83.
3. Jahangir, *Tuzuk-i-Jahangiri*, trans. A. Rodgers and H. Beveridge, Royal Asiatic Society, London, 1909, p. 96.
4. Daud Mishkati, *Asrar-ul-Abrar*, Research Library, Srinagar, f. 73.
5. M.L. Kapur, *Studies in History and Culture of Kashmir*, Jammu, 1976, p. 179.
6. Shrikanth Kaul, (ed.), *Rajtaranagini of Jonaraja*, Hoshiarpur, 1966, st. 707.

   श्री जैनोलाभदोनाख्य:सुत्राणो भवन् भवान् ।
   चिरं राज्यं क्रियादेवं राजास्याशिषमन्यधात्॥
7. J.P. Fergusson, *An Historical Introduction*, 1961, p.33 "Indeed history can give few examples where the policy of the father was so comptelely reversed by the son as was the case with Sikandar and Zain-ul-Abidin."
8. Srikanth Kaul, *op.cit.*, Stt. 765 to 770.

9. Jonaraja, *op.cit.* Bombay edition, 1898, stt. 1052-53, 1077-91; *Baharistan-i-Shahi* (anonymous), Research Library, Srinagar, pp. 46, 53; N.K. Zutshi, Sultan *Zain-ul-Abidin of Kashmir*, Jammu, 1976, p. 69.
10. Muhammad Qasim Firishta, *Tarikh-i-Firishta*, Lucknow, 1905, Vol. IV, p. 469. Sultan publicly announced, "Each individual worshipped his God agreeably to the faith in which he was educated."
11. Jonaraja, *op.cit.*, st. 1048; Baharistan, *op.cit*, p. 46; Firishta, *op.cit.*, p. 469.
12. Jonaraja, *op.cit.*, stt. 1049-50; Khwaja Nizamuddin Ahmad, *Tabaqat-i-Akbari*, edited by B. Dey and H. Husain, Calcutta 1927-35, Vol. III, p. 654.
13. Nizamuddin, *op.cit.*, p. 655.
14. Srikantha Kaul, *op.cit.*, p. 107, He expresses doubt, "Owing to their (Hindu) rigid system of ceremonial purity and notions of defilement, many Hindus could not have profited by the opportunity of coming back of their original fold."
15. Nizamuddin, *op.cit.*, p. 655; Baharistan, *op.cit.*, pp. 53-54; N.K. Zutshi, the biographer of Zain-ul-Abidin, is of the view that many Hindus returned to their original faith., p. 70.
16. Nizamuddin, *op.cit.*, p. 654; Jonaraja, *op.cit.*, stt. 755, 775-76; Baharistan, *op.cit.*, p. 46; Srivara, *Jain- Rajataranagini* edited by Srikanth Kaul, Hoshiarpur, 1966, I, IV, st. 2, V, stt. 80, 88, 100-101.
17. Ibid.
18. Srivara, *op.cit.*, Calcutta Edition, 1835, English tr. by J.C. Dutt as *kings of Kashmira*, I, V, stt. 56-58.
19. Firishta, *op.cit.*, p. 464.
20. Srivara, trans. by Dutta, p. 143, Also text, I, V, st. 61.
21. Abul-Fazl, *Ain-i-Akbari*, English tr., vol. II by H.S. Jarrett, Calcutta, 1949, p. 383.
22. Jonaraja, *op.cit.*, Bombay edition, st. 1078.
23. *Tarikh-i-Kashmir*, (Intikhab) Epitome of the Persian tr. of the *Rajtaranginis* of Jonaraja and Srivara (microfilm), Research Library, Srinagar, MS., f. 70a.

24. Baharistan, *op.cit.*, p. 46, "All those temples and idol-houses of the infidels which were broken and razed to the ground during the reign of Sikandar were repaired and rebuilt by the Sultan.
25. Sir Kantha Kaul, *op.cit*, stt. 872-74.
26. Ibid., st. 889.
27. Ibid., st. 834.
    समिज्जिते शयादेशे क्रूरादेशो महीपतिः।
    सुवर्णबुद्धप्रतिमां यवनेभ्यो ररक्ष सः ॥
28. *Baharistan, op.cit.*, p. 46.
29. Srivara, i, iii, st. 46.
30. Ibid.
31. Ibid., I, iii, st. 53, 58; Tuzuk, *op.cit.*, II, pp. 167-68 and note.
32. Srivara, trans. by Dutta, I, IV, stt. 1-2, 4, 8, 12.
33. Ibid., p. 124. The Sultan, "dismissed the devotees after having laden them with quilts, attendants, money and walking staves."
34. Jonaraja, Bombay edition, stt. 1233 sqq.
35. Srivara, I, V, stt. 88-95, 99-100.
36. Ibid., (Dutt), p. 134. "It snowed and the Gods", Srivara writes, "as if pleased with his (Sultan's) piety, showered flowers on him."
37. Jonaraja, *op.cit.*, stt. 973.
38. Ibid., p. 107.
39. Shri Ram Sharma, *The Religious Policy of the Mughal Emperors*, Oxford University Press, 1940, p. 50.
40. Nizamuddin, *op.cit.*, pp. 652-53.
41. Jonaraja, Hindi tr. by Raghunath Singh, Varanasi, 1972, st. 771 and note.
42. Jonaraja, *op.cit.*, Bombay edition, stt. 824-27.
43. Ibid., st. 972.
44. Haider Malik Chadura, *Tarikh-i-Kashmir*, Research Library, Srinagar, pp. 45-47.
45. Jonaraja, *op.cit.*, st. 823.
46. Srivar, I, V, stt. 76-78, VII, st. 114.
47. *Research Biannual* (J K), No 1, Vol. 1, 1976, Benevolent Badshah by Prof. K.N. Dhar, p. 29.
48.. Srivara, V, stt. 85-86.

49. G. Buhler, Report of a Tour in search of Sanskrit Manuscripts made in Kashmir, Rajputana and Central India, *Journal of the Royal Asiatic Society*, Bombay, Extra number (XII), 1877.
50. G.L. Kaul, *Kashmir Through the Ages*, VIIth edition, Jammu, 1963, p. 52.
51. Srivara, (Dutt), III, stt. 236-40.
52. Mirza Haider Dughlat, *Tarikh-i-Rashidi*, Eng. Tr. by E.D. Ross and N. Elias, London, 1895, p. 434.
53. *Baharistan*, *op.cit.*, pp. 53-54.
54. *Taufat-ul-Ahbab* (anonymous), Transcript, chapter IV, f. 106 a.
55. *Tarikh-i-Rashidi*, *op.cit.*, p. 434.
56. Jonaraja, *op.cit.*, stt. 962-63.
57. Nizamuddin, *op.cit.*, p. 656.
58. Jonaraja, *op.cit.*, st. 853; Haider Malik Chadura, *op.cit.*, p. 47.
59. *Journal of the Bombay Branch of the Royal Asiatic Society*, Vol. XLVIII, 1879, p. 284.
60. Nizamuddin, *op.cit.*, p. 657.

# 19

# RANJIT SINGH IN KASHMIR — A CRITICAL APPRAISAL

The intolerable and insufferable Afghan rule in Kashmir made the History to repeat itself,[1] when a Kashmiri Pandit, Birbal Dhar, invited Maharaja Ranjit singh to conquer the valley. The victorious generals of Ranjit Singh, Diwan Chand, Zaffar Jang and Phula Singh Nihang entered Srinagar on July 15, 1819. The Maharaja ruled Kashmir through the office of the governors.

Secularism was the prime characteristic of Ranjit singh's rule. *Dharmarth* fund established under his instructions was for every faith without any distinction of belief.[2] The religious intolerance in Kashmir was not his fault, but that of his governors.[3] Maharaja has given specific orders to his commander Diwan Chand, when marching into Kashmir to create an atmosphere of communal harmony.[4] Maharaja's wrath had acted as a deterrent in saving the Khanqah Muhalla Mosque at the hands of Phula Singh, the Akali and Nihang leader[5] from desecration and destruction.

The Shia Sunni clash during the Muharram festival,[6] when the Shia community was persecuted, and their women molested, raped and killed, angered the Maharaja so much against Bahama Singh, his governor in Kashmir, for dereliction of duty, inefficiency, and unpreparedness to tackle the emergency, that he recalled him immediately.[7] His standing orders were that the people of Kashmir should be made happy, as their happiness would bring to his "kingdom prosperity and felicity".[8] The ban on the *Azan* might be a diplomatic measure to placate Hindu and Sikh sentiments.

A salutary feature of the administration was linking of the Kashmir valley with the Punjab and other parts of India. Trade, commerce and intercourse which had come to a grinding halt since 1753, the year of the establishment of the Afghan rule, was geared up once again. The Gilzai Pathans and Durrani Afghans monopoly over the exports had ended. The Kashmiris resumed control over their trade. The export of the products like shawls, woolen rugs, saffron, fresh and dry fruits, vegetables, zera, papier machie articles, wooden boxes, wicker baskets, opium, and wine etc., and imported goods like salt, sugar, tea, chinaware, copper and brass utensils, medicines, and spices etc., once again came into their hands. The *Rehdari*[9] obstructions on the free movement of goods was removed after the political subjugation of the hill states and Derajat in 1831. It speeded up trade and commerce, and also provided the Kashmiri labour class avenues for employment. The Kashmiris also developed a habit of going down to the plains during winter season—a habit which is still very persistent. Now-a-days a Kashmiri feels cold more acutely than a non-Kashmiri. Kashmir became a trading centre. It was connected with Tibet and Central Asia via Ladakh, with the Punjab via Jammu, Muzaffarabad and Rajouri, and with Kohistan, Derajat, Peshawar, Kabul and Iran via Karna, Muzaffarbad and Hazara.[10]

The Kashmiri merchants became an affluent community with an international credibility. Moorcroft testifies it that while he was in Kashmir the merchants from Delhi, Banares and Kashmir, "Tendered their services to advance whatever cash I might require for my bills on Hindustan."[11] Many Kashmiri merchants had also settled in Calcutta, Delhi, Lucknow, Agra and Banares.[12] The Kashmir traders were used by the East India Company as their spies in Kashmir, Yarkand, Bokhara, Kashghar and Russia.

Maharaja Ranjit Singh himself was very much interested in the promotion of shawl trade — a rich source of revenue. When Maharaja came to know that the Persian shawl merchants were planning to leave Kashmir, he asked his favourite Kashmiri merchant, Samad Joo, to search them out and persuade them to start their business again. The government in Kashmir was ordered to do its best in rehabilitating them. He ordered the recall of the governor Kirpa Ram for his dereliction and profligacy. His salary was debited to pay up the salaries of the court officials.[13]

The social order remained unaffected due to the secular attitude of Ranjit Singh. Still certain practices crept in as is natural with a new system. The prohebition over the cow slaughter, revival of *Sati* system and sale of children were some of the new features introduced into Kashmir with the new rule.

*Begar*[14] in Kashmir known as *Kar-i-begar* or *Lam* was already prevelent. Hari Singh Nalwa tried to eradicate it, but was unsuccessful. The Sikh administration found it financially advantageous in times of peace as well as war. Sale of children was associated with the economic distress, following famine or floods made its ugly appearance during Ranjit Singh's rule. The parents sold their children to save themselves from the starvation. Jaquemont writes that about eight years old girls, promising to turn out charming maidens were sold to the trafficker's from the Punjab and India for twenty to three hundred francs. He further says that Kashmir was drained of its beauties.[15]

The Sikh administrators did not get enough time to encourage the study of the Sikh scriptures or learning of the Gurmukhi being pre-occupied within the short span of twenty years, either in administrative problems or to meet the financial demands of Ranjit Singh, or self indulgence in the beautiful vale of verdure and lovely maidens. But the Kashmiris on their own inclination carried on literary pursuits. Pandit Ram Lekhari in 1824 compiled *Ekadeshi* prefaced with the *tika*[16] of Japaji and wrote the *Granth Sahib* and *Ramayana* in the Gurmukhi script. Mirza Ghulam Mehdi Mujrim's *Diwan-i-Mujrim* composed in 1830 is an excellent work of great historical importance, portraying the condition of the people of his time. *Masnavi* of Khazir Shah depict the true and pathetic picture of the times. Hamid-ul-lah's *Bebujnama*[17] is a valuable source of information on the Sikh rule. Pandit Birbal Kachru's *Majmu-ut-Tawarikh* is a scholarly epitome on the philosophy of Hinduism and

Islam. The Muslim scholars have portrayed a gripping picture of the sufferings undergone by their co-religionists.

The revenue administration of Ranjit Singh was far from satisfactory. It made no provision to meet the emergency. The chief weakness of the system lay in the fact that the revenue was not assessed on the spot, but in Lahore after comparing some of the return of the Afghan times, making no allowance to the deplorable condition of the state and the people. Thus the principle of assessment was defective.

Second, no attempt was made to check the emigration of the agriculturists living on the borders of Kashmir due to the fear of the Sikh rule.[18] Third, nothing was done to improve the lot of the agriculturists, the backbone of the agrarian industry.[19] Fourth, official hierarchy was immoral and corrupt.[20] Coupled with the Nature's wrath, the peasantry lived in an animal existence.

Consequently revenue dwindled. In Akbar's time it was one crore rupees annually. The last Afghan ruler collected sixty two lakhs, and Ranjit Singh was to be contended with only ten lakhs[21]. He made no concessions even during the famine. When the Maharaja was requested by Suraj Behari, the revenue officer, to remit the revenue considering the devastating famine, he totally refused to oblige. He ordered that Suraj Behari should make good the loss. This has resulted in the bankruptcy of his biggest officials.[22]

Ranjit Singh tried his best to impart a good administration to Kashmir, but could not succeed. He ruled Kashmir through the office of the governors, but did not delegate them full authority. He was the fountain of power and authority. The governors derived power from him. He always suspected them of embezzlement. Strangely enough a ruler of the calibre of the Maharaja Ranjit Singh could not distinguish between conscientious and corrupt governors. He suspected even Colonel Mehan Singh, his best governor, of dishonesty. The Maharaja even wanted to remove him from his office.[23] Such as attitude towards the best of his governors, who gave Kashmir an interval of prosperity and plenty corroded the morale of the officers.

Ranjit Singh's government in Kashmir was imperialist by nature. It was manned by the Sikhs and the Punjabis. According to R.K. Parmu, "Politically and sociologically Kashmir remained during this period a Punjabi colony, for all that a colony meant in those times, just as previously she had been an Afghan colony, and before the Aghans a Mughal colony."[24] The interests of the masses were neglected. There started a process of exodus of the Kashmiris from Kashmir to different parts of India. The people from rural areas flocked to the cities. Agriculture was abandoned. From a flourishing country Kashmir turned into a "barren land of hardly several lakhs".[25] The Sikh government had no respect for the life of the Kashmiris. They were governed by the same attitude as later on was withnessed in the British India. If a Sikh killed a Kashmiri the maximum punishment for him was to pay a fine to the government between sixteen to twenty rupees, out of which four and two rupees were paid respectively to the Hindu and Muslim families of the deceased.[26] Hamid Ullah, in his '*Bebujnamah*' says that the administration from top to bottom was corrupt.[27] Justice was bought and sold.[28] The book in some repects may be compared to the Persian chronicle '*Siyar-ul-Mutakhrin*' of Mirza Ghulam Hussain in portraying the condition of the times.

To alleviate the sufferings of the people in Kashmir Ranjit Singh issued directives to his top officials to remove forthwith all restrictions including the duties on the free movement of the cereals to Kashmir. The corn merchants were directed to send their stocks directly.[29] Those guilty of hoarding were put behind the bars.[30]

The mass exodus of the Kashmiris focussed a remarkable quality of expressing their grievances through non violent means. The Kashmiris left the valley on account of unemployment and devastating famine, and went around the cities of Punjab and British India crying for bread. These peaceful marches may be called the Kashmiri version of *satyagrah*. This was the second mass protest of the Kashmiris. The first had taken place during the reign of Shahjahan in 1631.[31] These peaceful marches to ventilate their grievances against maladministration and oppression are unique in the history of India – where the population is generally docile and submissive.

For the good and efficient government in Kashmir. Ranjit Singh, had followed the Mughal practice of appointing two officers in the provinces, with very good intentions, governor and diwan, who would be a check on each other. With every non- Sikh governor of Kashmir Ranjit Singh appointed a trustworthy Sikh diwan to assist him and also to keep a watch on him.[32] But his arrangements could not succeed in Kashmir. The reason was that both the officers did not match each other in calibre, power, and diplomacy. Hari Singh Nalwa got Birbal Dhar, his capable Kashmiri diwan, dismissed for his insubordination.[33] Dewan Chunni Lal[34] was overmatched by his rash and overbearing revenue minister Kumedan Gurmukh Singh, who usurped all the powers. He seldom exercised restraint. In a cow killing incident, he persecuted innocent Muslims.[35] Even the God fearing and intelligent governor, Diwan Kirpa Ram, fell a victim to the charms of Kashmir – women, wine and music[36], leaving the entire administration to the care of Sheikh Ghulam Moly-ud-Din.[37] Luckily he was a trustworthy, competent and loyal officer.[38] During the governorship of Kunwar Sher Singh, his diwan Wasakha Singh exercised all power and authority, diverting his master's attention from duty to dissipation.[39] Thus the principle of check and balance between the officers was defeated.

Ranjit Singh was not always discernible in the appointment of governors. Moti Ram, his first governor was recalled for his inefficiency after one year in office, still he was made the governor for the second time as a measure of experiment. Hari Singh Nalwa as an administrator was a good choice, but his orthodoxy made the choice wrong and impolitic. Similarly selections of Chunni Lal and Sher Singh were not based upon sound judgement.

The term of the governors was very short for the smooth running of the administration and stability. Except Mehan Singh the average term of governors a was about two years. The governors when they got familiar with the conditions of the state, and able to cure the ills, were recalled.

Another feature of the rule was the establishment of the Kashmiri colonies in different parts of India. Unsuitable conditions, harsh administration and natural calamities forced the Kashmiris rich and poor alike to leave their country and settle outside in groups. Thus sprung up new Kashmiri colonies in Bhadarwah, Kishtwar, Jammu, Reasi, Punch, Rajouri, and Mirpur in the neighbouring hills states, in Simla, Bilaspur, Chamba, Mandi, Rampur and Nurpur in the Punjab Hills, and in Lahore, Amritsar, Sialkot, Hoshiarpur and Gurjanpur in the undivided Punjab[40]. They created a place for themselves by the dint of their hard labour, intelligence, scholarship and skill.

Ranjit Singh aspired to give a good administration to Kashmir. His secularism was the most prominent feature of his rule – there was no desecration of Muslim religious places and shrines or conversion. The Kashmiris regained control over trade and commerce lost during the Afghan rule. The country would have prospered if the chain of natural calamities would not have conspired to wreck it. His lust for money had a very demoralising effect upon governors, who could not undertake constructive measures and nation building projects as they had to send a large sum of money to appease the Maharaja. Vigne is also correct when he says that fear of the British imperialism was one of the deterrent factors to the prosperity of Kashmir.[41] A prosperous Kashmir would have been snatched away by the East India Company. Nevertheless it is true that with the end of the Sikh rule the medievalism came to a close in Kashmir, and modernism started creeping in,[42] as during this period most of the European travellers visited the valley who unveiled to the East India Company its natural beauty, charm and unlimited resources. To quote Prof. Gurcharan Singh, Ranjit Singh was a :

> "protector of the poor and the weak – he established a state where the strong were just and the weak secure – during his life he belonged to all men. After death, he belongs to the ages."[43]

## References

1. In 1753 the people of Kashmir being fed up with the rule of Abul Kasim Khan had invited Ahmad Shah Abdali, the ruler of Afghanistan, to conquer Kashmir. Vide Hassan Shah Maulvi, *Tarikh-i-Kashmir*, (in Urdu), Srinagar, 1960, p.435.
2. *Maharaja Ranjit Singh, First Death Centenary Memorial* - 1883, reprinted, 1970, p. 1., "He gave largess ---- without any considera-

tion as to man's caste, creed or colour. Faith – even his own – did'nt hem in his charity".

3. Punjab government Records, Vol. III, p. 3; Bhagat Singh, *Sikh Polity in the Eighteenth and Nineteenth Centuries*, Delhi, 1978 p. 293, Moti Ram, the Governor of Kashmir, put several men to death for killing cows.
4. Sohan Lal Suri, *Umdat-ut-Tawarikh, Chronicle of the Punjab from the Birth of Guru Nanak*, 1469 to *Annexation of the Punjab by the British*, 1849, translated into English by Y.S. Suri, 4 volumes (only vols III & IV have been translated from Persian into English), II, p. 259. (Persian)
5. R.K. Parmu, *History of the Sikh rule in Kashmir*, Srinagar, 1977, p. 155.
6. The first month of the Islamic Calender. The first ten days of the month, observed in commemoration of the martyrdom of Hussain, the second son of Hazrat Ali by Fatima, daughter of Prophet Muhammad. These days are observed by the Shia Muslims as the period of mourning. Mourning some times leads to clashes between Shias and Sunni's, two subgroupings of Islam; Pir Ghulam Hasan, *Tarikh-i-Hassan*, Srinagar Research Publication Department, Folio 208, (Persian) *Tarikh-i-Kalan*, scribed by Mir Ahmad s/o Noor Mohammad, The author says Shias were treated as a community separated from the Muslims. (Punjab State Archives, Patiala) (Persian Manuscript).
7. Naba Shah, *Wajiz-ut-Tawarikh*, f. 59b. (Manuscript), J.K. Government, Research Dept., Srinagar.
8. *Umdat-ut-Tawarikh, op.cit.*, III, p. 184. ; Edward Thoronton, *Gazetteer of the Countries Adjacent to India on the North-West including Sindh, Afghanistan, Baluchistan, the Punjab and the neighbouring states*, London 1841-44, Vol I, pp. 9, 36; William Moorcroft Collection, India Office Library, M.S.Eur D 260, folio 6.
9. Permit for travel.
10. R.K. Parmu, *op.cit.*, p. 303; William Moorcroft, MS Eur D 263, folio 9.
11. W. Moorcroft and C. Treback, *Travels in the Himalayan Provinces of Hindustan and the Punjab in Ladakh and Kashmir*, ed. H.R. Wilson, II, 1837, Reprinted 1970; p. 103, Diary of Kasid Pandit

quoted by D.P. Masson in *The State of Jammu and Kashmir*, Calcutta, 1899, Part I, pp. iv-v.

12. *Umdat-ut-Tawarikh*, III, p. 14. Ranjit Singh told Mian Samad "The sarkar was going to pay still more attention to them and they must feel easy at heart under all circumstances and that those who had left those Kothis must be searched out and persuaded to put up there again."
13. *Ibid.*, II, p. 392.
14. Forced, Paid or unpaid labour, M.A. Stein, Tr. *Kalhan's Rajtarangini*, Vol. I, p.209; R. Walter Lawrence, *Valley of Kashmir*, London, 1895, p. 412; William Moorcroft, MS EURD 264, p. 119; R. Legan, *Report on the Financial Condition of the Kashmir State*, Bombay, 1891, p. 29.
15. Victor Jacquemont, *Letters from India Describing a Journey in the British dominions of India, Tibet, Lahore and Kashmir*, London, 1834, II, p. 91, W.G. Osborne, *The Court and Camp of Ranjit Singh*, London, 1840, pp. 85-86. " Lahore Durbar, used to receive in tribute from the Governors of Kashmir beautiful girls and were kept by Maharaja Ranjit Singh or his courtiers." Rev. Joseph Wolff, *Travels and Adventures*, etc., London, 1861, p. 396.
16. Commentary.
17. *Bebuj* is a Kashmiri term meaning lawlessness. The idiom means story of the lawlessness, by this phrase Hamid-ul-lah designated his tract depicting immediate results of Sikh rule.
18. Parmu, *op.cit.*, p. 284.
19. Lala Ganeshi Lal, *Siyahat-i-Kashmir*, (Persian), Punjab State Archives, Patiala, p. 32. "The chief revenue and judicial functions of the Kashmir province were administered by a set of natives. Pandits have grown rich at the expense of the Mohemmedans and the people at large", W. Moorcroft, MS, EUR D. folio 264.
20. Moorcroft, *op.cit.*, II pp. 123-124; *Tarikh-i-Kalan*, *op.cit.*, f. 135.
21. G.T. Vigne, *Travels in Kashmir, Ladakh, Iskardo, the Countries adjoining the mountain course of the Indus and Himalayas*, London, 1842, II, pp. 118-19. "The first consequence of the oppressive nature of Ranjit Singh's government is, that the inhabitants have been constantly leaving the valley for many years back; the next has been that their masters have found it necessary to prevent their leaving it without assigning some sufficient reasons. The revenue

in Akbar's time amounted to more than three million of *Kirwahs* of rice – and he commanded that the crops should be equally divided between the government and the husbandman. The returns amounted, so I was informed, to more than a crore of small rupis, or a million sterling; and subsequently, in the time of Pathans to fifty or sixty lakhs of small rupis – Nawab Jabar, told me that when he was the governor collected 62 lakhs of small rupis, equal to more than 4,00,000 sterling. It has now in successive years dwindled down to 14 to 15 lakhs nominally, although in fact Ranjit, who always took care for a much larger sum from the government was obliged to be contended, I believe with something less than 10."

22. Baron Charles Von Hugel, *Travels in Cashmere, and the Punjab*, 1844, Reprint New Delhi, 1972, p. 58.
23. Abstract of intelligence from, dated 18-24 Sept., 1839, Pol. Cons. dated November 7, 1836, No. 45; *Umdat-ut-Tawarikh*, III, p. 504.
24. Parmu, *op.cit.*, p. 274. 2 E "Evidently, the relationship between the rulers and ruled was guided by the colonial maxim, "All that is yours is mine and that is mine is my own", D.C. Sharma, *Kashmir under the Sikhs*, Delhi, 1983, p. 273, "So Kashmir was ruled like a large Prison and no one was allowed to leave the valley without pass-port and the payment of one *tanga* per head".
25. *Ibid.*, p. 275.
26. Moorcroft, *op.cit.*, II, pp. 293-94.
27. Parmu, *op.cit.*, p. 4.
28. *Ibid.*, p. 141.
29. *Umdat-ut-Tawarikh*, III, p. 182.
30. *Ibid.*
31. R. K. Parmu, *History of Muslim Rule in Kashmir*, *op.cit.*, Delhi, 1968, p. 275.
32. *Umdat-ut-Tawarikh*, II, p. 337.
33. Maulvi Hassan Sah, *Tawarikh-i-Kashmir*, Vol. III, Srinagar, 1960 (Urdu), p. 522; Kirpa Ram, *Gulzar-i-Kashmir*, Lahore, 1870, "Pandit Birbal Dhar depending wholly on the Maharajah's kindness, did not show obedience and courtesy to Hari Singh Nalwa due to him."
34. Griffin, *Ranjit Singh*, 1911, p. 196.

35. Khalil Mirjanpuri, Tarikh-i-Kashmir, ii, J&K Govt., Research Dept., Srinagar (Persian Manuscript), ff. 175a - 175b.
36. Wajiz-ut-Tawarikh, *op.cit.*, p. 95b.; *Tarikh-i- Hassan*, *op.cit.*, vol. II, p. 762 (some parts of this stupendous volume have been published by Research Publications Dept., Srinagar).
37. Parmu, *History of the Sikh Rule*, *op.cit.*, p. 145.
38. *Gulzar-i-Kashmir*, *op.cit.*, p. 145; Hassan, *op.cit.*, p. 254.
39. Parmu, *op.cit.*, p. 158.
40. Cf. Parmu, *op.cit*, p. 176.
41. Quoted in Parmu, *op.cit.*, p. 314.
42. D.C. Sharma, *op.cit.*, p. 279.
43. Quoted in *Illustrated Weekly of India*, Jan. 11, 1981.

# 20

# CULTURAL ETHOS OF THE LADAKHI WOMEN THROUGH THE EUROPEAN TRAVELLERS

Woman, the perennial eve, held guilty for seducing Adam from the proverbial garden of Eden, has been since then a target for much calumny and slander. There has been no end to her exploitation. She has been given so many appellations by the opposite sex—better half, fair sex, feminine beauty, softer sex etc., but how much they were and still are profaned is anyone's guess. Every faith has persecuted them. In England the Tudor King Henry VIII being enamoured by a court lady Annebolyn divorced legally married and faithful wife Cathrine. The Muslim Sultans filled their harems with numerous concubines, besides four legal wives. The Hindus, burnt alive widows on the pyres of their husbands, giving it the colour of *Dharma* (Religion), but the material gain was the motivating factor. Similarly the institution of *Devdasis*, where young and charming girls were married to Gods, to become unwed wives of the priests of the temples. This is the saga of a woman, written with blood, tears, moans and wails.

But there is a relieving picture also—found on the roof of the world—Ladakh, a land where fairies congregate. The freedom enjoyed by the women in Ladakh surprised almost all the European travellers. Drew says, that the social liberty of the Ladakhi women was the same as of workmen's wives in England. The women moved about unveiled, freely mixing with the male members. They shared with them without inhibition toil, business and pleasures.[1]

Alexander Cunningham is of the opinion that the average height of the women in Ladakh is rather small than large.[2] The Buddhists in the colloquial language were called Bhots.[3]

**Dress, Makeup & Ornaments**

Their dress was simple. The dress was made of home made woolen cloth, which was coarse, thick, and loosely woven to keep them warm.[4] The women wore a gown, the skirt somewhat gathered into plaits generally of blue, red, green and yellow colours, but sometimes patterned and sewn together. Over the shoulders they wore a kind of shawl, of the sheep skin with the wool inside which was fastened with a loop and button on the right shoulder. Its outer part was covered with coloured cotton or woolen cloth with China Satin or Benaras brocade, according to their means.[5] They wore stockings of three types, of sheep's wool fetted, of sheep's wool knit, and of goat's wool knit. First was the most common. The Ladakhis generally are very proud of their boots, which is quite natural for a country like Ladakh, a land of rocks and stones and biting snow during winter.[6] The soles of the boots were of thick leather, like those of the Chinese, while the leg part was either of leather or of strong stiff cloth. The common women wore bright coloured shoes, whose seams were embroidered. The women of means had the boots of the Russian or Chinese leather. The ornamented boots came from Lhassa and Kashmir.[7]

The outstanding feature of a Ladakhi women's appearance was the extraordinary arrangement of hair and head dress, called *Perag*, the first part of the word being an old name for turquoise.[8] The hair was braided into inumerable plates.[9] There were hair dressers in the towns, but in the villages the women obliged each other. The hair was washed once in a month.

The perag consisted of a central elongated piece of leather, covered with red cloth, cut in the shape of a cobra with the expanded hood on top, shaped in such a way as to get fixed on forehead, and the tail on the back.[10] In reality the front part over the forehead resembled the head of a Cobra. On the bright red background rows of turquoise matrix were sewn, often ending in front with a chased gold and silver ornament, inlaid with small turquoises.[11] Small girls started wearing *perag* at the age of five or six, bearing single row of turquoises in front ending in cowrie shells in the back. Sometimes a large red correlian was also added.[12] The unmarried girls wore cowries. By the time a girl grew up, she ought to have a good sized *perag*, to be carried as a dowry. In fact it served the purpose of a bank for she invested money in turquoises which were an asset during old age or widowhood. While the eldest son inherited all the landed property, the eldest daughter inherited all the ornaments. Richly ornamented and turquoise studded *perags* generated a great jealousy,

> "and a lady with a very resplendent *perag* is often one of suspicious morals".[13]

Ganpat calls the *perag* "an heirloom".[14] Ladakhi women were very fond of ornaments. Earrings, necklaces and amulets boxes (Tabiz) made of chased gold were worn. Bracelet-cuffs were made of chased silver.[15] The most costly ornament, was the collar, encasing the neck, which was a stiff band of silver or gold, more or less wrought, bound with strings of coral, pearls, or silver beads, and studded with turquoises in the shape of flowers.[16]

The Muslim and Christian women had given up the *perag* but in the matter of dress they displayed exquisite taste and refinement than their Buddhist sisters.[17] They wore fine printed clothes much more expensive than the turquoises. The Muslim women had discarded also heavy collar necklaces for light and simple one.[18] During the gala occasions the Ladakhi women used the pulp of a fruit for the facial make up. It imparted a kind of glaze to the face, the small seeds of the pulp, which got stuck on the face, thought to improve the texture of the skin.[19]

**Dance:**

The dancing women wore similar dresses, but sometimes they wore long gowns of different colours, instead of the jacket and petticoat.[20] Their caps in winter were of oblong white sheep wool covered on the outside with large squares of green and red cloth. In summer they were replaced by fringed caps with Kashmiri or Yarkandi embroidery, or beautifully worked Chinese silk. Perhaps the ordinary women's dancing had a slight religious touch symbolised by their gestures of salutation, plucking of the flowers, the opening out of the bud into flower, and presenting it to God.[21] The rest of the dance was very slow, graceless, and monotonous, but not to the Ladakhis. In the peacock and pigeon dances both males and females danced together. The ladies looked quite picturesque in their dresses. At the beginning and end of the dance they knocked their wristlets in respectful salute to the king. The upper class families had to provide a woman dancer, who had to dance during the festivities at the New Year and festival of *Dasmoche*. Such women were very much respected, and were not selected for their beauty, bloom or youth. In the peacock and pigeon dance both males and females danced together.[22]

## General Characteristics

Temperamentally Ladakhi ladies are very laborious and active.[23] Cunningham says, that as porters they carried very heavy loads with ease and cheer. A girl of sixteen or eighteen carried box weighing sixty pounds over the high passes of Kanawar. "I have had practical proof of this superiority amongst the *Botis* of Lahul, Kanawar, and spiti. In 1846, the short Lahuli women carried with the greatest ease day after day, the roof of my tent, which the taller and finer looking men of Kullu and Shimla refused on account of its weight. Again in 1847, the Kanawari and Spiti women carried loads at which the pampered collies of Shimla had grumbled"[24]. According to him their physical strength is the result of salubrious climate of their elevated country and partly to the former infusion of Hindu blood.[25] Drew also says, that the women with sixty pounds of baggage on their back made twenty-three or twenty-four miles a day, lightening their burden in the company of their cheerful disposition and singing songs.[26]

Ganpat says, that they worked in the fields as the agriculture was the only profession they were engaged in.[27] It was a common sight to see the figures of women in dull, drab and ragged garments and gaudy *perags* of turquoise with conical baskets upon their back, laden with fruits or manure, or perhaps with the most precious and darling possession ------- a Ladakhi baby. Their hard labour and perseverance had turned the patches of stony Ladakh into a carpet of emerald. Moorcroft also testifies it. He says, that they are also very expert in wool picking.[28]

One of the outstanding features of the Ladakhi life is that their food habits are very good and simple, nevertheless nutritious and wholesome. The staple food of the people is barly meal. Except tea, they produce everything required, for their unostentatious life.[29] Cunningham, says that meat was seldom tasted by the poor classes except on occasions of rejoicing such as birth or marriage. Tea was getting popular, but the poor section of the society could ill afford it.[30] Women without any inhibition drank *Chang*, which is a must for the cold climate of Ladakh.

Every women kept a maid servant, except when very poor, who served for one or two years to collect some money for dowry. The servants' work was very light—only to light the fire, as the cooking was done by mistress. The Ladakhis call the servant "a fire blower".[31] The servant after getting married kept for herself a servant.[32] They are very cheerful, willing and good tempered. They are ever ready for a laugh. Scolding and railing are almost unknown amongst them.[33] The three characteristics most noticeable in Ladakh are "cheerfulness, honesty and willingness to work". Courage perhaps also, not the courage of fighting man so much as the courage of sturdy animals. They will face hard work and exposure to height and cold, and go on laughing.[34] 'Comfort' word is not in their grain.[35] Murder was unknown, infanticide undreamed of, and jealousy did not seem to exist.[36] Drew says, that simplicity and clumsiness are their characteristics.

> "There could hardly be two national characters more opposed than these of Ladakhis and the Kashmiries; the latter, quick, versatile, and plausible, and former slow, inept and much given to truth telling"[37]. Moorcroft says, "that the Ladakhis are in general, a mild and timid people, frank, honest and moral when not corrupted by communication with the dissolute Kashmiris. They are indolent, exceedingly dirty, and too apt to be addicted to intoxication."[38]

Drew, when he came to Ladakh as the Governor, was very much impressed by their ceremonial welcome. At every village, the villagers collected at the entrance of the village, with the musicians in attendance playing on *flageolet* and *tom tom*. The women in their brightest petticoats and gayest ornaments were drawn up in line, each holding a vessel containing either barley meal, or milk, or *chang*, or some other thing to eat or to drink, not in large quantity like the traditional *Indian dali*, but as a token. He adds:

> "lastly some of the women carry earthen vessels in which burn chips of pencil cedar. As one comes up, all place their vessels on the ground, and make profound and not undignified bows."[39.]

The Ladakhi women wore tattered dresses. They did not even wear the dresses they brought as trousseau. They treasured it for their daughters. With a gaudy and variegated *perag* their tattered dresses presented a total contrast.[40] She never mended her dress, and wore it until it fell to pieces. To Ganpat this unmindfulness to the dictates of fashion, is "strange in a daughter of Eve."[41]

Ladakhis are a religious community. *Om Mani Padma Haun* is always on their lips, either in prayer or work.[42] A European noted that an old woman never went beyond "Om Mani Pad", and wrote "let us hope the fraud on heaven was passed over".[43] The women were also ordained as nuns. Most Buddhist families like to have one representative in the church. In the absence of a son a daughter must join the church. She began her monastic life early. Her hair was shorn, she donned the clerical red dress, and wore a tight fitting red or yellow hat with the sides turned up. She was honoured with the title of *Abi Tomo*, (Grand Mother). Generally the nuns lived with their own family, but sometimes they were segregated, as in Lamayuru, where there was quite a little nun village.[44] Ganpat says, that the life of a nun :

> "is in many ways comparable to that of the religious order we call 'lay sisters' in Europe. She takes a very minor part in any religious services—equivalent to that of the congregation in Europe and she is chiefly engaged in much more menial tasks—cooking, sewing, etc.—as may be necessary for the monastery."[45]

They did not perform any ritual in Ladakh, but in the Central Ladakh like the Lamas they were invited to read from the holy books in private houses. They remained unmarried, and were generally very ignorant.[46] Drew says, that they were not allowed to enter the image room of the monasteries.[47] In Ladakhi language the nuns are called Chumo.

**Observations:** From the above accounts it is clear that the women enjoyed a privileged position, at present unspoiled by the concepts of civilisation, glamour and spohistication. A society undefiled by the notions of selfishness, possession or jealousy. A society where parents and elders were not left out in cold. Neve says that the Buddhist women enjoyed much freedom, in comparison to Muslim women, who were subjected to polygamy and *mutah*. Shias defend the *mutah* marriages, by saying that they were permitted by the Prophet, but the Sunni version is that they were afterwards disallowed by the Prophet.[48] Vigne says, that the marriage ceremony of Little Tibet[49] differs from that of other Muslim countries. First, in going of the husband personally to see the prospective bride instead of sending a friend or relative. He had also the option of rejecting her, if he did not like her. Second, on the day of marriage the bride came to bridegroom's house, instead of bridegroom going to her house.[50] About polyandry— it is not good to taste as polygamy— nevertheless it was prevalent in India—mythological example is that of Dropadi, who had five husbands. But the only daughter in family preferring monogamy is a proof that by nature they were not voluptuous or polyandrous. A society, where the child irrespective of its sex or birth is loved deserves laureles. The Europeans, who had projected a true image of the society, said nothing of the immorality of the nuns—which is a common drawback of this institution. It is a footnote in favour of the chastity and sobriety of the Ladakhi women.

Nevertheless it was not totally a free society for the girls or boys, as they too often were not permitted to marry according to their choice. The eldest son inherited the property. If the sister was eldest, she passed over for the brother next to her, who inherited the property. The sons were more prized than the girls, which is evident by giving the sons a girls name to cheat the DEATH. Where women are happy which is evident from their health, singing, dancing and laughing—heaven dwells there. All the luxuries and material comforts are nugatory to this bliss. Ganpat very aptly says:

> "I become more of a Gandhi-ite in my leanings to his utterly impracticable things to pit against modern civilization, but nevertheless they are fascinating beyond everything, and of all places I know I have never found any so friendly to dreams as the byways of Lamaland".[51]

## References

1. Frederic Drew, *The Jammoo and Kashmir Territories*, London, 1875, p. 280.
2. Alexander Cunningham, *Ladak*, 1854, p. 290.
3. F. Drew, *op.cit*, The word Bhot means Buddhist, or perhaps more particularly, Buddhist Tibetan. The Ladakhis are called Bhot by themselves and their neighbours.
4. Frederick Drew, *op.cit.*, p. 240; A. Cunningham, *op.cit*, pp. 301-302.
5. William Moorcroft and George Trebeck, *Travels in the Himalayan Provinces of Hindustan and the Punjab of Ladakh and Kashmir*, London, 1841, Vol. I, pp. 324-325.
6. Moorcroft, *op.cit.*; F. Drew, *op.cit*, pp. 240-241.
7. Moorcroft, *op.cit.*, p. 326.
8. Major M.L.A. Gompertz, (popularly known as Ganpat), *Magic Ladakh*, 1928, p. 57.
9. A. Reeve Heber and Kathleen M. Heber, *Himalayan Tibet and Ladakh*, London 1923, Indian Reprint, New Delhi, 1976, p. 181.
10. Ibid., pp. 126-127.
11. Ibid.
12. Cunningham, *op.cit.*, p. 802.
13. Heber, *op.cit.*, p. 128.
14. Ganpat, *op.cit.*, p. 68.
15. Ibid., Heber, *op.cit*, p. 128.
16. Moorcroft, *op.cit.*, p. 328.
17. Ganpat, *op.cit.*, p. 153.

18. Moorcroft, *op.cit.*, p. 328.
19. Ibid., Ganpat, *op.cit.*, p. 69.
20. Ibid., p. 328; Ganpat, *op.cit.*, p. 69.
21. Cunningham, *op.cit.*, p. 302.
22. Heber, *op.cit.*, pp. 210-211.
23. Cunningham, *op.cit.*, p. 69.
24. Ibid.
25. Ibid.
26. Frederick Drew, *op.cit.*, p. 248.
27. Ganpat, *op.cit.*, p. 143.
28. Moorcraft, *op.cit.*, p. 322.
29. Ibid., pp. 328-29; Frederick Drew, *op.cit.*, p. 247; Ganpat, *op.cit.*, p. 64.
30. Cunningham, *op.cit.*, p. 303.
31. Ganpat, *op.cit.*, p. 151.
32. Ibid.
33. Moorcroft, *op.cit.*, p. 122.
34. Ganpat, *op.cit.*, p. 60.
35. Ibid; Frederick Drew, *op.cit.*, p. 239.
36. Ganpat, *op.cit.*, p. 66.
37. F. Drew, *op.cit.*, pp. 239-240.
38. Moorcroft, *op.cit.*
39. F. Drew, *op.cit.*, p. 253.
40. Ganpat, *op.cit.*, p. 151.
41. Ibid., p. 152.
42. Andrew Wilson, *The Abode of Snow*, London, 1885, p. 257.
43. Ibid., p. 267.
44. Heber, *op.cit.*, pp. 136-137.
45. Ganpat, *op.cit.*, pp. 123-24.
46. Heber, *op.cit.*, p. 137.
47. F. Drew, *op.cit.*, p. 255.
48. Arthur Neve, *Thirty years in Kashmir*, London, 1913, p. 219. The Koran says, "forbidden to you are married woman, except those who are in your hands as slaves. And it is allowed besides this to seek out wives by means of your wealth and give those with whom you

have cohabited their dowry. This is the law. But it shall be no crime to you to make agreement beyond the law, *Surah IV*, 288.

49. Iskardo.
50. G.T. Vigne, *Travels in Kashmir, Ladakh, Iskardo*, London, 1842, p. 259.
51. Ganpat, *op.cit.*, p.155.

# 21

# TRADE AND COMMERCE IN LADAKH

Present name of Ladakh comes from the Tibetan word La-tags. But in the past it was known by other names also, as for example Maryul,[1] Kha-Chan-Pa,[2] kie-Chha,[3] and M-lo-pho.[4] It is also called Moonland, as earth and sky seem to meet here. The territory of Ladakh is one of the most elevated regions in the world. Leh, the capital of Ladakh, is more than eleven thousand feet above the sea level and some parts of the northern district of Nubra are two thousand feet above the sea level.[5] The passes that lead into Ladakh on its southern frontier are more than sixteen thousand feet above the sea level. It is a queer admixture of desert and valleys, which are long and flat at 15,000 feet above the sea level. Mountains that surround stand at 20,000 to 21,000 feet in height.[6]

Infertility of the soil is the cause of its thin population. Still the Ladakhi people by nature are mainly agriculturists.[7] The small holdings and short time for agriculture due to severe winter is compensated by its geographical situation. Placed in the centre of Asia, it had been a commercial thoroughfare between Tibet, Turkistan, China and even Russia on the one hand, and Kashmir, the Punjab and the plains of India on the other.[8] Ladakh's trade was of a varied nature. It was an import and export centre. It imported articles for its own use from India and China, and also exported articles from Kashmir and other Indian provinces to China and vice versa. The mountains of Ladakh contain huge deposits of mineral wealth, but it was not exploited fully in the nineteenth century.

Yak is the most prized animal in Ladakh.[9] Its long hair, after being fleeced, was manufactured into blankets, coarse woolens and socks. It was kept for home trade and not for export. From Balti, or little Tibet, came vessels of gritstone for cooking, water pots and dried fruits, especially apricots were exported, partly for consumption at home and partly for export along with those of indigenous products. Balti apricots are superior to the Ladakhi apricots.[10] Apricots were ordinarily bartered for wool. The two seers of Balti apricots fetched a seer of goat's wool, and one seer of apricots were exchanged for two and a half seers of sheep's wool. The main articles of import from Kashmir and the Punjab were shawls, chintzs, copper tinned vessels for cultinary purposes, as cauldrons, chang pots, dishes, plates, teapots, spoons and grain, intended mainly for consumption at home and Tibet. "Ghee" or butter and raisins were imported from the southern provinces of the Himalayas in exchange for salt, borax, sheep's wool, and gold dust.[11]

Charas, a narcotic preparation made from rubbing of hemp and bhang is brought from Yarkand.[12] About 500 maunds were imported annually at the overage price of three rupees per seer, amounting to Rs. 24,000 or £ 2,400. About 300 maunds of charas was consumed in Ladakh.[13] A small quantity of tobacco was imported from Bisahar[14] and Kashmir. A large quantity of tobacco was imported from Yarkand, its annual supply being stated at 4,000 maunds, or 128,000 Ib., whole of which was consumed in the country.[15] This proves that the consumption of intoxicating drugs in Ladakh was more than normal.

### Export of Home Products

The main products of Ladakh for export were wool, tea, dried fruits, borax and sulphur. Wool was on the top of the exporting list. Wool, in Tibetan *bal*, was the chief product of Ladakh.[16] It was of three kinds: first, goat wool or *le-na*, which was used for the shawls, second sheep wool or *bal*, which was used for blanketing, coarse clothing and stuffing pillows and mattresses, and third was the prized *tus*. This wool fleeced from *asali tus*, a wild goat, was exported in smaller quantity to Kashmir. It is of a light brown colour, known for its warmth and softness.[17] Tea stood second in order of the items of export. Although its consumption in the country was considerable, nevertheless it was exported to Kashmir and the Punjab.[18] Dried fruits were exported in abundance from Ladakh. They consisted of apricots and small seedless raisins (commonly called currants). The export of the indigenous produce of Ladakh fetched Rs. 80,000 or £ 8,000[19] or thereabouts.

Minerals like borax and sulphur were also exported. The borax and sulphur mines are found together in the Puga valley,[20] near the bank of Rulang-Chu, a small stream full of hot springs, before it joins the Indus on its left bank, at a great distance from Leh.[21] The borax is ejected from the bed of the stream by the numerous hot springs at various temperatures from 80°upwards. Salt is found along both banks of the stream for about two miles along with chloride of soda. It is in a damp state owing to the vapours emitted by the hot springs. In collecting borax, the surface of the salt, which is generally of light pink colour, but sometimes also green, is carefully scrapped. Afterwards, the material is smeared with fat to prevent loss by evaporation. In that shape it was transported across the Himalayas to the plains. Borax is used in preparation of certain medicines and to add glaze and lustre to gold, silver and pottery.[22] The quantity of the borax annually exported was stated at 500 maunds, or 16,000 lbs. It fetched a sum of Rs. 500/- at the rate of sixteen seers per rupee.[23]

Sulphur is obtained from the Puga sulphur mine,[24] situated at a short distance from the stream, at the foot of a gypsum cliff. The mineral is found in the form of a thin lamina disseminated throughout the rock. In all the laminas there are numerous and detached crystals, of all sizes, from that of a grain of sand to one-eight of an inch. In detaching the sulphur, crystals are mostly reduced to powder. A small quantity of gypsum rock is also mixed with the powder. It is later exported to India. Cunningham is of the opinion that annually about 250 maunds equal to 1600 lbs. were actually exported.[25]

Ladakh acted as a commercial centre for export and import between the Chinese provinces of Yarkand,[26] Khotan[27] and Kashghar[28] and India. The foreign trade of Ladakh was principally in transit through the town of Leh, the sole market or entrepot. The different communication lines from Yarkand, Chinese Tibet, Kashmir and the Punjab converge on Leh.[29] The main articles of trade export from China were tea, shawl-wool and borax. Besides these, a number of articles were exported from China to India, via Ladakh.[30] An interesting example is that of *gur* or coarse sugar, exported from Kashmir through Ladakh to Yarkand, where after undergoing a tedious journey of two and a half months it was refined and crystallised and given the shape of sugar candy, which again was imported back to Kashmir. Tea imported to India from China was of three varieties — two of black and third of green colour. Their names consecutively were - *Zungcha, China Chum,* and *Chopinz.* It was sold in India for four rupees a seer, or 4 Sh. a pound (English). The medicines Touzu and Tedock were also imported.[31]

The Indian exports to China via Ladakh and Yarkand were also considerable. Kashmiri Shawls of inferior quality were very much in demand. The fine Kashmiri shawls famous in the world for their embroidery and softness were not imported due to prohibitive prices. Cheap shawls with large patterns were preferred in the Yarkand market. Their prices ranged between Rs. 50 to Rs. 300 per pair, the average being about Rs. 100/-. The total value of the shawls imported to Yarkand was about Rs. 50,000 or £ 5,000.[32]

Like the shawls, brocades of the cheap variety was preferred in the Yarkand market — ranging between Rs. 50 to Rs. 300 each. About 400 pieces were exported annually, which at an average rate of Rs. 100/- each, made the total amount to Rs. 20,000 or £ 2,000[33].

Spices to the value of about Rs. 1000/-, or £ 100, were said to be annually imported into Ladakh of which Rs. 800/- worth was exported to Yarkand.[34]

Saffron was exported to Yarkand from Kashmir via Ladakh. About twenty maunds, or 640 lbs. were annually exported, at the rate of Rs. 40/- per seer. The total trade proceeds was about Rs. 12,800/- or £ 1,280.[35]

Cloths of all coarser sorts and bales of flowered cotton and bright coloured chintzes were imported from India. The annual amount of about 100 maunds or 3,200 lbs. of cloth was imported valuing Rs. 10,000/- or £ 1,000. A small quantity was kept for domestic use and the rest was exported to Yarkand.[36]

From Ladakh to Yarkand and through it to other, provinces of China, the Indian exports generally consisted of madder, pearls, English Calicoes, Dacca Muslins, Chintzes Kimkhab or Zari, shields, indigo, senna, sugar, tabsir and silica found in Bambru resembling the opal in appearance, lemon juice and opium, etc.[37]

Cunningham is of the opinion that the whole value of foreign trade of Ladakh's home produce did not exceed Rs. 80,000/- or £8,000.[38] Yearly imports and exports to the Chinese territories were to the tune of Rs. 2,67,650/- or £ 26,765 and Rs. 2,16,000/- or £ 21,600/- respectively.[39] Similarly Indian imports and exports were to the tune of Rs. 2,20,200 or £ 22,020 or $ 23,800/-. It meant that both China and India exported more and imported less.[40] Very heavy duties were imposed on the merchandise by the Ladakhi officials.[41] During the middle of the nineteenth century the total duties levied was Rs. 18,000/- per annum.[42]

**Coins**

In Ladakh coins from the nighbouring states were found, on account of its being a trading centre, e.g., the golden tiles of Bokhara and Kokand (or Kokan), the sycee silver and pierced copper coins of China, the thin silver pieces of Nepal, the copper dumps of Bishar, Mughal rupees, the Nanak Sahi and Govind Sahi rupees of Ranjit Singh and broad rupees of the British India, bearing the head of the Queen of England. The only Ladakhi coin minted in Kashmir was the silver Jud or Jao, which was worth one quarter of a rupee. The Nepal coins were of silver, each worth two Jaos of Ladakh.[43]

**Weight & Measure**

The weights of Ladakh were almost the same as that of India — *Batti* and *Man* or Maund. *Batti* was equal to two Indian seers or thirty-two *Chhataks*. *Man* was equal to eight *battis* or sixteen seers, as was the small maund of India.[44]

For weighing heavy produce especially the grain, the universal measure was *Khal*. It was of two kinds — the *Dek-Khal* and the *Shor-Khal*, meaning "Weight *Khal*" and Measure *Khal*".[45] The common *Khal*, whether by weight or measure, was the well-known quantity of a sheep's load, *luk-khal*, equal to *eight battis* or one maund of sixteen Indian seers, or thirty two English pounds. When a large measure was to be mentioned, *Khal* was preceded by a prefix, a *Ta - Khal* (horse Khal), or *Yak - Khal*, which was equal to four maunds, or 128 lbs.[46]

Ladakh was the leading commercial centre for central Asia. It catered to the needs of China, Tibet, Turkistan, Kashmir, the Punjab and Northern India. Leh was the commercial heart of Ladakh. Different lines of communications from Yarkand, Chinese Tibet, Kashmir and the Punjab, converged upon Leh. Four roads lead from Leh to Yarkand across the Karakoram range. Thus Leh was connected on all sides by the roads.[47] The importance of Leh as a trading centre was obvious, due to its gravitating position, as the meeting place of the great empires of Asia. Russia and Britain were both interested in it for its trade and commercial potential,[48] and wished to monopolise it.[49]

Trade and commerce in Ladakh suffered from many drawbacks. There were no manufacturing industries. Though there were flocks and herds in abundance, which if properly developed would have made the country a manufacturer of the wool industry. Ladakhi women knew weaving, but only half of their number was employed in manufacturing, as they had to look after household work also.[50] Similarly there were vast resources of mineral wealth in salt, borax, natron and gold,[51] which was not fully exploited. Means of communication even in the nineteenth century were not modernised and other new routes were not explored. They presented a medieval outlook in the modern age.

A quite unexpected phenomenon was that the trade and commerce in Leh was in the hands of the merchants from the Punjab, Kashmir and Kashghar.[52] The shopkeepers in Leh were either half castes or foreigners. Drew explains it in the light of Ladakhi's natural inclination for the soil. "They (Ladakhis) form a peasantry tilling their own land."[53] Mostly the barter system was in practice.[54] The traders from the south generally exchanged their goods with the men from the north, similarly the traders from the Punjab got the needed articles from Yarkand at Leh. They arrived in July and left in November, due to intense cold.[55]

Thus Ladakh with all the advantages remained poor and its people were consequently illiterate. Progress and illiteracy go ill together. In present times one sees educated Ladakhis, mostly women, dominating the path markets in the big cities of northern India, along with the Tibetan refugee women, especially at Srinagar and New Delhi, which proves that they have a natural talent of a good salesman.

## References

1. Low land or Red land. Cosma de Koros spells the name Mar-Yul, the "Low Country." Hienn Tsang, in 640 A.D., calls it Ma-Lo-Pho or Mar-Po, that is "red", vide Alexander Cunningham, *Ladak*, 1854, Indian Reprint, 1977.
2. Snow land, this name was also used by the Chinese travellers.
3. Fa-hsien in 400 A.D. called it by the above name.
4. See F.N.I.
5. William Moorcroft and George Trebeck, *Travels in the Himalayan Provinces of Hindustan and the Punjab in Ladakh and Kashmir*, London, 1841, Vol. I, pp. 259-60.
6. Cunningham, *op.cit.*, pp. 41-74.
7. *Gazetteer of Kashmir and Ladak,* herein after Gazetteer p. 532; Frederic Drew, *The Jummoo and Kashmir Territories*, 1875, p.245. "Almost all the Ladakhis are engaged in agriculture; the number of artisans is very small indeed, and of shop-keepers of that race there are hardly any; the shopkeepers of the town of Leh—the only town in the whole of country - are either half-castes or are strangers. Thus the greater part of the population of Ladakh is connected with the soil. They form a peasantry tilling their soil."
8. *Gazetteer*, p. 532.
9. *Gazetteer*, p. 94; Cunningham, *op.cit.* p. 209.
10. Moorcroft Trebeck, *op.cit.*, p. 357. "The Ladakh apricots are much cheaper and are commonly sold in ass loads, each load weighing about sixty seers or a maund and a half pakka."
11. *Ibid.*, pp. 357-58.
12. Cunningham, *op.cit.*, p. 244.

13. *Ibid.*
14. *Ibid.*, p. 245.
15. In British India.
16. Cunningham, *op.cit.*, pp. 238-39.
17. Moorcroft, Trebeck, *op.cit*, pp. 348-350. "Beside the fleece of the domesticated goat, that of the wild goat, under the denomination of Asli Tus, is exported in smaller quantities to Kashmir. It is of a light brown colour, and exceeding fineness, and is worked into shawls, a species of soft cloth called Tusi, and lining for shawl wool stockings; very few shawls, however, are made from this material ....... In general the pickers of the shawl wool are paid by the hair, but in this case the hair was considered unfit for making into ropes. Shawls made from this material would be much softer, lighter and warmer, than those of ordinary fabric. When without being picked the *Asli Tus* is worked into Tusi; it forms a warm, soft cloth, of a drab or grey colour, which is much worn in the hills. It is manufactured at various places in the Punjab. A piece bought at Amritsar for ninety rupees was sold at Delhi for two hundred and fifty, but the Tusi cloth which comes to Hindustan is made from a mixture of the *Asli Tus* with other wool. This article must be always high priced from the difficulty of procuring the animal that produces it, the wild goat rarely venturing within gun-shot during the day, and being obtained only by snares at night when they come down from the mountains to browse in the valleys."
18. *Ibid.*, p. 350.
19. Cunningham, *op.cit.*, . 240.
20. *Gazetteer*, p. 671, Lat. 78° 25'. Long. 33° 15'. Elev. 15,200'. It is on the right bank of the Puga rivulet. It is a halting place on the route from the Isomorari Lake to Leh. The route from Leh to Hanle and Gardok also passes through it. There are sulphur mines and borax fields here. Hot springs occur in the bed of the rivulet for a length of about two miles, and its banks are quite white with saline matter that is being continually precipitated.
21. G.T. Vigne, *Travels In Kashmir, Ladakh, Iskardo*, London, 1842, II. p. 343, Leh is well known to be the principal place as rendez-vous for merchants travelling to and from Yarkand. The roads from Nurpur, Jammu and Kashmir, lead directly from it. There is a nearer way, I believe, by the plains of Chang Thung, to the north of Ladakh, but the jealousy of the Chinese is such that

they have closed it.; *Gazetteer*, Lat. 34° 10′. Long. 77° 37′. S.lev. 11,538′. The capital town of Ladak.

22. *Gazetteer*, p. 30.

23. Cunningham, *op.cit*., p. 240; Moorcroft & Trebeck, *op.cit*., p.355, It (borax) is bought in Bhot at thirty-two battis, or one maund and twenty-four seers, Delhi weight, for a rupee. By refining it loses half its weight, but the thirty-two seers sell for five or six rupees. There is a kind of smuggling trade carried on. The shepherds of these provinces receive a gratuity for pasturing the flocks of Katoch, Chamba, on the borders of Lahoul, but they sometimes take half the flocks with them to Bhot for borax, instead of leaving them to graze on mountains, and are thus enabled to sell it at a lower price (Bhot is one of the names of Ladakh).

24. See F.N. 20.

25. Cunningham, *op.cit*., p. 40.

26. H.W. Bellow, *Kashmir and Kashghar*, London, 1875, p. 249. Yarkand is one of the ancient cities of Tartary, and was in remote times a royal residence of the Turkish princes of the Afrasyab dynasty..... Yarkand would be Tartar form of (Sanskrit) Hari Khand, "The dwelling of Hari", *Gazetteer*, Lat. 38° 21'. Long 77° 28. A province in the dominions of the Amir of Kashgar, lying north of Ladak, and separated from it by the Karakoram and Western Kuenlun ranges.

27. Ibid., Lat. 37° 10'. Long, 79° 27'. A province in the Chinese Empire lying to the north of the Eastern Kuenlun range, which here forms the boundary of Ladak.

28. A commercial centre of Chinese Turkistan.

29. *Gazetteer*, p. 563.

30. Cunningham, *op.cit*., p. 241; Vigne, *op.cit*., p. 345; (1) Charas or Bang, an intoxicating extract of hemp; (2) Silver in bars or ingots, called Kuru and Yambu. Kuru is a Turkish name; the Tibetans call them Yam-Bu; (3) Felts of various kinds; (4) Suklát, a kind of camlet made of camel's hair; (5) Tea, both black and green; (6) Sugar candy; (7) Russian leather, called Bulgár; (8) Sable - Skins, called Kūndūz; (9) Gama, or black leather; (10) Kimasan, or golden coloured leather, about eight inches wide; (11) Sāgri, a green leather; (12) Lāka, a peculiar cloth made of hemp bark; (13) Velvets, both coarse and fine; (14) Mashru, or coarse silk cloth of

three kinds; (i) Badshahi; (ii) Alchinbar, made at Alchi or llitsi; (iii) Kotani, made at Kotan; (15) Siling, a soft and fine silky woollen of two kinds; (i) Shirūn; and (ii) Gorūn; (16) Parcha Samsūn, coarse cotton cloths; (17) Parcha Zukh, coarse cotton cloths; (18) Silk both raw and manufactured; (19) Gold; (20) Gold thread, called Zirru, both genuine and false; (21) Silver; (22) Silver thread; (23) Turquoises, from Persia, through Bokhara; (24) Carpets, from Kotan; (25) Rewand-Chini, or rhubarb (26) Chob-Chini, or China- root; (27) Gol-i-Dal-Chini; (28) Zeddary, Nirbisi from Nepal; (29) Coral, Munga; (30) Mushkanafa; (31) Tobacco; (32) Raisins; (33) Pistachio Nuts, Pista; (34) Soap; (35) Bādiāṇ Khitai-Chinese aniseed, which is bruised and put into tea; (36) Mamira, a yellow root said to be a cure for bad eyes; (37) Galer Patt par (neck stone), good for swollen necks. (38) *Mulhatti*, Liquorice-root, used for coughs; (39) Daryahi; (40) Ponies; (41) Salt, from the lakes of Chang-Thang.

31. *Ibid.*, Vol II, pp. 344-45.
32. Cunningham, *op.cit.*, pp. 246-47.
33. *Ibid.*
34. *Ibid.*
35. *Ibid.*, pp. 247-48.
36. *Ibid.*, pp. 247-48.
37. Vigne, *op.cit.*, p. 345. It is supposed by the Asiatics to possess great medicinal properties (But Vigne doubted it); Cunningham, *op.cit.*, p. 243-47.

    List of Indian Articles carried to Yarkand: (1) Laki, or skins of red leather. These are goat-skins tanned and coloured at Nurpur (British India). There is a great demand for them all over the hills, but more particularly in Ladakh and Yarkand, where bright-coloured leathers are generally employed in the manufacture of boots, and of bridles and trappings of horses. About 200 maunds, or sheep-loads (6,400 lbs weight) of these skins are said to be annually imported into Ladakh; which at the mean rate of one pound per skin, and of one rupee each, are worth Rs. 6,400 or £ 640. Half of this quantity (100 maunds) or 3,200 skins, worth Rs. 3,200/- or £ 320 are exported to Yarkand; (2) Cotton, flowered chintzes; (3) Cotton, coarse (ghāra); (4) Thin (gazi); (5) Chintzes of all kinds; (6) Silk, lungi of Multan; (7) Shawls, mostly coarse; (8) Jāmiwar, or shawl cloth figured in breadths; (9) Broacades, mostly coarse; (10) Turbans; (11) Opium; (12) Indigo; (13) Heron-plumes, kalgi, generally made of the feathers of the jungle fowl; (14) Shoes from Nurpur; (15) Pearls of all sizes upto one hundred rupees each; (16) Otter skins; (17) Turmeric; (18) Cardamums; (19) Ginger; (20) Cloves; (21) Black pepper; (22) Honey; (23) Tamarinds dry; (24) Sherbet, lemon; (25) Coarse sugar, *Gur*; (26) Narcachor, the root of a reed, used both as a scent and as a medicine.

38. Cunningham, *op.cit.*, p. 240.
39. Vigne, *op.cit.*, p. 345.
40. Cunningham, *op.cit.*, pp. 248-253.
41. *Gazetteer*, p. 563.
42. Cunningham, *op.cit.*, p. 251.
43. *Ibid.*, pp. 253-54; Moorcroft & Trebeck, *op.cit.*, Vol. I, p. 353.
44. Cunningham, *op.cit.*, p. 255-56.
45. Moorcroft & Trebeck, *op.cit.*, Vol. II, pp. 70-71. The whole revenue of Spiti is collected in grains by a measure called Khal, equal to eight pakka seers and of the value of thirteen annas. The highest tax paid by any one is fifteen khals, and the lowest seven.
46. Cunningham, *op.cit.*, p. 256.
47. *Ibid.*, pp. 147-48. The different roads that lead to Leh on all sides are the following: (1) The western road from Kabul and the Punjab through Kashmir; (2) The south-western road from the central Punjab through Jammu, Kishtwar, and Zanskar to Leh. A branch of this road runs from Zanskar through Rukchu to Leh; (3) The southern road from Lahore and Amritsar, through Kullu, Lahul and Rakchu to Leh. A branch road from Bisahar, via Spiti, joins this road at Garo; (4) The south-eastern road from Lhasa to Garo and Indus to Leh. A branch from India, via the Niti Pass, joins this road at Garo; (5) The eastern road from Chinese Tartory, through Rudok and valleys of Chushal an Sakte to Leh; (6) The northern road from Yarkand and Kotan, over the Karakorum mountains, and down the Shayok and Nubra rivers to Leh. The old route, which is now closed by glaciers that dam the stream, followed the Shayok from its source to Sessar, and thence either continued down that river, or across the mountains and down the Nubra river to Leh; (7) The north-western road from Balti, via the Shayok and Indus rivers, to Leh.

48. Moorcroft & Trebeck, *op.cit.,* Vol I, pp. 328-59.
49. *Ibid.*
50. *Ibid.*, Vol. II, p. 73.
51. *Ibid.*, Vol. I, p. 358.
52. *Gazettteer*, p. 563.
53. Frederic Drew, *op.cit.*, p. 245.
54. Moorcroft & Trebeck, *op.cit.,* Vol. II, p. 71. Salt, wool, tea, turquoises, sheep, and goats are important from Chanthan, and are paid for with grain, woollen cloth, and a few horses; from Bisahar and Kulu come iron, cooking utensils, brass, copper; tobacco, rice dried fruits, tea cups, timber, amber, and glass beads, which are paid for with grain, horses, and woollen clothes of the district, and with the salt & wool of Chanthan, although the latter is an illicit export. The iron and metal vessels of the south are sent to Leh in exchange for tea, coarse cloth, coral, and dyeing drugs, etc.
55. *Gazetteer*, p. 563.

# 22

# BAHIS OF KASHMIR (Matan and Koti Tirth)

Recently with emphasis on socio-economic history the importance of *Bahis* maintained in different regions of India by different castes and categories have come to limelight. In this context also comes the *Bahis* maintained by the *Pandas* (priestly class) at Matan[1], which is also called Bhavan in Kashmiri Bavan[2]. This *Tirtha* is one of the most sacred pilgrimage centres in Kashmir on the way to the Amarnath cave. *Vishnu Surya*[3], under the form of *Martand* is worshipped here. On account of its sacred origin, Hindus every year visit this place to gain eternal peace in the next world. They also visit this place to perform *Shradh* to their dead so that their souls rest in peace and attain salvation. In this respect the place has the same significance as that of Gaya, Hardwar, and Sangam. The rush of the pilgrims is more during the *Malmas* and *Bhanumas* or *Adityamas*, which in the cyclic order falls around after two and a half years. Traditionally it is held that *Shradh* performed during this period has more religious merit and excellence. Another reason for attraction to this place is its being on the way to the holy cave of Amarnath, where thousands of pilgrims from India and abroad throng in the month of *Shravan* to see ice *lingam*, which waxes and wanes with the appearance of the moon. The holy mace of Lord Shiva, which is carried from the city of Srinagar to Amarnath has its first important camp at Matan, which adds to the socio-religious importance of Matan.

These circumstances helped in the emergence of a set of professional priests called *Pandas*. Quite ingeniously they have maintained the records of the pilgrims and visitors. They charm the pilgrims and visitors with their tact, poise, and submission. They make adequate arrangements for the stay and comfort of their clientele (*yajman*). They say that in their *Bahis* they have records of more than thousand years on the *birch bark* (Bhoj-Patra). But they do not show them. On reliable information, they do not have records more than three hundred years, as during the upheaval of Sikandar's time when many priests ran away for fear of life, the records might have perished. It is said that all had fled except eleven families. Now it has become a proverb in Kashmiri language to indicate scarcity.[4] Those who suffered but stayed in Kashmir are called as *Malmasis*, and those who returned in Zain-ul-Abidin's time when peace and order was restored[5] are known as *Bhanumasis* (pronounced in Kashmiri dialect as *Banamasis*). Malmasis take *Bhanumasis* as aliens. Even their calendar registers variations[6].

**Bahis**

Older *Bahis* or record books are stated to have been maintained on birch bark. *Old Bahis* are of hand made Kashmiri paper and mounted with leather binding. Modern *Bahis* are of mill made paper mounted with leather or rexine binding. The length and breadth of *Bahis* generally is 30'' by 9 to 12''. They keep it folded so as to reduce it to half of its size. They note down the details about the visitors and pilgrims on the *Bahis*. The language written on the *Bahis* is in *Sharda* script. Sometimes they persuade the prominent and influential visitors and pilgrims to write in their own languages. Therefore, following scripts and languages find place in the *Bahis*: Sharda, Modi, Lhanda, Sanskrit, Persian, Gurmukhi, English, Gujarati, Marathi, Dogri, Pahari, Devnagiri, Bengali and Sindhi, This indicates that people mostly came from Northern India. When the recording of the pilgrims began hardly fifteen to twenty families were in the profession, gradually their number increased to one hundred and fifty. Therefore, the families branched off and also shared the *Bahis* in terms of families, sur names, or habitat. In early times the Pandas used to generally record the *Saptarśi Samvat* or *Laukika Smavat* which was current in Kashmir. Later on they switched to the *Bikrama Samvat* and occasionally recorded the Saka, Hijra and Christian era too. The dates when recorded by the pilgrims/visitors are written according to their choice. Pandas have divided between themselves areas and specific families, which is going on undisturbed from generation to generation. Broadly speaking an entry would record a detailed bio-data of their clientele. They record the bio-data of each Yajman in three to five or seven lines utmost.

**Following is the list of prominent families covered by the Bahis :-**

**A. Royal Family Outside India :**

Nepal—Baskar Nath has the *Bahis* of the Maharaja of Nepal.

**B. Pilgrims Outside India:**

Chinese pilgrims—Sham Lal Lamba has the *Bahis* of the Chinese pilgrims.

**C. Royal Families from the erstwhile Princely State of India:**

(i) Badri State—Pandit Dinanath has the *Bahi.*

(ii) Bikaner State—Sham Lal has the *Bahi* of Rathors[7].

(iii) Chamba State—Lakshmi Nathji Gora has the *Bahi.*

(iv) Chinani State—Shivaji Madhusudan has the *Bahi.*

(v) Darbhanga State—Baskar Nath has the *Bahi.*[8]

(vi) Himachal State—Lakshmi Nathji Gora has the *Bahi.*

(vii) Kapurthala State—Lakshmi Nathji Gora has the *Bahi.*[9]

(viii) Jaipur State—Sham Lal and Badri Nath Tikku have the *Bahi* of Kachwahas.[10]

(ix) Jammu and Kashmir State—Dina Nath Kachru has the *Bahi* of the Dogra family.[11]

(x) Jodhpur State — Balkeshwar has the *Bahi* of Rathors[12].

(xi) Khurva State—Dinanath Kachroo has the *Bahi.*

(xii) Patiala State—Lakshmi Nathji Gora has the *Bahi*[13].

The Royal families after their signatures also affixed their seals.

**D. Prominent Dignitaries :**

(i) Birlas—Som Nath Musa has the *Bahi.*

(ii) Nehrus—Balkeshwar Sher has the *Bahi.*

(iii) Tagore—JaiLal Khah has the *Bahi* bearing the signature of Rabindra Nath Tagore and details about his visit.

**E.** S. N. Musa had the *Bahi* of the pilgrims coming from Hyderabad State.

**Few Peeps into the Contents :**

**A. Nepal Royal Family :**

(i) Maharaja Veer Jang Bahadur Shah—He came to Bavan in the month of *Baisakh* 1985 Bikrimi. He was on a tour of Kashmir. Details about him are in the Nepali (Gorkhali) language on the *Bahi.*

(ii) Hem Shamsher Jang Bahadur Rana—He visited Bavan on August 4, 1936.

(iii) Jagat Shamsher Jang Bahadur Rana—He visited this place in August 3, 1938. Details about him are in Sharda script. He signed in English.

(iv) Daman Shamsher Jang Bahadur Rana—He was the Counsellor General for Nepal in India. He visited Bavan on June 13, 1945. He was on a tour.

(v) Veer Vikram Shah Mahendra—He visited Bavan in 1963 A.D. He was on his way to the holy pilgrimage of Amarnath cave.

(vi) Gajendra Bahadur Raj Bahadur—He was the Minister for Foreign Affairs, Nepal. He visited the place on May 3, 1969. He was accompanied by B.P. Pande, Nepalese Ambassador in India (New Delhi).

(vii) Kirti Nidhi Bisht—He visited Bavan in May 1, 1972.

**B. Royal Family from the Princely State of Jammu and Kashmir : Dogra Period :**

(i) Mian Surat Singh—Grandfather of Maharaja Gulab Singh came here in 1876 Bikrimi. He performed *Shradha* to his dead father and grand-father. He stayed in a camp (tent) near the sacred *Tirtha.*

(ii) Maharaja Gulab Singh—Visited Bavan on 29, *Sawan*, 1899 Bikrimi. Details about his visit and stay are in Persian. He signed in *Dogri*.

(iii) Maharaja Ranbir Singh—Visited the place on 29, *Haar*, 1907 Bikrimi. Details about him are written in Persian. He signed in Dogri.

(iv) Maharaja Partap Singh—Visited the place on 17 *Jeth*, 1961 Bikrimi. He performed *Shradha* to Ranbir Singh and Gulab Singh. He signed on the *Bahi* in English and Dogri. Details about him are written in Urdu.

(v) Raja Amar Singh—son of Ranbir Singh, stayed at Matan for three days from 26 *Haar* to 29 *Haar*, 1956 Bikrimi. He accompanied his brother Raja Ram Singh and performed *Narayan Bali*.

(vi) Sukh Dev Singh—He was the son of Raja Baldev Singh of Poonch. He performed *Shradha* to his father and grandfather on 2, *Jeth*, 1976 Bikrimi.

(vii) Wazir Lakhpat—Resident of Kishtwar, was the son of Shobha Ram. He visited the place in 1878 Bikrimi.

(viii) Gopal Swami Ayangar—He was the Prime Minister of Jammu and Kashmir State. Visted the place on April 6, 1937.

**C. Royal Families From the Princely States of India Other than Jammu and Kashmir :**

(i) Maharaja Babu Ram Narayan Singh—He was from Badri State U.P. He visited Bavan in 1943 Bikrimi, while on his way to visit the holy cave of Amarnath.

(ii) Raja Baldev Singh—He was from Kamaka State, Jaipur. He came in 1943 Bikrimi. He signed both in Hindi and English.

(iii) Maharaja Gopal Singh—He was from Khurva State, Ajmer. He visited Bavan on 10 *Asuj*, 1957 Bikrimi. He signed in Hindi.

(iv) Maharaja Bhawani Singh—He was from Jhalawar State, Rajputana. Visited Bavan on May 17, 1900 A.D. Details about him are in English.

(v) Maharaja Jiwan Singh—He was from Kishen Garh State, Ajmer. He was the son of Prithvi Singh. He visited Bavan in 1959 Birkrimi. Maharaja Raghu Nath of Ajmer was also with him. Signatures are both in Hindi and English.

(vi) Maharaja Rameshwar Singh—He belonged to Darbhanga State, Bengal. He visited Bavan in *Shaka*, 1842.

(vii) Rani Girija Devi—Rajkumari of Ajar Garh, Bundelkhand. She came here in 1926 A.D. with her two brothers.

(viii) Maharaja Bajrang Bahadur Singh—He was from Badri State, (U.P.). He was the son of Maharaja Krishna Prasad Singh. He visited the place in *Jeth* 1987 Bikrimi. He signed in English.

(ix) Maharaja Visheshwar Singh—He was from Darbhanga State, Bengal. He was the son of Maharaja Rameshwar Singh. He visited the place in February 7, 1939.

(x) Kunwar Devendra Narayan Singh—He was from the Kerva State, U.P. He was the son of Durga Narayan Singh. He visited the place on August 17, 1962.

**D. Visitors From Punjab and North West Frontier Province of British India :**

(i) Hari Chand Mehra—He came to Bavan in Bikrimi 1965 from Peshawar, accompanied by his mother Lajwanti.

(ii) Rai Bahadur Kidar Nath Khanna—He also came to this place from Peshawar during Pratap Singh's time.

(iii) Sardar Hari Singh—He was the chief of Wehali, District Jehlum. He visited Bavan in *Haar*, 1969 Bikrimi.

(iv) Rai Bahadur Tirth Ram Shah—He was the resident of Nawa Shahar, District Hazara. He visited Bavan on 16th *Sawan*, 1971 Bikrimi.

(v) Diwan Kishen Kishore—He was the son of Diwan Bhagwan Dass of Dadiwalia, Lahore. He visited Bavan in 1974 Bikrimi. He signed both in English and Urdu.

(vi) Mukund Lal Malhotra—He came to visit Bavan in July 27, 1917 from Sialkot.

(vii) Fateh Chand Sahani—He was the resident of Jala Pura Jeta, Gujarat, and visited Bavan on September 17, 1932.

(viii) Roshan Lal Mehra—He came from Peshawar in 1996 Bikrimi, with his wife Satya.

**E. Nehru Family :**

(i) Bansi Dhar (Koul), Nehru-He visited the place in 1945 Bikrimi. He came alongwith Narayan Koul.

(ii) Bishambar Nath—He visited the place in 1945 Bikrimi.

(iii) Nand Lal—He was the brother of Moti Lal Nehru, and son of Gangadhar Nehru. He visited Bavan in *Ashvin* (Kashmiri *Asuj*) 1960 Bikrimi, and performed *Shradha.*

(iv) Moti Lal Nehru—came to Bavan thrice. He signed in Urdu on the *Bahi.*

(v) Kunwar Bahadur—Judge, Chief Court, Punjab. He was the son of Bansi Dhar Nehru, and came to Bavan in *Ashvin* (Kashmiri Asuj) 1961 Bikrimi. He signed in English.

(vi) Shanti Dhar—She was the daughter of Rattan Narayan Nehru. She visited Bavan in 1983, 1987, 1988, 1989, 1991 and 2001 Bikrimi.

(vii) Radha Mohan Nehru—He visited Bavan in *Shravan* 1988 Bikrimi.

(viii) S.R. Pandit—He was the son-in-law of Moti Lal Nehru, and visited Bavan in *Jeth* 1991 Bikrimi. He signed in Hindi.

(ix) Brij Lal Nehru—Son of Nand Lal Nehru. He visited Bavan in January 20, 1935 and August 11, 1940 A.D. In 1940, he came alongwith Shobha Nehru, his daughter-in-law, to see only the place.

(x) Jawahar Lal Nehru—He visited Bavan on February 23, 1940 A.D., then on June 15, 1942 alongwith Feroze Gandhi and Indira Gandhi. Feroze signed in Urdu on the *Bahi.* He came again in July 11, 1962 A.D., along with Indira Gandhi, Sanjay and Rajiv. Bakshi Ghulam Mohammad, Prime Minister of Jammu and Kashmir State, accompanied them. From Bavan they went to see the ruins at Martand. They were on a tour to Pahalgam.

(xi) Kamala Nehru—She visited Bavan on June 8, 1940 A.D. on her way to Pahalgam.

(xii) Sarojvati Nehru—She visited Bavan in June 15, 1941.

(xiii) Rameshwari Nehru—The wife of Brijlal Nehru and mother of B.K. Nehru, visited Bavan in 1943, A.D.

(xiv) Krishna Nehru (Hatti Singh)—Daughter of Moti Lal Nehru. She visited the Bavan on *Jeth*, 2002 Bikrimi.

(xv) Indira Gandhi—She visited Bavan in 1945 A.D. (earlier she had accompanied her father on June 15, 1942 A.D. and husband on July 11, 1952 A.D.)

**F. President of India :**

Rajendra Prasad—He visited Bavan on October 10, 1955, accompanied by his wife Raj Bansi Devi. He performed *Puja*. He signed in Hindi.

**Bahis at Koti Tirth :**

Professor P.N. Pushp, ex-Director, State Archives, Jammu and Kashmir, told me that the *Bahis* are not only kept at Matan, but also at some other *Tirthas* of Kashmir like the Koti Tirtha[14]. He salvaged some loose sheets of the Koti Tirtha *Bahis* from some apothecary (in Kashmiri called as *Buhur*), who was selling medicines wrapped in the *Bahi* Paper. He purchased them. The *Bahis* entered the bio-data of their *yajman* in the following order :- (see pages 156, 157)

The entries show that the Pandas wrote the bio-data in *Sharada* script, but the pilgrims signed in the script of their choice. Photostat sheets No. III and IV depicts that Karam Chand, son of Kishen Chand of Bira, records in his own hands in Urdu the fact that he has appointed Ishar Dass as his *Purohit* at the Koti Tirtha. On the same sheet Kan Chand, an official in the court of Gulab Singh, records in his own hand in the Persian language the fact that he appoints Budhram, son of Sadram for purposes of *Puja* and *Shradha* etc. at the *Tirtha*, dated *Bhadon* 15, 1907 Bikrimi (in Persian). The document also bears three signatures in *Sharda* and five seals of which as many as four are in Persian languages. Sometimes they per-

| | Name | Surname Caste | Gotra | Residence | Father's Name | Grand Father's Name | Grand Father's Surname | Brother's Name | Sometimes Sister's Name | Uncle's Name | Son | Particular purposes if any | Date |
|---|---|---|---|---|---|---|---|---|---|---|---|---|---|
| 15 | Shiv Charan | Kanya Kubja Brahmin | Upmanyu | Bhesuna | Tilak Nath | Khusalasi | Iswari Prasad | ,, | ,, | Chande Din | ,, | .. | ,, |
| 16 | Shiv Charan | ,, | Kashap | ,, | Durga Prasad | Adomal | Dachyant | (i) Madware Lal<br>(ii) Gaya Din | ,, | (i) Ram Din<br>(ii) Oganu Prasad | Ayodya Prasad Bhagwan Din | Father's *Pind Dan* | ,, |
| 17 | Ram Sevak | ,, | Bhardwaj | Fathehpur | Bhasawan | Jaya Ram | ,, | (i) Ganga Din,<br>(ii) Ram Gulam | ,, | ,, | ,, | ,, | ,, |
| 18 | Ram Kumar Brahmachari | ,, | ,, | Amagkathe Lamal Dal Bengal | Nand Kumar | ,, | ,, | ,, | ,, | ,, | ,, | ,, | ,, |
| 19 | Shri Nath | ,, | ,, | Village Sripur Bengal | Bhola Nath | ,, | ,, | ,, | ,, | ,, | ,, | ,, | |
| 20 | Thakur Das Brahmachari | ,, | Kashap | Sakle Amapur Hyala Bharasatha | Thakur Chetam | Bhairav Chandra Hor | ,, | (i) Isar Chandrahora<br>(ii) Mit Ram Chandra hora<br>(iii) Som Chandrahora | ,, | ,, | ,, | ,, | Samvat 2145 Bikrami |

## Continuation of the Table on page 156

| | | | | | | | | | | | | | | | |
|---|---|---|---|---|---|---|---|---|---|---|---|---|---|---|---|
| 21 | Radhika Prasad | Brahmin Ray | ,, | Calcutta | Ishwar Chandra Roy | ,, | ,, | | ,, | ,, | ,, | ,, | ,, | ,, | Date |
| 22 | Manomali Bandopadyaya | Kanya-kubja | Shandilya | Calcutta Village—Swakhachyar | Ganga Narayanam | Ram Prasad | Ram Ram | | ,, | Madhu Sudan | ,, | ,, | ,, | Pilgrimage to Amarnath | (Samvat 1920 Bikrami) |
| 23 | Chandra Mohan | ,, | ,, | Calcutta Village–swakhachyar | Narve Kanto | Atma Nandan | ,, | ,, | ,, | ,, | ,, | ,, | ,, | Pilgrimage to Amarnath | (Shravan Samvat 1920 |
| 24 | Kanchand | ,, | Kashap | Bira | Sohan Lal | Roshan Rai | ,, | ,, | ,, | ,, | ,, | ,, | ,, | Shradh | ,, |

formed *Shradh* of four or five deceased relatives (See sheet No. III).

## Conclusion

*Bahis* if properly scrutinized could provide missing links in tracing out the genealogical tables of the families listed in them. Badri Nath Kachroo, a *Panda*, who also works as the Manager of the Broca Press, Srinagar, told me that the records in the *Bahis* are accepted by the law courts in the Kashmir Valley. Many a times the litigants have produced them to stake claim to ancestral parentage. He has also got genealogical records of most of the prosperous Punjabi Hindu families, e.g., Sahanees, Chopras, Khannas, Aroras etc., who had migrated from Pakistan and settled in Kashmir. He was asking prohibitive price for selling the *Bahis* in his custody. The *Pandas* in Kashmiri are called as *Pand*, they are well to do. Now-a- days they have diversified their professional activities to other fields as well. They are at present occupying responsible position in government establishments and even are engaged in trade. The *Pandas* are generally endogamous i.e., marrying within the circle of their professional connections. The Kashmiri Pandits generally do not enter into matrimonial alliance with them in view of the fact that they accept alms (*dakshina*) in lieu of religious services. The younger generation is feeling restless and has given up the profession for the stigma attached to it and also their inclination for government jobs. They Went to open a new chapter for themselves. The *Bahis* are now lying uncared for.

Prof. Pushp who lent me the sheets to get photostated told me that he had once talked to the *Pandas* of Matan about the desirability of getting a few selections from the *Bahis* microfilmed. They had point- blank refused to oblige. Secrecy appears to be trick of their trade. They think that if the contents of their profession are publicised they would lose their clientele. Their almost computerised efficiency in tracing out the ancestry of the pilgrims from their *Bahis* is simply breathtaking.

The *Bahis* under a close research would provide valuable clues to social, economic and cultural ethos of the society covered. They also provide evidence to social mobility of the Indians for religious purposes, when otherwise they were generally immobile. The women who were kept within four walls of the house, were taken out for sacred pilgrimage to Bavan and Amarnath cave by their male folks. In this context it would not be amiss to cast a glance at the spectrum of geographical variety covered by these *Bahis* discussed above.

The records are, no doubt, scratchy and disjointed, still their historical value could not be discounted. There is an apprehension that with indifference to this profession among the younger generation, the *Bahis* may fall into the hands of scrap dealers. Institutions like the National Archives could take timely steps even now to salvage whatever is still lying in dark corners.

## References


1. Vishva Bandu, Ed., *Rajatarangini* of Kalhan, Hoshiarpur, 1963, p. 136.
   सो ऽ खण्डिताश्म प्राकारं प्रासादात्तर्व्यधित्त च
   मार्तण्डस्यादभुतं दाता द्राक्षास्फीतं च पत्तनम ।14।192
2. M. A. Stein, ed., Kalhan's *Rajatarangini or Chronicle of the Kings of Kashmir*, Bombay, Education Society's Press, 1892, Vol. I, p. 141; ~Abul Fazl Allami, *Ain-i-Akbari*, Asiatic Society of Bengal, Calcutta, Vol. II, p. 358.
3. M. A. Stein, *op.cit.*, The Tirth of Martanda is also mentioned in the *Nilmata Purana*, Stanza 1036, among places sacred to Surya.
4. *Kasheeri ruda Kahai Ghari*.
5. Jonaraja, *Rajatarangini*, Bombay Edition, 1896, St. 1048; N.K. Zutshi *Sultan-Záin-ul-Abidin of Kashmir*, Jullundur, 1975, p. 69.
6. Pandit Anand Koul, *The Kashmiri Pandit*, Calcutta, 1924, Appendix IV and V, pp. 86-88.
7. *Imperial Gazetteer of India*, Oxford, 1908, XIII, pp. 382- 99.
8. *Ibid.*, XI, p. 163, An State in Bengal, which traces its origin to Mahes Thakur.
9. *Ibid.*, XIV, pp. 408-16. Sardar Jassa Singh was the founder of the State.
10. *Ibid.*, XII, pp. 382-99.
11. *Ibid.*, XIV, pp. 49-50.
12. *Ibid.*, p. 182.

13. *Ibid.*, XX, pp. 31-50.
14. In Varamul (Old Varāhmūla) now called Baramulla.
15. See photostat sheet No. 1. (see page no. 160A, B.)
16. *Ibid.*
17. *Ibid.*
18. *Ibid.*
19. *Ibid.*
20. *Ibid.*
21. Sheet No. II. (see page no. 160, C, D.)
22. *Ibid.*
23. *Ibid.*
24. Sheet No. III & IV (see page no. 160 E, f.)

Sheet No I – 160–A

[illegible]

[illegible]

[illegible]

[illegible]

[illegible]

[illegible]

[illegible]

[illegible]

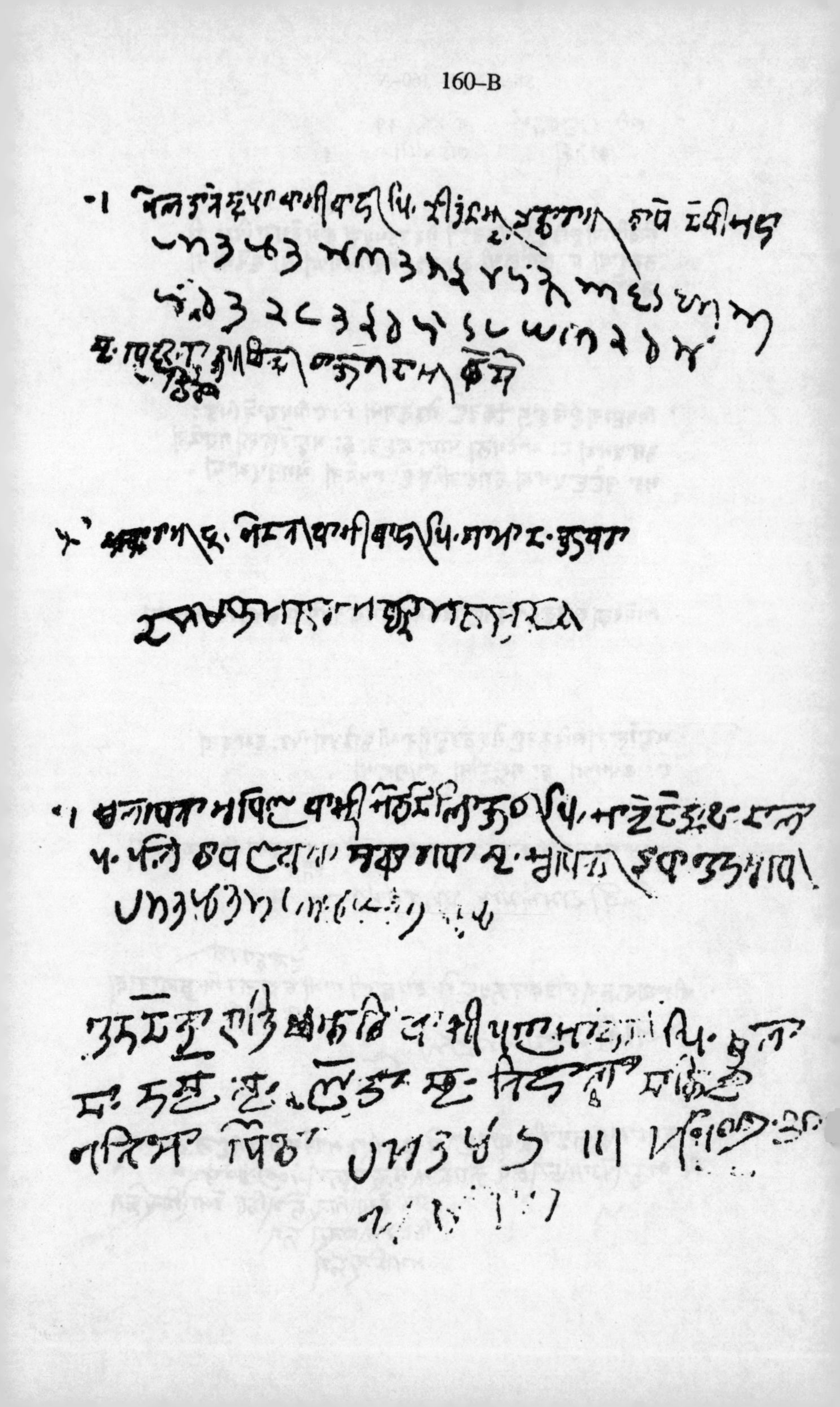

Sheet No II – 160–C

160 D

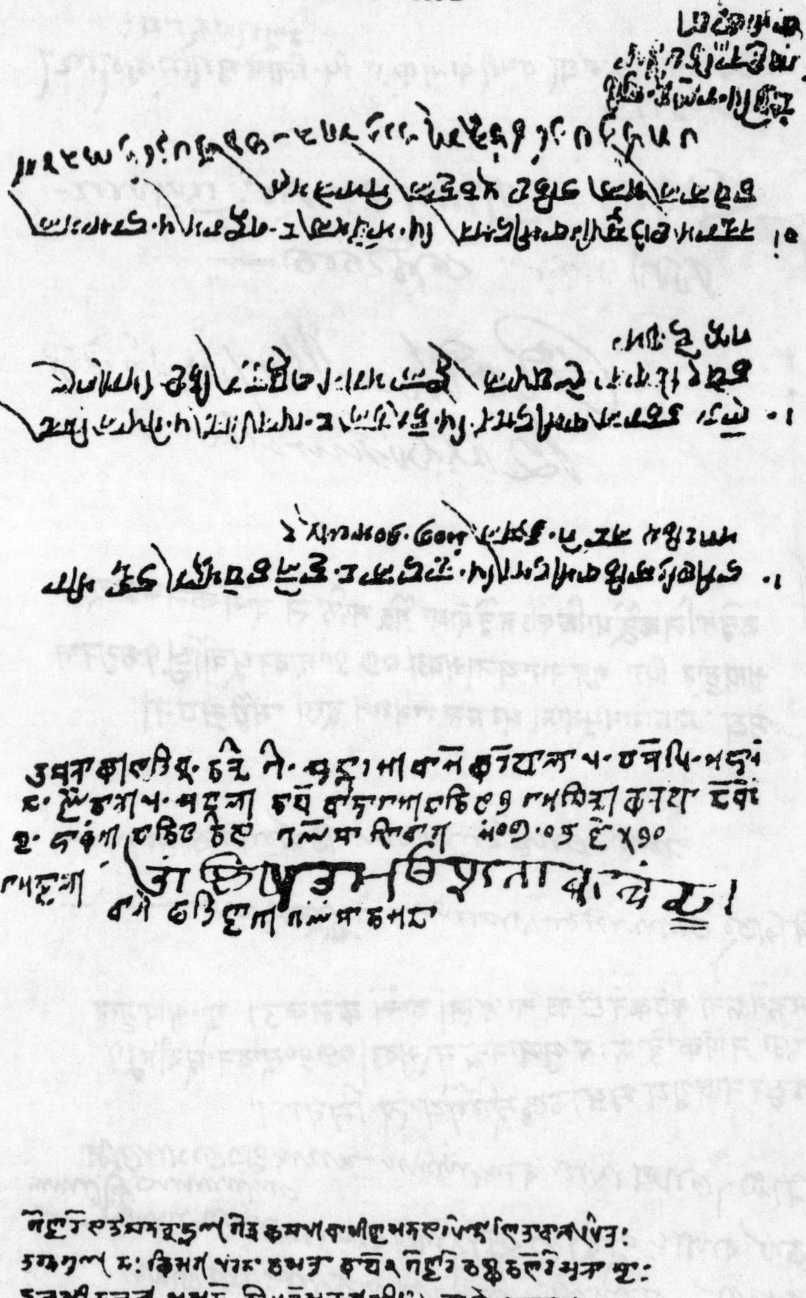

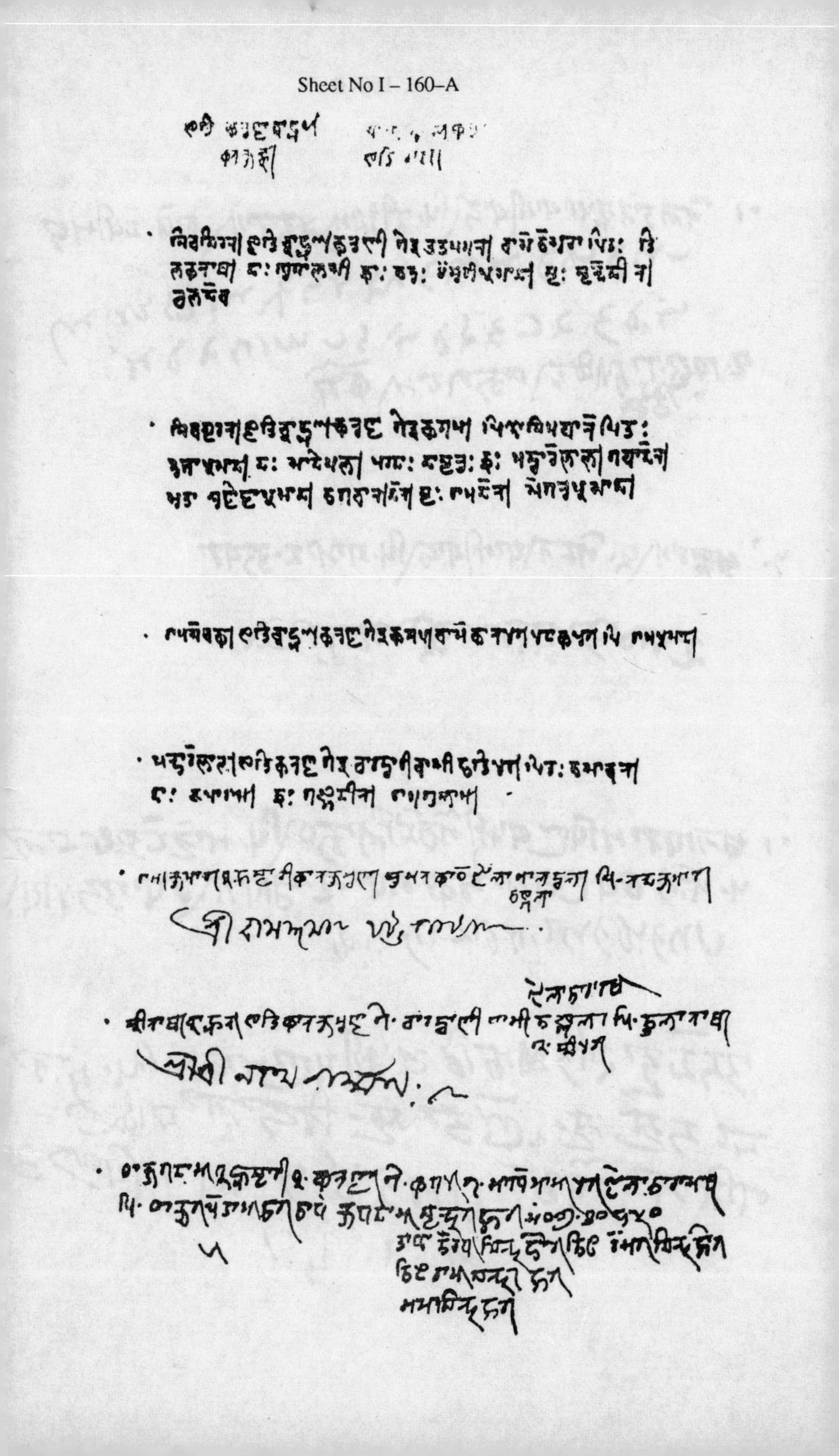

Sheet No I – 160–A

[illegible]

[illegible]

[illegible]

[illegible]

[illegible]

[illegible]

[illegible]

[illegible]

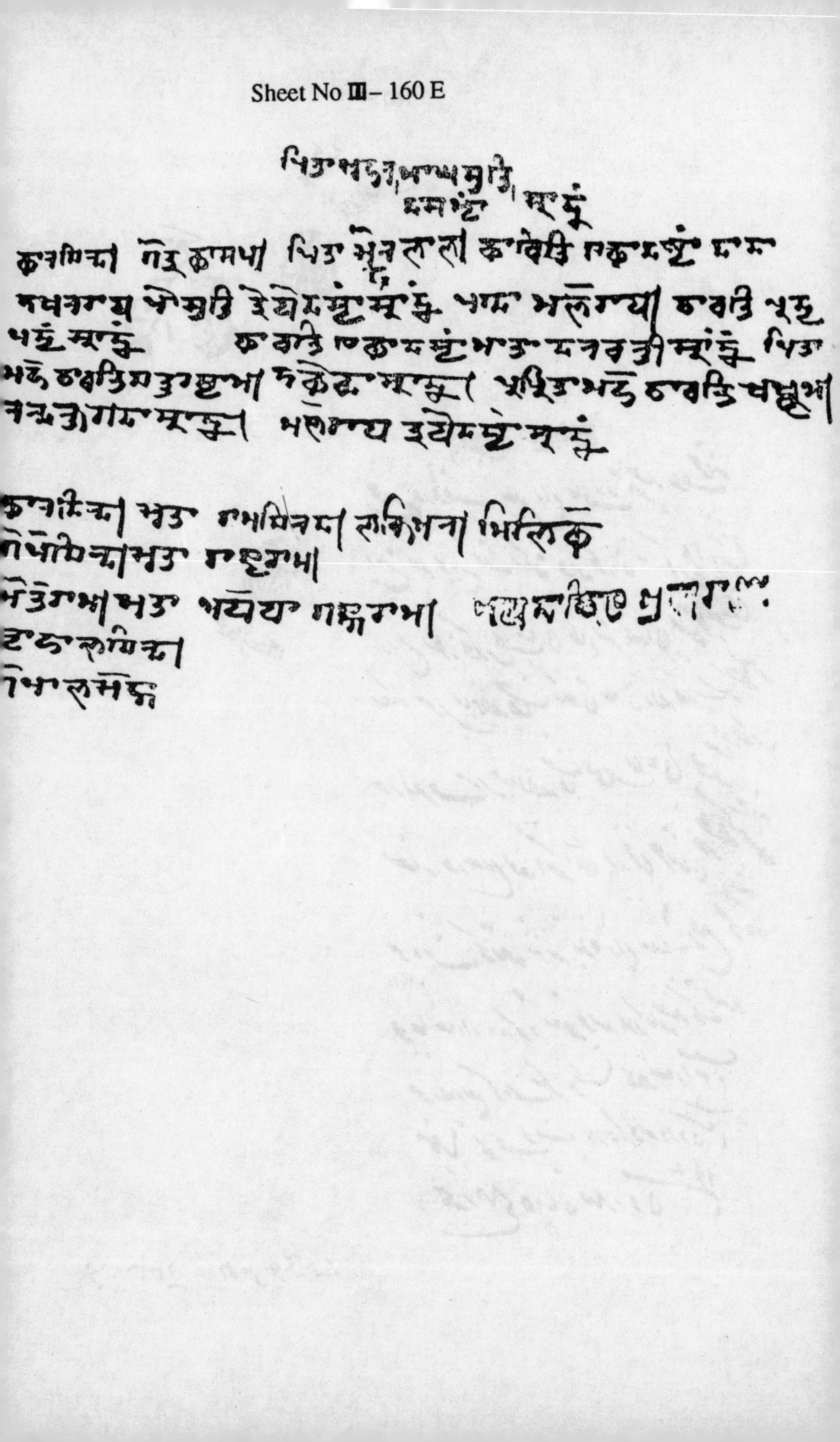

Sheet No III – 160 E

[illegible]

160 F

[illegible]

# 23

# NATIONAL ANTHEM AND JAMMU AND KASHMIR

At the Delhi Darbar of 1902 it came to the notice that the Ruling Chiefs of India were received so far as musical honours were concerned with a general salute[1], as the ruling chiefs possessed no national anthems of their own. Under the orders of the government of India the British national anthem was for His Majesty, the king, and in his absence only to the Viceroy.[2]

The first Astt. Resident, Captain R.C. Trench, informed the chief minister of Jammu and Kashmir, Daljit Singh, that in British India national anthem was being played on occasions prescribed in para 1773 of the King's Regulations and that the same should be observed in the state.[3] On enquiry from the secretary to the Commander-in-chief, it had been ascertained that in the Indian states the military band played the national anthem of the state on occasions as prescribed in the said Regulations. It was not, however, known as to what practice was observed by the police band in respect of playing national anthem. The matter was submitted to Maharaja Partap Singh for further orders with the recommendation that both the military and police bands of the state should closely follow the same procedure as laid down in the King's Regulations with regard to playing of the national anthem.[4] The Maharaja accepted the recommendations and passed the following order :

"The procedure as laid down in the King's Regulation with regard to the playing of the national anthem should closely be followed by police bands of the state as is being done by the military band."[5] The copy of the order of the Maharaja was forwarded by the Chief Minister's registrar to Captain R.C. Trench[6].

The Maharaja entrusted the task of composing the national anthem to C.J. Barrow, Director of the Music, in the state. The latter composed it in 1911, which was highly appreciated[7]. As it was a new air, and the officers and public were unaware of it, therefore the office of the Commander-in-Chief advised that the civil and military officers and the general public of the state should be trained to rise and salute when the national anthem was played[8]. In order to make people familiar with the music, it was proposed that the Director of Music or the officer conducting the band would raise a small flag, bearing the state coat of arms, at the time, which would be an indication that the Kashmir National Anthem was being played.[9] The Resident of Kashmir had already informed to the secretary of the Maharaja that the Europeans would rise when the anthem was played for His Highness the Maharaja Sahib Bahadur.[10]

In 1912, the government of India called for copies of airs adopted by the Indian states for salutes on ceremonial occasions, and these airs were played by British bands at the reception of respective princes/chiefs during the Imperial Coronation Darbar at Delhi in 1911. Those chiefs who had adopted no ceremonial air or anthem were received with a general salute only.[11] This music was also played for the salute of any senior inspecting officer.[12]

In view of the above order the initiative was taken by C.J. Burrow to collect the national anthems of the ruling princes and publish them in a book form.[13] Accordingly, he submitted the proposal to the government of India, which permitted him to communicate with the states directly on the matter. C.J. Burrow approached the Maharaja Partap Singh, as he was the first ruling prince of the Indian states to have his national anthem composed by him, to be patron of his new scheme. Maharajah acceded to his request.[14]

C.J. Burrow's plan was to publish national anthems in sets of books for different states. It would facilitate the military bands accompanying guards of honour to play music for the national airs of the Ruling Chiefs. It would thus be possible for every Indian Chief to have the pleasure of being received with his own national air, which was of as much importance as the artillery salute accorded to him.[15]

On receiving an order from the military department of the government of India for submitting a progress report on his proposal 'Indian States and National Anthem', C.J. Burrow requested to the Maharaja Partap Singh, as the primary patron of the project to write favourable remarks on the progress report.[16] The Maharaja complied with his request and wrote the following remarks :

> "I congratulate Mr. C.J. Burrow, Director of Music, on the progress made. He has brought his wide experience which he gained in the course of his long and good services in the state to bear upon the undertaking in which I wish him all success".[17]

When the news of the national anthem of J and K spread, the Maharaja Partap Singh received a request from the Maharaja of Holkar to have national anthem of Kashmir State, so that the Maharaja Holkar's band might be able to play the anthem on ceremonious occasions in the event of His Highness' visit to his state. Maharaja of Holkar also offered to furnish J and K state with the full and parts of the Holkar state anthem in exchange.[18] Maharaja of J and K obliged the Maharaja of Holkar and forwarded 37 parts of the Kashmir state National Air for full military band.

Thus, the state of Jammu and Kashmir and its ruler, Maharaja Partap Singh, played a pivotal role in getting the national airs of the Indian states published and played by the military band on ceremonial occasions.

## References

1. State Archives Jammu, C.S. Old Records, File No : 134- J-9/of 1913.
2. Ibid., Memo. No. 588, Rai Sahib Dewan Amar Nath C.I. to Chief Minister of J & K State, 19.12.1913.
3. Ibid., 1911—58/E—19; 1912—36; 1913—134/ J-9; C.S. Old Records, File no. 58/E - 19 - 1911, Dated 26-7-11.
4. Ibid., Copy of order no. 792, Dated July 31, 1911.

5. Ibid., Dated August 1, 1911.
6. Ibid., D.O.—No. E $\frac{11}{11}$, Dated August 10, 1911.
7. Ibid., Pol. Dept. File No. 36 of 1912; Ibid., Copy of a Memo No. 949 M, Dated Sept. 22, 1913 submitted to the Maharaja Sahib Bahadur.
8. Ibid.
9. Ibid.
10. Ibid., D.O./No. 374, Dated Sept. 9, 1913.
11. Ibid., File No : 134/J-9/of 1913.
12. Ibid., Memo No. 915, Dated 21.2.1913.
13. Ibid., Memo No. 588, Dated 17.12.1913
14. Ibid., C.M.'s letter no. 10821 of April 7, 1913.
15. Ibid.
16. Ibid., Memo No. 588, Dated 17.12.1913; Memo no. 915.
17. Ibid.
18. Ibid., Acc. No. 2824, Dated 26-7-1917.

# 24

# EDUCATIONAL AND SOCIAL REFORMS AMONG KASHMIRI WOMEN (1900-47 A.D.) : A CONSPECTUS OF NEW SOURCE MATERIAL

### The Missionaries As An Agent To Social Change

The first lady missionary to go to Kashmir in 1894 was a young girl named Miss Irene Petrie. She died of typhoid in Leh in 1897 at the altar of her duty.[1] It is interesting to note that while the boys school began with Pandits, the girls education began with the Muslims. The Hindu parents needed much persuasion to send their wards to the Schools.[2] After the death of Miss Petrie, the girls' education was continued by Miss Frances Mackay in private houses until 1909. In 1909 Dr. Kate Knowles ran a small school at Habakadal in Srinagar, in addition to her medical work as a consultant for all Mission Schools in Kashmir. It had 17 pupils on its rolls.[3]

The founding of the CMS Girls School is normally taken as October 1912, when Miss Violet Fitze opened the Memorial School CMS at Fateh Kadal better Known as Miss Fitze's School.[4] In 1914 she reported that there was not a single Kashmiri women teacher.[5]

Miss Fitze's mission to educate and enlighten the Kashmiri women was beset with difficulties. But with undaunted spirit, she taught her students the lessons in cleanliness, honesty and social intercourse in their own language 'Kashmiri'. For the first time a Hindu girl Tulsi studied with the Muslim girls. There was such a change in her that amidst sobs she said while leaving the school that if she was ever a mother, she won't say that her children should not mix with the Muslims.[6]

Miss Fitze gave to the Hindu widows an identity of their own. They were made economically viable by engaging in the brass industry and other crafts. She had sanguine hopes for a bright future for Kashmir, which she characterised as 'arriving'.[7] Her mission was taken up with unmatched dedication by Miss M.P. Mallinson in October 1922[8]. By inculcating in women the idea of self-respect, she ushered in a new era in Kashmir. Besides teaching, she also unhinged their minds from the shackles of superstitions, and time worn customs. She taught them to be clean, smart and the advantages of ventilation[9]. She wrought a change in dress as the common *pheron* was not conducive for school activities.[10] She also motivated the girls to discard nose ring, huge heavy earrings, wooden clogs, as for leather pollution shoes could not be worn. She also created an aversion against the child marriage, so that the girls were made happy and cheerful. She happily reported about a party thrown by the Lady Wood at the Residency for the CMS Girl Students :

> "The Girls went off in the school shikaras, attired in their clean school pherons, fearfully proud of being paddled along by three of the Residency Boatmen...... Drinking tea and tucking into a spread of Kulchas — sweets and fruit to the strains of the club gramophone, running races on the springy turf under the chenars, then a glorious red in their autumn glory; choosing prizes from undreamt of possessions, such as brooches, little mirrors, horses and coloured handkerchiefs, and finally going away with bags of sweets and bunches of flowers was all too wonderful for words".[11]

Thus her mission was successful. Again, she proudly wrote :-

> "Yes, freedom for the women and girls of this fair land, freedom from dirt, disease and '*dastur*', especially the evil customs of

> child marriage, of the joint family system and its disastrous results".[12]

Her students' handwork were exhibited at the All India Educational Exhibition, held in Srinagar in 1942, where they were very much appreciated.[13] Thus the Missionaries initiated a process of social change which suited to the ethos and culture of Kashmir. It earned the handsome encomiums from the government, which was sceptic in the beginning.[14]

The other equally important philanthropic work undertaken by the Church of England Zenana Missionary Society (C.E.Z.M.S.) in cooperation with the C.M.S. was the opening of the *Zenana* hospitals in Jammu & Kashmir State. Maharaja Partap Singh also changed his stand towards them. They constructed Diamond Jubilee Zenana Hospital in Srinagar, which received grant from the royal treasury to help maintain its upkeep and establishment.[15] Dr. Neve's efforts are worthy of emulation. On November 25, 1899, he wrote to the Darbar for a site at Sarul in Anantnag to rebuild the John Bishop Memorial Hospital. There is a thick file on this matter in the State Archives, Jammu, which proves his dedicated persuasion to get the land allotted for the hospital. A copy of the agreement with signatures between A. Neve, TRCS, Senior Medical Missionary, Church Missionary Society, Kashmir, and Maharaja Partap Singh is still with the S.A.J.[16] In this connection H.V. Cobb, Assistant Resident's remarks are very significant :

> "As I think you know I am not very much in *sympathy* with missionary work pure and simple. But when it is coupled with really first class medical work as in the case with the Neve's institution, I cannot help thinking it deserved the support of all creeds and classes, may all—Hindus, Mussalmans and Christians — find a common foot-hold in what a celebrated French author describes as the religion of human suffering."[17]

Even the Swiss Missionaries Messrs Danial Voumard and Robert Berger were granted permission for the welfare activities in Khaplu Baltistan and Srinagar. Sisters of Mercy were granted permission to establish hospital in Baramulla.[18] Besides the Missionaries also established King Edward Zenana Hospital, a Female Hospital, and Leper asylum, respectively in Jammu, Gilgit and

Srinagar.[19] The government consistently gave adequate facilities for getting medicines and other items for use in the missionary hospitals. The government nevertheless kept them under perfect surveillance.[20]

**The Government Enterprise To The Social Change in Kashmir**

The Christian Missionaries acted as a catalytic agent to the government in bringing social change through education. The Administrative Reports issued by the Darbar throw ample light on this aspect. The Reports are generally annual but some were half yearly, two yearly or three yearly as well.

**A. Administrative Reports**

AAR (Annual Administrative Reports) from Samvat 1947 (1890- 91 A.D) to Samvat 1950-60 (1901-04 A.D.) draw a blank. But in Samvat 1961 (1904-05 A.D.), the famale education figures in. The state provided funds for establishing two girl schools in Srinagar, one for the Hindus and the other for the Muslims to be managed by the leading men of both the communities separately under the supervision of the State Educational authorities. This means that there were separate schools for Muslim and Hindu girls.[21]

Female education in Kashmir as in other parts of India suffered from popular prejudices.[22] Apart from public apathy, there was a lack of trained teachers inspite of the offer of high salaries by the state. Almost every AAR complains about it during our period of study.[23] The school at Baramulla was closed on account of this during winter.[24] There were no good buildings and funds.[25]

Free education was a salient characteristic of the educational policy of the government,[26] and scholarships were given as an incentive. Even *khillats* were presented for the trained teachers.[27] During 1911-12 A.D. an impetus was given to female education by deputing a lady teacher with an award of a scholarship for Rs. 18 per mensem, to the Female Normal School at Lahore. One of the most encouraging features of the year was the appointment of a lady Inspector in the grade of Rs. 100-10-150 per mensem for supervising girls education.[28] The government during 1927-30 A.D. sanctioned 10 scholarships of Rs. 10 per mensem and of Rs. 40/- per mensem for each girl wishing to study within the state and colleges outside the state respectively.[29] The AAR from 1926-27 showed that females belonging to the educationally backward communities, viz., The Muslims, the Rạjputs and the Sikhs were steadily progressing. A chart is given which shows percentage of increase in their number of the scholars being 21, 16 and 3 respectively.[30] Covered motorbuses were engaged at places to carry girls to schools and back to their homes.[31]

The government followed the policy of the British government in adopting the grants-in-aid system.[32] The management committees of the aided schools were taking active interest in the promotion of education among the girls and they were helped with the technical advice, such as method of teaching, discipline etc. by the Inspectresses of the schools.[33] Thus the coming of the private enterprise was a laudable feature.

Training schools for the teachers were also opened. AAR for 1915-16 is a landmark in the progress of female education. An Educational Conference was held in Srinagar in September 1915, to discuss the school curriculum, use of vernacular medium and school hygiene etc. The Conference came to the conclusion that the curriculum required careful revision with a view to render instruction more practical and useful.[34]

AAR for the year 1931 is very important. It lays emphasis not only on education but on the general development of the woman's personality. Women's Welfare Associations were established, chaired by the Minister-in-charge of the Municipalities. The Kashmir Association was inaugurated in 1927. Each Association was divided into 4 sections (1) Educational (2) Health (3) Industrial (4) Recreation.

In Srinagar, under the auspices of the Educational Section, the work of education was taken up independently. It imparted free education. Education for the adult women was a priority. Volunteers were enlisted to teach women in their homes. Education in the vernacular was emphasised and for this text books in Kashmiri were prepared. A women's league was founded with the object of band-ing women together for self development, social service and social reform. In the Health section, maternity and child welfare work was vigorously undertaken both on the educational and practical side.

In the Industrial section, the object was to teach crafts to widows and destitute women to earn their livelihood. For recreation a park was presented with swings and sea-saws by the Maharaja to the women.[35] The AAR given in the footnote supply a detailed statistical information regarding the stratification, classification, scholarships, attendance, training of teachers, refresher courses, expenditure and curriculum etc.[36]

**B. General Records**

The General Department records housed in the State Archives, Jammu, testify that the government was interested in the welfare of the women. It kept a watch on the activities of the women's welfare association.[37] The government of India was also apprised of the welfare activities of the State.[38]

The Darbar looked to the maintenance of the widows of its employees as was the case with the widow of the late Pandit Narendra Nath kaul.[39] The government also gave appointments to widows, and confirmed those appointments which were made by Maharaja Partap Singh.[40] The government also gave menial allowance to the female employees of the Jammu municipality.[41]

The females were appointed in the *Zenana Deorhi*.[42] The Maharaja gave orders to appoint widows on the female establishment of the palace.[43] They were also granted leave.[44] The wives and widows of a foreign nationality married to the State subject were recognised as State subjects and were granted State subject Certificates.[45] The government in compliance with the women convention of 1930 held under the auspices of the International Labour Organisation at Geneva issued orders to the effect that women would not be employed in underground works and this condition was binding to all future mining leases.[46] The cases of abduction of the women from Kashmir province to the British territory for the purpose of prostitution were brought to the notice of the government.[47] The government took action against some notorious traffickers in Srinagar under Section 108-A-CR.P.Code.[48]

### C. The Census of India

The Censuses of India for the period under study, provide an authentic record of literacy in the city of Srinagar and Kashmir.[49] It is a ten yearly record. In the beginning of our period, i.e, in 1901, in the city of Srinagar, the total number of literates was 8326, in which the number of males was 8276 and that of females was 50.[50]

In 1911 the Census has recorded number of literates per thousand for each sex. They report :

> "From the point of view of education, Kashmir is the most backward part of India. The total number of literate persons is less than 65 thousand and their proportion per mile is only 38 in the case of males and one in that of females."[51]

The 1921 Census records:

> "The local distribution of literacy among females closely follows that of the males, on an average there is one literate female to over 15 literate males. The proportion of literate women to the total female population aged 5 and over, is 3 per thousand. Female education among women is negligible. Under the 1921 Census, neither a Hindu nor a Muslim female knew English, but a Sikh women was literate in English."[52]

Census Report for the year 1931 for Kashmir province says:-

> "For 114,807 male literates there are only 9,078 female literates in the State which means that for every hundred male literates only 8 female literates are to be found. This is not a very good state of affairs though comparison with 1921 figure reveals an increase of 127 percent in the ranks of literate females."[53]

Following table shows the number of female literates in 1921 and 1931.[54]

| Kashmir Province | Female literates in 1921 | Female literates in 1931 | Percentage of Increase |
|---|---|---|---|
| | 1,141 | 1,175 | 65 |

Under the last Census in 1941 during our period of study, the percentage of literate females was 46.27, whereas that of the males was 53.73.[55] Thus the literacy among the women was increasing in comparison to males.

**D. Government Reports**

(i) Sharp Report

The photostat copy of the Sharp Report is in the State Archives of Srinagar. It is a note on the Education of Jammu and Kashmir State written by H. Sharp, the then Education Commissioner with the government of India. He submitted a Report in 1916 A.D. after visiting all the educational, technical and training institutions in the State. He recommended some suggestions which were accepted by the Maharaja but the Education Department was too slow and tardy in implementing it. All India Muslim Kashmiri conference criticised the Government for its indifference.[56]

(ii) Glancy Commission

His Highness Hari Singh appointed a Commission on November 12, 1931, under the presidency of Mr. B.J. Glancy of the Political Department of the government of India with four non-official representatives of Hindus and Muslims of Jammu and Kashmir province as members to inquire into the grievances of the different communities. The Commission among other things made recommendations for the Education of the women.[57]

(iii) Ganga Nath Report

In July 1943, His Highness Maharaja Hari Singh appointed a Commission of Enquiry, under the Presidentship of R.B. Ganganath, Chief Justice' to formulate a policy for the future and evolution of an organised scheme for the administration of J & K. It consisted of principally non-official members of the Praja Sabha and others representing different interests and communities.[58]

It is a voluminous Report dealing in detail with every aspect of administration.

The Report Says:

> "Social and Economic conditions appear to have combined to relegate the female sex to a position of definite inferiority and therefore the number of females in independent occupation is

> very small.....This is also reflected in almost a complete absence of consciousness among them. Their franchise compares unfavourably with the of males."[59]

About the pardah system, polygamy and child marriage, the Report says that it was not widely prevalent in Kashmir. The menace of child marriage in a very small proportion still was haunting the society in spite of the Infant Marriage Act of 1929. It gives year wise figures of educated girls from 1927 A.D. to 1942 A.D. , and recommends the training of women teachers to accelerate the female education. Again, it says:

"On the whole women have not taken any prominent part in public life, though of late they have been asserting themselves in certain restricted affairs."[60]

The most interesting feature of the Report was that all the members either withdrew themselves in the middle or refused to sign it, and it only bears the signature of the President of the Commission.[61]

**E. Indigenous Enterprise**

During 1900 A.D. and around it the private enterprise was conspicuous in its absence , due to the uncongenial atmosphere rendered by Afghan and Sikh rule.[62] It was believed that a women was no more than a sex object designed to give pleasure to men, bear children and fit only for the domestic chores.[63] The age old *Pathshalas* and medieval *maqtabs* for the female education had become imperative due to the unsettled times and obscurantist attitude of men. The Administrative Reports draw a blank in this regard.[64] This is also testified by the government Reports. H.Sharp appointed by the Maharajah Hari Singh to report about the education in the State of Jammu and Kashmir in 1916, says: "At the 1911 census it was found that 0.1% of the female population was literate. The people are highly conservative regarding the pardah system; and the problem of girls education is here, more than elsewhere in India, a social question".

> For the *Pathshalas* and *Maqtabs* he says: "The idea of girls education is totally lacking...... I am informed that some of the

private *Pathshalas* and *Maqtabs* are attended by girls, although I saw no girls in the institutions of this kind which I visited".[65]

Even Sir Ganga Nath Report (November 1944) says that the figures taken from the educational institutions

> "indicate that there is complete lack of private enterprise in the matter of providing indigenous schools for the girls".[66]

## F. Female Dropouts

Annual Administrative Reports give indication that there was considerable drop out.[67] This is also borne out by the Census of India.[68] Early marriage was the main cause besides this there were other snags relating to, "Priest, Prestige and Pisa (Money)'.[69] The Priests were dead against the education. The Prestige of the people stood in the way of sending their children to the schools, 'for great folk must not send a child to you (the Christian Missionaries) but you must go to her'. Pisa, which in Kashmir is called 'Ponsa', you

> 'throw money about, and the parents pour their children in your school.'[70]

Annual Administrative Reports do not give the year wise figures of drop outs.

## G. National Conference's New Kashmir

The Charter of Rights was prepared to establish an egalitarian society in Kashmir. It has a section named Women's charter which aims to impart to the women political, economic, social, legal, educational and cultural rights to enable,

> "her just and rightful place in society, and her co-operation in the mighty and responsible task of nation-building."[71]

## H. Unpublished Manuscripts

(i) Tarachand Wazir's Autobiography

Though mainly important on account of a detailed and authentic material on sericulture industry in Kashmir, (as he was the Director, Sericulture , J&K Government) it throws ample light on the social system of the Pandits (Hindus). The manuscript could be had from his son, Shri Man Mohan Wazir, 31, Gupkar Road, Srinagar. The autobiography if published would be a great help to Scholars.

(ii) Ghunwanti's Diary

It contains songs which throw light on the customs, dress, social evils like dowry etc. The lady is very aged, and keeps the diary tueked away. It is written is *devanagari* scripts in Kashmiri language. Her address is : R/o Karphali Mohalla, Srinagar.

**I. Public Consciousness**

No social change in the status of women could have taken place if the public consciousness towards it would not have been aroused.[72]

Hindu Social Reform Movements: The inspiration for eradication of social evils and emancipation for the women came from India.[73] The Arya Samaj at first established its branch at Jammu in 1892, and afterwards also moved to Srinagar.[74] The Arya Samaj in the beginning was unable to make any dent but around 1915,[75] the Kashmiris were attracted towards its programmes. Soon after the Arya Kumar Sabha was founded. Its main planks were :[76]

(i) To raise the status of women;

(ii) Education of women;

(iii) To abolish the evil institution of child marriage;

(iv) Re-marriage and rehabilitation of widows.

Under its motivation during 1920-30, the Arya Samaj celebrated the marriages of half a dozen widows.[77] However, it could not make further progress due to its *shuddhi* and *Sangathan* and political activities.[78]

Dogra Sabha: In 1903 the Dogra Sabha, a socio-political organisation was founded at Jammu by Lala Hansraj.[79] It also established its branch office at Khwaj Adda, Srinagar.[80] Its main aim was that the social evils should be eradicated through the state legislation.[81]

The Dharm Sabha: The Dharm Sabha was a social organisation established for the eradication of Social evils and removing the indignities of the women. Its founder members were orthodox and conservative.[82]

Fraternity Society: The establishment of this Society was founded by the progressive youths, a reaction against the orthodox and conservative members of Dharm Sabha.[83] The progressive elites among the Kashmiri Pandits joined this society. Prem Nath Bazaz was the moving spirit of the new wave. The workers went from door to door to dissuade the Kashmiri Pandits from unnecessary rituals and to cut axpenditure on marriages.[84] They were nick-named as *'Hund Kath'* (progeny of widows) for propagating the widow remarriage.[85] P.N. Bazaz approached Mahatma Gandhi, who appreciated his stand,[86] and exhorted both the boys and young widows to make bold and set an example to the society through their re-marriage.[87] But the Society failed even to make any breakthrough in the field of women education,[88] what to say about the widow marriage.

Women Welfare Trust: Annie Besant, the President of the Theosophical society, was interested in the valley. During her visit in 1905 to the valley won the progressives among the Kashmiri Pandits to her ideology.[89] Inspired by Annie Besant's Indian women's Association, the Kashmiri Theosophists started Women's Welfare Trust, a non-official organisation in 1926, for the emancipation of women.[90] Tara Chand Wazir was its President and D.N. Dhar, the Secretary. Shri Kanth Toshkhani and Aftab Kaul Nizamat did a Yeoman's service to the Trust. Prem Nath Bazaz joined it in 1930 as supervisor. The number of schools run by the Trust rose to ten.[91]

For the rehabilitation of the young widows in their 20's Seva Sadan was established.[92]

Women's League was established for the training of women through debates and discussions to the social problems and evils associated with it.[93]

Yuvak Sabha : Failure of the Fraternity Society to face the challenge of times led to the birth of 'Yuvak Sabha', under the Presidentship of Prem Nath Bazaz.[94] This Sabha was a dynamic body. Now the women also came forward and raised their voice against dowry and unnecessary expenditure in marriages.[95] They succeeded in changing the dress of the Kahsmiri Pandit females from costly *phiran, tarang,* and *pooch,* to saree, blouse and petticoat.[96] Their crowning achievement was the Widow Marriage Act of 1933, which legalised the marriage of the Hindu widows.[97]

The Kashmiri Pandits' Social uplift Association: This association was organised for the allround development of women's personality.[98]

Muslim Socio-Religious Reform Movements: The Muslim reform movements were late arrivals due to their being a backward and poor community. After some time they also came under the impact of the west through education.

Anjuman-i-Nusrat-ul-Islam, Srinagar : Founded in 1905 by late Mirwaiz of Kashmir Moulvi Rasool Shah, this was the earliest and most important socio-religious organisation,[99] with its official organ *Halat-o-Rou-i-Dad.*[100] Its leaders stressed upon improving the moral tenor of the society.[101] The learning of education was, therefore, "A duty on every man and woman".[102] They aimed to remove social, educational and cultural disabilities of the society, and under the auspices of their Social Reform Committee stressed upon the eradication of social evils in connection with the marriage.[103]

Conflicts between the Anjuman and Ahmadias : Mirwaiz's unchallenged monopoly over the *Anjuman* was resented by the educated youth.[104] At this time the Ahmadias made their appearance in the Kashmir scene (1924). They stressed upon the education and national unity among the Muslims in Kashmir.[105] Mirwaiz was no match to their sharp wit, dialectics and debating capacity.[106] Hence, the period between 1920 to 1931 could be described as the period of conflicts and compromises.[107]

Anjuman-i-Hamdard Islam, Srinagar : This *Anjuman* was established by a few Punjabi Muslims during the First World War.[108] The aim of the Anjuman was to ameliorate the condition of the Muslims through education and vocational training.[109] It also opened free orphanages for the Muslim orphans children.[110]

Anjuman-i-Taraqqi Talim-wa-Ittihad : This was an organisation of the Western educated youth,[111] who had got disillusioned with the conservative ideology of the Anjuman-i- Nusrat-ul-Islam. Its aims and objects were the promotion of education and co-opertion between the people and educated community.[112]

Anjuman-i-Tahafuz-i-Namaz-wa-Satar-i-Masturat : It was started in 1923 as a socio-religious organisation.[113] Its social aims were:[114]

(i) The Muslim women should dress properly covering their heads and legs.

(ii) All traffic in women should be stopped and the marriage contracts should be duly registered in a court of law.

Anjuman-i-Hanifa : The Anjuman was started in 1924 at Anantnag.[115] Its social aim was to inculcate a literary taste among the people.[116]

Anjuman-i-Islat-ul-Muslimin : This *Anjuman* was set up in Srinagar at Sokalipora. Its aims and objects towards the women emancipation were. :[117]

(i) To carry on propaganda for the spread of female education.

(ii) To try to introduce effective reforms to check extravagance in marriages and other social ceremonies.

(iii) To carry on extensive propaganda for the maintenance of cleanliness and the observance of hygenic principles about houses, dress, and diet etc.

(iv) To improve the standards of living.

The Sikh Social Reform Movements: The Sikhs formed a minority in Kashmir. With the advance of education their leaders like their sister communities, also started reform movements to liberate themselves from the social disabilities.

Chief Khalsa Diwan : Founded on October 30, 1902, it supported the demand of the Sikh community to set up an educational committee so as to let the State government know the backwardness of the community. It also stressed upon teaching of Punjabi in the state schools.[118]

Khalsa Youngmen's Organization: Born in 1917, the Association worked hard for the educational uplift of the poor Sikhs through lectures. In its annual sessions, it directed the attention of the government to redress its distress and disabilities.[119]

Sikh Sahaik Sabha, Kashmir: Founded in 1920, it was recognised by the government in 1921.[120] It directed the attention of the government through, resolutions, and meetings to ameliorate the pitiable condition of this agrarian community.[121]

The Akali Movement : This association founded in 1924, was an off-shoot of the Punjab Akali Movement.[122] They became more conscious of their rights hence became more assertive.[123]

The Sudhar Sabha :The Sikhs of Badgham area formed this Sabha to follow the principles of Guru Maharaj, to preach social reforms, eradication of social evils and creating an awareness in the community for learning.[124]

Above material would help the research scholars engaged in the Social History of Kashmir.

## References


1. Mrs. Asheley Carus Wilson, *Irene Petrie Missionary to Kashmir*, 1900. Its only tattered copy is in the Seminar Library, Dept. of History, Kashmir University, Srinagar .
2. Violet Fitze Log Book for 1918 C.M.S. Archives, London. The log Books are records of the annual academic and extra-curricular activities. They recorded the progress of the C.M.S. Schools both for boys and girls in Kashmir and elsewhere. Formerly the copies of the log books were also available in the library of the Tyndale Biscoe Memorial Schools, but unfortunately due to the untimely death of its librarian, Smt. S. Thakur Das, the log Books notes could not be traced.
3. Ibid., Jerry Building in Kashmir, 1913 (Log Book).
4. Ibid., Road Making in Kashmir, 1912 (Log Book).
5. Ibid., Violet Fitze Log Book for 1918.
6. Ibid.
7. Ibid.
8. Ibid., A School Log Book : A School in Being, 1918.
9. Ibid., M.P. Mallinson,'s Log Book—1925.
10. Ibid., School Log, Character Building in Kashmir., p. 8 ; Ibid., Grinding Grit into Kashmir 1929.
11. Ibid., M.P. Mallinson's Log Book—1925.
12. Ibid., Some Progress is Seen—M.P. Mallinson's Report for 1942.
13. Ibid.

14. State Archives, Srinagar (hence SAS) Jammu & Kashmir Annual Administrative Report (AAR) for Samvat 1974, (1917 A.D.); Ibid., AAR, 1931 A.D., State Archives, Jammu (S A J).
15. For this one must consult the J & K Archives, stationed at Jammu. General Records, Index of Records, Volume V (G to P). Pol. Dept. Permanent Group — Records from 1922 A.D. to 1940 A.D.—Mission Hospital Zenana — Rainawari. Year 1936, File No. 246 / Accounts—37.
16. Ibid., Volume III (A to F) from 1868 to 1921 A.D. — year 1909, File No. 115/B-13.
17. Ibid., (B-13-1899) Extract from a letter dated 3rd May 1900 to the Vice President of the State Council from H.V. Cobb, Assistant Resident.
18. Ibid., Volume V (G to P) Pol. Dept., Permanent Group Records from 1922 to 1940 A.D. year 1934, File No. 239.; Ibid., From 1889 A.D. to 1938 A.D., Year 1928. File No. 11/212/G.
19. The Administrative Report at the J & K Archives, Srinagar for the year October 1927—Oct. 1930.
20. J & K Archives, Jammu See F.N. 18 for details—year 1934, File No. 239; Ibid., year 1937. File No. 29/D-18; Ibid., Year 1925 file No. 52/RC 3; Ibid., Vol. V (B) Pol. Dept. — Period Groups—Records—Jammu—1942 year—1939, File No. 2; Ibid., Year 1939, File No. 15/E-284; Ibid., Year 1939, File No. 16/E-282.
21. Jammu and Kashmir Administrative Report 1961 (1904-05) State Archives Srinagar (hence SAS); Ibid., AAR, for Samvat 1971 (1914- 15 A.D.)
22. Ibid., A.A.R. for Samvat 1976 (1919-20 A.D.); Ibid., A.A.R. for Samvat 1981 (1924-25 A.D.) Ibid., A.A.R. for 1920-23 A.D.
23. Ibid., AAR, Samvat 1976 (1919-1920 A.D.); Ibid., AAR Samvat 1977-99 (1920-23 A.D.); Ibid., A.A.R., Samvat 1982 (1925-26 A.D.); Ibid., A.A.R. Samvat 1884-85 to 1886-87 (1927-1930 A.D.)
24. Ibid., AAR, Samvat 1976, year 1919-20.
25. Ibid., AAR, Samvat 1981 (1924-25 A.D.); Ibid., AAR, Samvat 1982, (1925-26 A.D.)
26. Ibid., AAR, for Samvat 1969 (1912-13 A.D.); Ibid., AAR, Samvat 1980 (1923-24 A.D.).
27. Ibid., AAR, for Samvat 1975 (1918-19 A.D.).

28. Ibid., AAR, for Samvat 1968 (1911-12 A.D.); Ibid., AAR, for Samvat 1969 (1912-13).
29. Ibid., AAR, for Samvat 1984-85 to 1986-87, October 1927—October 1930.
30. Ibid., AAR, for Samvat 1983 & Ist six months of 1984 (1926-27 A.D.); Ibid., AAR, for Samvat 1990-91 & 1991-92 (1933-34 & 1934-35 A.D.) also gives a chart. The Report says that the progress of girl education is slow but steady.
31. Ibid., AAR, for Samvat 1990-91 & 1991-92 (1933-34 & 1934-35 A.D.).
32. Ibid., AAR, for Samvat 1993-94 (1936-37 A.D.).
33. Ibid., AAR, for Samvat 1968 (1911-12 A.D.); Ibid. AAR, for 1931.

    Ibid., AAR, for Samvat 1969 (1912-13 A.D.); Ibid. AAR, for 1931.

    Ibid., AAR, for Samvat 1971 (1914-15 A.D.); Ibid. AAR, for 1931.
34. Ibid., AAR, for Samvat 1972 (1915-16 A.D.); Ibid., AAR, for 1931.
35. Ibid., AAR, for the year 1931.
36. SAS/ AAR Samvat 1982 (1925-26 A.D.), Ibid., AAR, Samvat 1983 and Ist six months of 1984 (1926-27 A.D.); Ibid., AAR, Samvat 1984-85 to 1986-87 (Oct. 1927—Oct. 1930 A.D.); Ibid., AAR, Samvats 1987-88, 1988-89 (1930-33 A.D. ); Ibid., AAR, Samvat 1990-91 & 1991-92 (1933 to 1935); Ibid., AAR, Samvat 1992-93 (1935-36 A.D.); Ibid., AAR, 1993-94 (1936-37 A.D.); Ibid., AAR, Samvats1993-94 (1936-37 A.D.); Ibid., AAR, Samvat 1995-96 (1938-39 A.D.); Ibid., AAR, Samvat 1996-97, (17th October 1939 to 15th October 1940 A.D.); Ibid., AAR, Samvat 1998-99 (1941-43 A.D.); Ibid., AAR, Samvat 2000 (1943-44 A.D.).
37. SAJ/General Records, Index of Records, Vol. V, Q to Z. Pol. Dept. — Permanent Group — Records From 1922 A.D. to 1940 A.D. — Year 1929, file No. 119/HE/9.
38. SAJ/General Records Vol. VI (a) General Dept., (1922-1940) File No. 1394/1-W year 1929.

    The Note was prepared by G.E.C. Wakefield, the Political Minister. The Women's Welfare Association should operate in both the cities of Jammu and Srinagar and constituted as follows :

    1. Political Minister—President For both the provinces.

2. Director of Medical-Vice President services.
3. Governor
4. President of the City Municipality.

5-8. Four Indian Ladies.

Sd/Harisingh.

No. 5424 Dated Srinagar — The 8th August 1930.

39. SAJ/General Records, Index Records Vol. VI A, General Dept. — Permanent Group—Records from 1922 to 1940 A.D. year 1922, File No. 26/R.G.-25.
40. SAJ/Ibid., Year 1930, File No. 1195/M.D. - 2.; Ibid., year 1931, File No. 4/M.K.-2.
41. SAJ/General Records, Development Secretariat 1889 to 1938 A.D. year 1920, File No. 15/C-83/76.
42. SAJ/Index of Records. Period Group 1907-1943 from letter A to Z. Block No. A 12-6 year 1925 File No. D.M. 19/84. Ibid., File No. D.M. 193/84 year 1925.
43. SAJ/Ibid., year 1927, File No. 190/84.
44. SAJ/Ibid., year 1927 File No. D.M. 180/84.
45. SAJ/General Records, Vol. V, (Q to Z) Pol. Dept. — Permanent group — Records from 1922 A.D. to 1940 A.D. year 1929 File No. 173 Jdl-9.; Ibid., year 1939 File No. 157/Jdl-3, years/1929 File No. 173 Jdl-8.
46. SAJ/Ibid., year 1930, File No. 105/MN-1.
47. SAJ/General Records-Vol. V. Police Dept. from 1892 A.D. to 1932 A.D., year 1922, File No. 12.
48. SAJ/Ibid., Vol. V, Q to Z, Pol. Dept. — Permanent group — Records from 1922 A.D. to 1940 A.D. year 1935, File No. 188.
49. They are in the SAS.
50. SAS/Census of India-1901, Vol. XXIII -A-Kashmir Part-II.
51. SAS/Census of India - 1911, II, Vol. I, Part-I Report.
52. SAS/Census of India 1921, IV, XXII, Kashmir Part -I.
53. SAS, Census of India, 1931, Vol. XXIV J & K State, Part I, Report.
54. Ibid.
55. SAS/Census of India 1941, Vol. XXIV J & K State Part II.

| Kashmir Province | Total Educated | |
|---|---|---|
| Total | Male | Female |
| 1,569,218 | 847,022 | 722,196 |
| Percentage of educated | 53.73 | 46.27 |

56. SAJ/File No. 2, Mis. 14 year 1920.
57. SAS/Glancy Commission Report.
58. SAS/AAR for the second half of Samvat 1998 and for Samvat 1999 (18 Months from 16th October 1941 to 12th April 1943 A.D.).
59. SAS/The Ganga Nath Report on Administration of Jammu and Kashmir State November 1944 (Typed copy).
60. *Ibid.*
61. *Ibid.*
62. *The Khadmat*, March 15, 1948.
63. Census of India, Jammu & Kashmir Report, 1931, Part-I, Volume XXIV, p. 263.
64. Triennial Administrative Report of Jammu & Kashmir State, Hindi Years 1958-60 (Middle of April 1901 to middle of April 1904)/SAS.
65. SAS/A note on Education in the State of Jammu & Kashmir, 1916.
66. Ganga Nath Report, *op.cit*.
67. See Foot Notes 22, 23, 24, 25, 26, 27.
68. See Foot Notes 51 and 52.
69. See Foot Notes 2 and 5.
70. *Ibid.*
71. This Booklet is in the office of the National Conference Mujahid Manzil, Srinagar, Kashmir.
72. Several Newspapers representing Hindu and Muslim view points were published; for the Hindu view point *Martand* (Its copies available at Sheetalnath, Sathu Srinagar) & *Ranbir* (copies available at the University of Jammu Library, Jammu Tawi), for the Muslim Consciousness, *Khidamat* (Available at Abi Guzar, Srinagar); *Khalid* and *Hamdard* (copies of both the News-papers are available at the information office, Srinagar); *Akhbar-Kashir, Bande Matram, Khalsa, Morning Post*, (Copies are available at the state Archives, Jammu); Anjuman-Nusrat-ul- Islam Kashmir, *Tarikh, Khadmat. Mansobee* in Urdu (pamphlet) *Muhsin-i-Qaum,*

Periodical (The copies are available at Mazi Hall, Mustaqbal, Rajauri Kadal, Srinagar.

73. SAJ/Captain Trench, Resident in Kashmir to Dewan Amar Nath, C.M. to Maharajah, September 16, 1910, File No. 215 of 1910.
74. National Archives of India (hence N.A.I.), Home Department, Political, November 1917, No. 7, Fortnightly Report for Second half of October, 1917.
75. Interview with Dina Nath Nadim, a prominent educationist, poet and freedom fighter, June 1986; SAJ/File No. 262/77-C of 1918.
76. Interview with Damodhar Hanjora, a prominent Social Reformer at Karan Nagar, Srinagar, March 1981; Interview with Dina Nath Hanjora, a prominent Social Reformer, at Chhanpora, Srinagar, March 1981; SAJ/File No. 261/28-C of 1917.
77. Census Report of India, 1931, p. 297.
78. SAJ/File No. 1-85 of 1923-24; File No. 157-C-11, Pol. Dept. of 1921, Government Records (Old English Records), Confidential Report From A.S.P. Jammu to S.P. Jammu, dated April 6, 1921;*Ibid.*, Hafiz Mohammad Ismail, Personal Diary, 1907-1950. Unpublished manuscript, July 30, 1923, March 23,1924 item 1; *The Muslim Chronicle*, weekly July 2, 1926, (National Library, Calcutta).
79. Interview with Dina Nath Nadim, *op.cit.*
80. Interview with Pt. Kashap Bandhu, May 1985, At Tral. A prominent Social Reformer and politician. His original name was Tara Chand Kaul. At the age of twenty he left Kashmir. At Lahore he edited *the Arya Gazette*. In 1931 he returned to Kashmir. Later on at the invitation of Shaikh Mohd. Abdullah joined National Conference. Died in 1986.
81. Hafiz Mohd. Ismail, *op.cit.*, October 14, 1926, item 4, and October 15, 1926, item 1.
82. Census Report of India, 1901, 1, p. 24; SAJ/File no. 52/L-11 of 1898.
83. Interview with Mohan Krishen Tikoo, at Sanatnagar, Srinagar, Sept. 15, 1985. Former Law Member of Jammu & Kashmir Assembly. A reformer, played an important role in the education of women in Kashmir. Served as a teacher in the schools run by the women's Welfare Trust.

84. Interview with Premnath Bazaz, (doyen among the Social Reformers, Journalist, Historian, and Freedom Fighter.) at Jawahar Nagar, Srinagar, June 1977; J. Manners to J.B. Wood, September 1917, Home Dept., Pol., September 1917, No. 62, NAI.
85. Interview with Pt. Nand Lal Wattal, A Social Reformer and Journalist, At Rajbagh, Srinagar, 1985.
86. Interview with P.N. Bazaz, *op.cit.*
87. Interview with Kashap Bandhu, *op.cit.*
88. Interview with R.K. Kak, (a famous Arya Samajist, Journalist and Social Reformer) at Regal Chowk, May 29, 1885.
89. Interview with P.N. Bazaz, *op.cit.*
90. Interview with Damodhar Hanjora, *op.cit*; Interview with Gwasha Lal Kaul, Journalist, and writer in 1981.
91. Interview with Prem Nath Thussoo, President of the Scout Movement, at Rainawari, Srinagar, June 20, 1985.
92. Interview with Dina Nath Nadim, *op.cit.*
93. Interview with Rattani Khar, teacher, Kashapa Girls School, July 6, 1985, at Srinagar.
94. Interview with Kashap Bandhu, *op.cit.*
95. Interview with R.K. Kak, *op.cit.*
96. Ghunwati's Diary.;*The Ranbir*, December 19, 1932; *The Tribune* (Lahore), September 25, 1931.
97. Interview with Prem Nath Bazaz, *op.cit.*
98. Interview with Kashap Bandhu, *op.cit.*
99. SAJ/File No. J-88 of 1924.
100. The Journal was published from Lahore, Himalayan Steam Press; After some times it was also published from Srinagar, Pratap Kashmir Steam Press.
101. Hafiz Mohammad Ismail, *op.cit.*, July 4, 1922, item 3, December 20, 1925, item 3; NAI/Home Dept. Pol., December 1914 No. 31.
102. Halat-o-Rou-i-Dad, *op.cit.* p. 41.
103. *Ibid.*, p. 63.
104. Hafiz Mohammad Ismail, *op.cit.*, July 24, 1921, item 1.
105. *Ibid., September 16, 1926, item* 2.
106. *Ibid.*, September 14, 1928, item 3.

107. Interview with Prof. Fida Mohammad Hasnain, Ex-Director of Archives and Archaeology, Jammu & Kashmir Government.
108. Hafiz Mohammad Ismail, *op.cit.*, October 16, 1918, item 2.
109. *The Zamindar*, Lahore, August 3, 1928.
110. Hafiz Mohammad Ismail, *op.cit.*, October 16, 1918, item 2.
111. SAJ/File No. 240/P-136 of 1918, Education Minister to Chief Minister, August 16, 1918.
112. SAJ/File No. J-88 of 1924.
113. SAJ/File No. 439 of 1923.; *Akhbar-i-Kashmir*, July 25, 1925, (Lahore).
114. SAJ/File No. J-88 of 1924; *Akhbar-i-Kashmir*, February 21, 1929, (Lahore).
115. SAJ/File No. 274 of 1925.
116. *Ibid.*, Interview with Fida Mohammad Hasnain.
117. Interview with Padamshri Begam Zafar Ali, an Educationist and Social Reformer, M.L.A., May 1986. The first Muslim woman who matriculated and came out of the house to serve as a teacher.
118. SAJ/File No. 216/A-92 of 1918.
119. SAJ/File No. 439 of 1924; *Ibid.*, File No, J-44 of 1924; *Khalsa Akhbar' Lahore*, Lahore 28, 1918; SAJ/File No. 216/A-92 of 1918.
120. SAJ/File No. 259/62 of 1920.
121. *Ibid.*
122. SAJ/File No. 439 of 1924; *Ibid.*, File No. J-44 of 1924.
123. SAJ/File No. B-89/A of 1924; *Ibid.*, File No. 435 of 1924; *Ibid.*, File No. 389 of 1925; *Ibid.*, No. G-104 of 1925.
124. *Khidamat*, January 28, 1947 and March 15, 1948.

# 25

# 13TH JULY 1931 IN KASHMIR ------ A UNIQUE SAGA OF THE FREEDOM STRUGGLE AND COMMUNAL OUTRAGE : A CONSPECTUS OF NEW SOURCE MATERIAL

The State of Jammu and Kashmir came into existence as a sequal to the defeat of the Sikh power in the first Anglo Sikh War. The new state was born as a result of the Treaty of Amritsar, which was concluded between Raja Gulab Singh of Jammu and the East India Company on March 16, 1946.[1] The early Dogra rule was very oppressive.[2] The Kashmiris felt that they were treated as a conquered people.[3]

The British intervention in the Kashmir politics was a blessing in disguise, as in its wake came the Christian Missionaries. Moved by pathetic plight of the Kashmiris they started schools to educate them. To persuade them to attend the schools was an uphill task.[4] The greatest missionary of his times, Tyndale Biscoe, has penned a very graphic and pathetic picture of the unhygienic condition of the students. Their clothes were dirty and smelling. Mouth open, emitting 'most foul' breath due to pyorrhea. Almost all of them suffered from 'seald heads.'[5]

Gradually the missionary enterprise succeeded in imparting Kashmiris their identity, through education. The first to gain benefit were the Kashmiri Pandits, the Muslims, who were in majority, followed suit in a low gear. With the passage of time the Kashmiris could not remain immune from the wave of non- cooperation, Khilafat and civil disobedience movements sweeping over the British India[6]. In Kashmiri character there is an intrinsic quality of resistance, which could be understood in the second and third decades of the twentieth century by gleaning into the demographical structure. The Kashmiri Society consisted of urbanised Kashmiri Pandits, Kashmiri Muslims, and the Panjabi Commercial Community. The Pandits being educated were largely employed in the government offices, the Muslims by and large were an exploited agrarian society, and the Panjabi Hindu was an affluent class, imported into Kashmir by the Dogra Rulers.[7]

Among the Kashmiri Pandits with the education came the political consciousness earlier than their Muslim counterparts.[8] They vehemently protested against siphoning off of the higher government jobs to the British Indians to the detriment of their interests.[9] Their pleas and canvassing resulted in the implementation of the state subject law, a colourful victory of the Kashmiri Pandits.[10] This law is the precursor of the present Article 370.[11]

The Muslims also became politically conscious and brooded over their deprivation and sequesteration.[12] Sometimes the pentup anger and suspicion against the ruler explodes like a volcano at a trivial incident making the moment historic or turning point. Same phenomenon happened in Kashmir, when on July 13, 1931, a large crowd of the Kashmiri Muslims collected at the Central Jail, to hear the trial of a non-Kashmiri Afghan Abdul Quadir charged with the sedition. Mishandling of the situation led to an order of firing in which nine people were killed.[14] The day became famous as the beginning of the freedom struggle in Jammu & Kashmir.

## COMMUNAL OUTRAGE

The Muslims, who were at the Central Jail brought the dead and wounded men on *charpoys* in a procession. They carried a banner soaked in blood in front of the procession. Quite psychologically the gruesome scene excited the mob comprising of the Muslims. They thought of vengenance against the government. At a time when the passions were so excited that reasoning and discrimination were thrown to the winds, the government was equated with the Hindus.[15] Almost all the officials were Hindus and the Maharaja was also a Hindu, so they held the Hindus responsible for the actions of the government. The loot of the Hindu shops, i.e., Punjabi and Kashmiri Hindus had started. As is common in such incidents the anti-social elements joined the infuriated mob, in looting Maharajganj, a busy shopping centre, in the city of Srinagar. But at Vicharnag,[17] the loot was not the direct result of firing, as the plunderers came from Saura, a suburb of Srinagar, and not from the direction of jail. According to Pandit S.K. Khar, the looters were spurred by Shaikh Mohammad Abdullah' speeches, who told them:

> "The Pandits take all the employment and none was given to them".[18]

On the whole three Hindus were murdered, 291 were either beaten or wounded, and 54 shops were looted.[19]

## ASSESSMENT

The communal unrest and flash was sequel to both backlash and backwash factors inherent in the Kashmiri Muslim Society. The special privileges enjoyed by the Dogra Rajputs and the monopoly of the Kashmiri Pandits over the government services irked the pride of the majority community, who did not like to be dominated by the minority.[20] The agrarian structure comprised of the Muslims was mainly feudal, i.e., surfdom at the bottom and feudalism at the top.[21] Undoubtedly the new Maharaja Hari Singh promulgated an Agricultural Relief Act in 1927, but he could not chasten the exploitative bureaucracy in one day. Suspicion and distrust had taken the place of communal harmony.[22] *Shuddhi* and *tablig* were openly preached and advocated by the rival communities vitiating the atmosphere. Barjor Dalal, the Chairman of the Srinagar Riot Enquiry Committee, 1931, quoted the evidences in his report:

> "Mirza Ghulam Mustafa and Col. Ghulam Ali Shah have definitely stated that unless preachings exciting communal

hatred in mosques and temples are stopped with an iron hand the present communal tension will not end, ------- till eternity."[23]

They also highlighted Muslim backwardness in education by adducing facts and figures to prove their charge.[24] Mutual distrust had reached to such an extent that the injured and wounded patients during the July riots refused to be treated by a doctor of opposite faith, for fear of life.[25]

Maharaja's government was autocratic in nature, hence neither it had any forum to know the people's reaction towards the administration, nor it had allowed the formation of any political party through which popular grievances could be ventilated.[26] In 1924, Lord Reading, the Viceroy of India, visited the valley, the Muslims submitted a Memorandum, focusing their grievances and demands.[27] One of the main demands was that their employment in the state services should be in proportion to their population which was 95 percent.[28] They should be trusted with the important and key posts. The Muslim crowds exhibited black flags bearing inscriptions such as "Our mosques desecrated" and "How Long will Muslims be trodden down by the Hindus in this country"[29]

The memorandum instead of relief earned the displeasure of the State Council for its signatories[30]. They were expelled, exiled, dismissed, deported, their property confiscated and also were debarred from attending Royal Darbar and other state functions.[31]

The people of the valley did not take it lying down.[32] They intensified their propaganda, and won the sympathies of the Muslims of the state and British India. The press in British India specially in Punjab supported their cause.[33] The government of India connived at it, as the new Maharaja Hari Singh had turned out to be far less submissive and obliging than his predecessor.[34] Hence the outside intervention in the Kashmir politics generated communal fervour within the valley. The Reading Room Party acted as a catalytic agent to arouse communal passions.[35] Certain factors as the Recruitment Board, Maharaja's departure to Britain in September 1930, want of harmony in the cabinet, tolerance of Muslim agitation through Jammu Association[36] and papers printed outside the state,[37] the help given to the local agitation by outside Muslims,[38] the tragic and accidental happenings of the *Khutba*,[39] *Tauhine Koran*,[40] i.e., leaves of the Holy Quran found in a public latrine,[41] and mishandling of the Jammu deputation, provided grist to the mill of discontent.

The Kashmiri Pandits also became restless at the stir of the majority community. They demanded special minority rights and safeguards of which they had heard in British India. Employment was their only means of livelihood, therefore they looked with disfavour to the Muslim demand for reservations in public services. They advocated merit to be the criterion for the appointments.[42]

Infact the unprecedented and unpremeditated communal violence was a tug of war between the haves and have nots which was given a religious tinge to enlist mob sympathy. Premnath Bazaz holds both the Reading Room Party and Hindu indiscrimination responsible for all the unsavoury incidents.[43] This outburst was natural and necessary for breaking the shackles of obscurantist communalism and thereby to usher in secular politics. The blood oozed out of the martyrs and victims of the communal outrage did not go unredeemed. The metamorphosis of the Muslim Conference into the National Conference was its reward.

## References

1. C.U., Aitchison, *A collection of Treaties, Engagements and Sanads relating to India and neighbouring Countries*, Oxford, 1897, Vol. VIII, pp. 169-170.
2. IOL/G.G. to Secret committee, Sept. 19, 1846, Bengal India Secret Letters.
3. *Hamdard*, Special Number, July 31, 1938. (copies available at J & K Information Office, Srinagar).
4. CETB LOG BOOK, 1930, CMS, Archives, London. The Log Books are records of the annual academic and extra - curricular activities.
5. Ibid.
6. JKA/File No. 9 of 1920; NAI/Home Dept. Progs, Pol., July 1920, No. 105, Bannerman to Johnwood, July 16, 1920; NAI/Home Dept. Progs, Pol., June 1921, No. 12; NAI/Home Dept. Progs, Pol. August 1921, No. 18; JKA File No. 73 of 1922; NAI/Home Dept.

Progs, Pol. April 1921, No. 42; JKA/File No. 55 of 1922; NAI, Home Dept., Pol., Jan 1930, File No. 18, Fortnightly Report for First Half of January.

7. JKA/File No. 24 of 1891 (Old English Records), Kashmir Government Records; NAI/For Dept. Secret E. Feb. 1898; NAI/For Dept. Sec. E, July 1897; A plea for State Subject Definition and its genesis by the Dogra Sadar Sabha, Jammu, JKA/File No. G 514 of 1911.
8. JKA/File No. 40 - 5 - 18 of 1904.
9. NAI/Home Dept., Pol, Jan 1922, No. 18; JKA file No. 21/23 F-219 of 1909; Ibid., Memo by A Mitra, May 23, 1910.
10. Definition of State Subject. A Historical Review, *The Ranbir Weekly*, Jammu, May 20 and 27, 1935, p. 3 (copy available at the University of Jammu Library, Jammu Tawi).
11. Interview with Swaroop Nath Saraf, a prominent Social Reformer at Shopian, March 1981.
12. NAI/Home Dept., Pol., June 1924, File No. 25; Ibid., Dec. 1924, File No. 25; G.S. Raghwan, *The Warning of Kashmir*, Allahabad, Pioneer, 1931, p. 63.
13. *Kashmir's Journey to Freedom*, A Survey of Political Events in Jammu and Kashmir State since 1931, Jammu and Kashmir National Conference, Mujahid Manjil, Srinagar, KMR.
14. NAI/Home Dept., Pol., July 1931, File No. 18, From the Resident in Kashmir, No. F-9-C/30, Dated July 17, 1931.
15. JKA/Report of the Srinagar Riot Enquiry Committee, Srinagar, 1931., p. 13; *The Musalman*, July 30, 1931, p. 6, National Library, Calcutta.
16. "We are the worst sufferers. On the 13th July, 1931, The Muslims raided us, looted our houses, robbed us wherewithall, killed us and perpetrated horrible atrocities on our own. The incident at Vicharnag was a matter of History. Maheshwar Nath Kaul to Prime Minister, Maharaja's Government, May 21, 1932, *Kashmir Hindu Bulletin*, Vide, Ravinderjit Kaur, National Movement in Kashmir (1901-1931), an unpublished dissertation, at the Iqbal Library, University of Kashmir, Srinagar.
17. A locality in Srinagar.
18. JKA/Evidence Recorded in Public, SREC, 1931, witness No. 65, p. 177.

19. Sanatan Dharm Youngmen's Association, 1931, *Kashmir Hindus and the Recent Disturbances*, Foreword by Premnath Bazaz.;P.L. Lakhanpal, ed., *Essential Documents and Notes on Kashmir Dispute*, New Delhi, 1958, International Books, p. 272.
20. NAI/Home Dept., Pol., 1922, No. 847.
21. JKA/File No. 72/C-57 of 1920.
22. JKA/File No. 9/85 of 1924.
23. JKA/SREC Report, 1931, p. 17.
24. JKA/SREC Report, p. 44.
25. JKA/SREC, 1931, *op.cit.*, Witness No. 2, p. 14.
26. JKA/File No. 830 of 1922. In 1930. at Fatehkadal, Srinagar, Reading Room Party was founded with the permission of the government. Initially it was an academic body of the unemployed educated youths.
27. NAI/Home Dept. Pol., Dec. 1924, File No. 25, Johnwood to Patterson, Dec. 19, 1924.
28. JKA/SREC Report, p. 17; JKA/File No. T/81 of 1924.
29. NAI/Home Dept. Pol., Nov. 1924, File No. 25, Johnwood to Patterson, Dec., 1, 1924.
30. NAI/Home Dept., Pol., Dec. 1924, File No. 25, Johnwood to Patterson, Dec. 19, 1924.
31. NAI/Home Dept. Pol. Sept. 1925, File No. 112; Ibid., Home Dept., Pol. Dec. 1924, File No. 25. Johnwood to Patterson, Dec. 19, 1924.
32. JKA/File No. G/102 of 1924-25, Extract from the confidential diary of Supdt of Police, Kashmir Province, Period ending March 21, 1925.
33. *The Inqilab*, Lahore, Dec. 14, 1929. (NAI); *The Syasat*, Lahore, June 6, 1929, (NAI); *The Kashmir*, Lahore, June 28, 1920, (NAI)
34. *The Mulsim Outlook*, Lahore, June 1, 1928, (National Library, Calcutta).
35. NAI/Home Dept., Pol. June 1931, File No. 18, Fortnightly Report for first half of June. From the Resident in Kashmir, No. F-9- C/30 dated June 19, 1931.
36. JKA/SREC Report, p. 23.

37. Besides so many newspapers the *Siyasat* (NAI), *Muslim Outlook* (NAI) and *Inqilab* (NAI), played a very important role. They were published in Lahore.
38. *The Akhbar-i-Kashmir*, Lahore, June 28, 1925, p. 14 (JKA); JKA/ File No. G/102 of 1924-25; Ravinderjit Kaur, *op.cit.* p. 238; The Associations respectively were The Anjuman-i-Kashmiri Musalman, Gojranwala, The Youngmen's Muslim Association, Gujrat, and the All India Kashmir Muslim Conference.
39. JKA/Middleton Report on an Inquiry into Disturbances in Kashmir, p. 2.
40. *The Musalman, Calcutta*, July 28, 1931, p. 6 (National Library, Calcutta); NAI/Home Dept., Pol. June 1931, File No. 18, Fortnightly Report for the first half of June, letter No. F-9- C/30.
41. Mohammad Yusuf Saraf, *Kashmiris Fight --- For Freedom*, Vol. I, Lahore, 1977, p. 363 (its copy is in the private library of Late Shaikh Mohammad Abdullah).
42. JKA/SREC/1931, *Op.cit.*, Witness 80, p. 266.
43. Premnath Bazaz, *Inside Kashmir*, Srinagar, 1941, p. 132.

## ABBREVIATIONS

C.E.T.B. — Canon C.E. Tyndale Biscoe.

C.M.S. — Christian Missionery Society.

I.O.L. — India Office Library, Common Wealth Relations Office, London.

J.K.A. — Jammu Kashmir Archives.

N.A.I. — National Archives of India, New Delhi.

S.R.E.C. — Report of the Srinagar Riot Enquiry Committee.

# 26

# ROLE OF WOMEN IN THE FREEDOM STRUGGLE OF KASHMIR

'Man is born free, but everywhere he is in chains', so said Geneva born French philosopher Rousseau, whose call coupled with the other philosophers brought a revolution in France known as the French Revolution which gave to the world three cherished rights of mankind—equality, liberty and fraternity. Liberty is in the very veins of nature. A sapling grown in a pot remains stunted even with all the manure and care, whereas the same planted in an open space blooms into a majestic Chinar tree.[1] Man, who is the only creature gifted with intelligence and wisdom of all the animate species, strives for freedom at the cost of his life. The history of the world is replete with the glowing examples of the nations, who had attained liberty after great sacrifices. Very ably, the poet has depicted,

> "For Freedom's battle once begun bequeathed by bleeding sire to son, though baffled oft, is ever won."[2] The same is true to the freedom struggle of Kashmir.

The emerald green valley of Kashmir is a veritable heaven on earth. Beauty and grace both in nature and man has been generously showered upon this paradise by Almighty God. The happy vale was sold for seventy-five lakh rupees by Lord Hardinge, the Governor-General of the East India Company, to Raja Gulab Singh Dogra, as a reward for his perfidy against his Sikh master and the people of the Punjab.[3] The new masters of the newly created Jammu and Kashmir State ruled like despots, ignoring the natural aspirations of the people and their moral and material upliftment.

Being a protected state under the British Crown,[4] it was indirectly placed under the control of the government of India. On September 25, 1885, the day Partap Singh was formally installed as the Maharaja of Jammu and Kashmir the goverment of India replaced the 'Officer on Special Duty' by the British Resident in Kashmir, on the plea of reforming the administration.[5] The people of Kashmir were now subjected to the double tyranny and harassment of the dual control of the Dogra and the British. Every cloud has a silver lining. With the advent of the English Resident in Kashmir, also arrived missionaries. They were moved by the pitiable and pathetic condition of the people, labouring under ignorance. The worst sufferers were the Muslims, who formed the bulk of the population, which was generally speaking an agricultural community. The women were steeped in ignorance, superstitions and poverty. The missionaries started schools, and thence dawned upon the first ray of light and learning.[6] Thus the freedom movement in the state was the outcome of the impact of the West and the British India, which filled the Kashmiri mind with new aspirations and hopes. They also aspired for a respectable and decent life.

This was the time when the British India was passing through the crucial period on the way to liberation. Suffering had become the watchword of the freedom fighters. The Indian states no longer remained a mute witness to the metamorphosis going on in British India. The people of Kashmir rose from their age old slumber, and took up cudgels not only against the alien rule, but also against all exploiting agencies such as the jagirdars, landlords, capitalists, mullahs and corrupt officials.[7] The women of Kashmir, who had a long and illustrious history of being great scholars, Queens and administrators,[8] came forward to share the responsibility of freeing the motherland and to build a New Kashmir out of the ashes of the past'.[9]

The struggle for freedom and the demand for democratisation of the administration in Jammu and Kashmir goes back to the year 1930-31.[10] The origin of the discontent was purely economic, i.e., inadequate representation in the state services particularly and in the economic and industrial life of the state generally. The Muslim tillers, labourers and artisans were the excellent target of exploitation by the richer sections of the society, which overwhelming consisted of non-Muslims. They (the Muslims) were denied of the fruits of Western education under the constraints of circumstances, at last realised its importance. But to their utter dismay, they found that after obtaining academic degrees, the doors of the suitable jobs were closed for them.

Agrarian discontent and lack of suitable opportunities for the educated Muslims were the motivating forces of the Muslim masses to agitate against the despotic Dogra regime.[11] The year of 1924 was a landmark in the history of Jammu and Kashmir, when the Muslim leaders presented a memorial to the Viceroy, Lord Reading on his visit to Valley in 1924.[12] The process of presentation of demands and their half-hearted consideration by the government continued until 1930, when the Reading Room Party was formed by a few Muslim graduates to highlight the problems of the Muslim masses. Among those graduates was also Sheikh Mohammad Abdullah, who spearheaded the freedom movement. The movement received active approval and support from the neighbouring province of the Punjab, where under the guidance of Sheikh Mohammad Iqbal, the Kashmir Committee was founded to activise the struggle of the Kashmiri Muslims. Very soon Muslim Conference was founded in the State and Sheikh Mohammad Abdullah became its President.[13]

On July 13, 1931, there was a massive demonstration against the state government and the Maharaja. The Muslim demonstrators had gathered outside the prison walls, where the trial of a non-Kashmiri Afghan was taking place for sedition. They demanded that they might also be allowed to hear the proceedings. The Sessions Judge ordered the armed police to disperse the crowd. The police lathi-charged the crowd, which started pelting stones and throwing burning *kangries*, traditional Kashmiri weapon till today. Then the police opened fire with the result that twenty- one people reported killed by bullets and many received injuries.[14]

This was the occasion, when the poor women of the working classes of the Muslim society fought shoulder to shoulder along with their counterpart against injustice and misrule of the Dogra despots. This is a unique feature of Kashmir's freedom struggle, that during its first phase the women participants came from 'have-nots' section who could in no way be called as emancipated, enlightened and educated. The instinct was inborn, result of centuries of suffering, denial and torture. It may also be interpreted as traditional characteristic of the Kashmiri women's yearning for independence. During this period, the women processionists, many of them with suckling babies in their arms, passed through the streets raising slogans either against the oppressive Dogra regime or demanding the release of their imprisoned leaders and for the establishment of a democratic setup. They were surrounded by the armed police and were ordered to disperse. On their refusal, they were abused and molested. They used to appear on the streets in large numbers at a moment's notice. After a few days, the body of a Muslim women was recovered from the river in Srinagar.

The Muslim women took out a procession on July 24, which terminated at the Mazar-i-Shohda. They again came out in a procession on July 27, with about 5,000 carrying black flags. It was lathi-charged, in which 10 women were injured. Addressing the procession at Mazar-i-Shohda, a woman speaker said :

> "Our men should sit in their homes and wear *burqas* ... We are proud of our Punjabi Muslim brethren but so far they have merely confined themselves to merely issuing statements..... We request the members of the British Parliament to take our grievances to the League of Nations... We appeal to the army not to oppress women as it was no chivarly. But if they have any such instructions, they will find us ready to meet the challenge."[15]

In 1931, when the government had handed over the administration to the military command, on September 6, a crowd of women agitators was lathi-charged and their modesty was outraged. Some women were injured and fainted.. The brutalities perpetrated on defenceless women processionists were universally condemned, even by Hare Kishan Koul, the Prime Minister of the Maharaja. A few days later the women took out a very big procession, which was assaulted with gushing water from fire brigade hoses. They were drenched to the skin in September cold, stood the ground and held a meeting ventilating their grievances.[16]

**Women Martyrs in 1931 Upheaval**

In Shopian, Sajida Bano, aged 25 years, who had recently lost her husband, received a bullet wound in military firing. She was pregnant and died along with the child on the spot. The second woman to die was Jan Begam, widow of Abel Lone, aged 35 years, resident of Khwajapura in the locality of Nowshera, Srinagar, who was killed in a police firing. The third martyr was Begum Bohru, better known as Freechi, a specimen of the famed Kashmiri beauty, aged 30, widow of Khwaja Razaq Joo Bohru, resident of mohalla Jalal Sahib, Baramula, who died of a bullet wound received in military firing. Her offence was that she had hurled a kangri on the face of a police officer in course of a procession of women which disfigured him permanently. The fourth women to die was Fazli on September 24, 1931, when the military opened fire on a procession of women which was parading through the Maisuma Bazar, Srinagar.[17] Some of them were arrested and had to undergo imprisonment.

These women were forerunners of the educated women participants in the later phase of the freedom struggle. They attended the meetings organised by the Muslim political leaders or by the Muslim Conference. Their patriotism was fired by the speeches of Sheikh Mohammad Abdullah, who started with spell- binding recitation of the Quran before breaking into Kashmiri language. It is a sad commentary on the sagacity of the leadership, which failed to canalise the pent up energies of those women freedom fighters, released by the 1931 upheaval. They had silently suffered in their thousands, and passed into oblivion without any recognition or fame. Some of them had undoubtedly the potentialities of leadership, but in the absence of proper guidance and training such a valuable asset was lost to the national cause.

The last stage in the freedom struggle of Kashmir was from 1936 to 1946, with its spectacular turning into secular movement.

It was a struggle between 'haves' and 'have-nots', 'oppressed' and 'oppressors'. In 1939 the Muslim Conference was transformed into National Conference.[18] During this decade the women in Kashmir were engaged in the pursuit of education and learning to qualify themselves to join the mainstream of the national life.

The last phase of popular resistance against the state government in Kashmir was Quit Kashmir Movement started by National Conference in May, 1946.[19] The new slogan derived its inspiration from Mahatma Gandhi's Quit India Movement of 1942. Quite naturally the spokesman, author and architect of the new movement was Sheikh Abdullah, who had been honoured by the title of 'Sher-i-Kashmir' by his followers. He was arrested along with other leaders of the National Conference.[20] The women of Kashmir from all walks of life came forward with redoubled enthusiasm and energy in support of their beloved leader.

**Some Prominent Women Freedom Fighters**

Jan Ded was the heroine of 1931 upheaval. Being illiterate and belonging to 'have-nots', she could not rise to the height of national eminence. Her natural talents were not exploited. To fight against injustice and for attaining legitimate rights was in response to an urge within her. She was pragmatist, and was poles apart from many of the male political leaders of Kashmir in secularising the political atmosphere and shunning narrow communal loyalties. She was ebullient, outspoken and demanding. This incurred the wrath of the top Muslim leaders, and she had to retire from the active politics after 1934.[21] She is one of the many women freedom fighters, who found no place in the pantheon of the freedom fighters.

Zoni Gujree, a milk man's daughter drawn into the 1946 Quit Kashmir Movement, is a living testimony in proving that freedom's call was not restricted to the upper and educated sections of the female society. She typified the Kashmiri beauty, vivacity and elegance. She was at that time in her teens, and her husband was dead against her entrance to the political whirlpool. Wife of a poor, working man, politics was no luxury for her, home was to be looked after. Pressure and force could not confine her to the four walls of home. Breaking all the shackles she came out to defend freedom, sacrificing the demands of hearth and home. She was nine times put behind the bars, but no suffering could deter the freedom loving daughter of Kashir.[22] Her magnetic oratory drew large throngs of women agitators. Several times she was attacked by the armed police. At one of the assaults made by the military police at Fateh Kadal, she lost her only son aged 12 years, when a bullet struck the boy. During the tribal raid of 1947, she joined women's Defence force and received militia training at a place, where now stands the New Secretariat building. During this period she remained at the top with the sole aim and ambition to topple the Dogra regime, and to have a government in Kashmir by the people of Kashmir, for the people of Kashmir, and of the people of Kashmir, headed by their beloved leader Sheikh Mohammad Abdullah.

Her sacrifices to the cause of freedom were widely acclaimed and appreciated. She is awarded with the title of 'Zoni Mujahid' in grateful acknowledgment for her services. She has now retired from politics, and is now receiving a pension from the Freedom Fighters' Fund. She has been to Mecca thrice, and at present basking in the memory of bygone days.

Begam Akbar Jahan, wife of Sheikh Mohammad Abdullah, threw herself in the freedom struggle, after Sheikh and his colleagues were arrested during the 'Quit Kashmir Movement'. She kept the movement alive by her heroic courage. She broke the shackles of *purdah*, outdated customs and seclusion of the upper class women from the national life. She led anti-government demonstrations, and her greatest work was to boost up the sagging morale of the National Conference Leaders. She is the heroine of the Quit Kashmir Movement of 1946. Her delicate frame conceals an iron will and unbending spirit. She is a pretty daughter of an European man Harry Nedous from his charming Kashmiri Gujar Wife. She represents a happy amalgamation of the east and west. Being brought up in a home which represented a synthesis of love and mercy of christianity and the Islamic tradition of fear in God, she has imbibed the best of both the religions and cultures.[23] She in accordance with her upbringing brought the ideals of love and justice to all human beings irrespective of race, caste and creed. At the age of seventeen she passed Senior Cambridge Examination with distinction. She has throughout her life and still is waging wars against the dragons of communalism and chauvinism. Service above self and emancipation of women are her life mission. She not only fought against the Dogra oppression, but also collected donations from the people in aid of the victims of the Dogra persecution. She came into contact with the Indian National Leaders.[24] Mahatma Gandhi and Jawaharlal had a great respect for her heroism, secularism, patriotism and devotion to duty.

During Pakistani invasion she was foremost in the Women's Wing of Peace Brigade, which fought Pakistani invaders. In 1947, when the country was groaning under the grip of communal frenzy, she carried the torch of peace and love to far flung areas of the State.[25] She soothed every afflicted heart with the balm of love and peace. She rehabilitated the victims of the partition with a mother's care and love. It was only due to her tireless efforts that the state of Jammu and Kashmir was saved from madness of communal riots. She is awarded the title of Madar-i-Meharban (kind mother) by the people of Kashmir, to whom she is sacred as a benign mother. She is Shakti (strength) to her husband in accordance with the Indian tradition and culture. What Sheikh Abdullah is today, is due to her unflinching devotion in the days of his trial and tribulation. She was elected to the Parliament. She speaks in Kashmiri, Urdu and English with equal command and ease.

Fatima, a peasant women, is an immortal martyr of the Quit Kashmir Movement, who laughed at death to propagate the message of freedom. She was shot dead at Anantnag by the Dogra forces in May 1946, while leading a procession to voice protests against the repressive policy of the Maharaja. The Dogra forces had occupied the town and armed soldiers were parading through the streets with pointed bayonets fixed on their guns. Some people took out a procession in defiance of the military orders. Fatima, also joined at the head of the women processionists. In the crowd her slogans were the loudest, and for this she was made particular target of attack.[26] Her martyrdom is a lighthouse to the freedom fighters of Kashmir.

Another freedom fighter of the Quit Kashmir Movement is the educationist, Miss Mahmuda Ali Shah. She is one of the first highly educated woman of Kashmir, who had gone to England for studies. She is M.A., B.T. (Punj.) Dip. Education (Leads). During her student days at Lahore, she joined the "Punjab Students Federation", which was fighting against the British Imperialism. She often addressed the meetings. In Kashmir she founded "Free Thinkers Society" which gathered under it the intellectuals of the state. This was the time when the freedom movement in Kashmir had risen to unprecedented heights under the leadership of Sheikh Abdullah. She joined the freedom movement under him, and rejected the two nation Theory under his tutelage. The slogan of National Conference in those days was ; "*Uttho, Meri Duniya Ke Garibon Ko Jaga Do*".... which epitomises the aims and objectives of Kashmir's freedom struggle. Nature has gifted her with regal charm and administrative capabilities. Though she had joined the state service on June 22, 1940, yet the young girl fired with the zeal of liberty found the call of nation irresistible. She staked everything and threw herself in the Quit Kashmir Movement of 1946. Again in 1947, she was in the forefront of women's resistance against the tribal raid. She did a great service in bringing normalcy to the State, when whole of the sub-continent was gripped into communal frenzy. With the same zest she served the people during 1965 Pakistani aggression.

After 1947, she left politics and dedicated her life to the cause of women education. She became the Principal of the state's first College of Women in Srinagar on November 13, 1953.[27] The college flourished under her care and supervision in all the field of activity both curricular and extra-curricular. The college was visited off and on by the dignitaries of the world over, who had highly commended the working of the institution. She visited USSR in 1956 as a member of GOI sponsored Educational Study Delegation. After her retirement she had returned to political field again and is actively associated with the Congress I.

Zainab Begam is one of the first Kashmiri women to discard *purdah.* She came to prominence during Quit Kashmir Movement. She threw her heart and soul together to the freedom movement and afterwards to political activity, in response to the call made by their beloved leader, Sheikh Abdullah. During this period she along with her brother, afterwards the chief minister of the state, late G.M. Sadiq, fought against the Dogra rule under the auspices of the National Conference. Like other members of the National Conference she had also to undergo suffering and torture. She organised Women's Resistance Force during Pakistani raids and invasion of Kashmir in 1947 and 1965.

Afterwards she left the National Conference and joined the Congress. She is associated with various social organisations. In 1972, she was elected member to the State Legislature from the Amirakadal constituency.[28] In 1975, she joined Sheikh Sahib's cabinet as Minister of State for Social Welfare. At present she is actively associated with the Congress I. She is a powerful orator.

Sajida Zamir Ahmad was another educationist, who was also associated with the freedom movement in its later stage. She is B.A., B.T., M.A. (Edu.) London. During the Pakistani agression in 1947, she joined Women's Defence Corps. She worked actively in the various refugee camps. Her soft and affable nature restored the confidence in uprooted and forlorn mass of humanity.

She is a woman of head and heart. She took active part in National Cultural Front. She was amongst first Kashmiri girls to go on stage, playing key roles. She also took part in the film Mahjoor. She is associated with several important bodies. She attended 13th General Conference of UNESCO in Paris as youngest member of the Indian Delegation in 1964. She has contributed six feature articles on Kashmir's contribution towards secularism.

She joined State education service in 1943 and made rapid strides. She was the Principal of T.T. College during 1961-67. In 1967, she was promoted to Jt. Director Women's Education. She was the first woman of the state who became the Director of Education in 1971.[21] At present she is secretary to the department of Tourism.

Woman along with man, from time immemorial, has formed an integral part of social structure. She always comes to his rescue whenever exigencies of the situation demand it. This is evident from gleaning through the role of Kashmiri woman in the freedom struggle of Kashmir. They in spite of their seclusion for years together, had miraculously risen to respond to the call of freedom, at the cost of their lives and comforts of family. They smiled at the embrace of death.

## References

1. Chinar is found only in Kashmir in the Indian sub-continent.
2. Articles in the *Civil and Military Gazette*, 11-10-1897, vide Dept. Home (Edu. A), Progs., 19-31, July 1898 (Confidential).
3. S.N. Gadru, (ed.) *Kashmir Papers*, New Delhi, 1975, p. XVI; Arthur Brinckman, *The Wrongs of Cashmere*, London, 1868, pp. 7, 8.
4. Bikram Jit Hasrat, *Angol Sikh Relations*, 1799-1849, Hoshiarpur, 1968, p. 297.
5. National Archives, Foreign Dept. Progs. Sec. E, May 1884, No. 354.
6. Prem Nath Bazaz, *Daughters of Vitasta*, New Delhi, Pamposh Publishers, 1959, p. 222.
7. R.L. Handa, *History of Freedom Struggle in Princely States*, Central News Agency, New Delhi, 1968.
8. P.N.K. Bamzai, *A History of Kashmir*, Metropolitan Book Company, Delhi, 1962, p. 185.
9. P.N. Bazaz, *Daughter of Vitasta, op.cit.* p. 245.
10. Joseph Korbel, *Danger in Kashmir*, Princeton, 1964, pp. 16, 17.
11. P.N. Bazaz, *History of Struggle for Freedom in Kashmir*, Delhi, 1954, p. 138.
12. Ibid.
13. R.L. Handa, *op.cit.*, p. 250; Mohammad Yusuf Saraf, *Kashmiri's Fight - For Freedom*, vol I, 1819 - 1946, Lahore, 1977, p. 482; *Hindu Daily Tribune*, July 28, 1931.
14. Sadr-ud-Din Mujahid, *Azan*, 13th July Number, July 1968; Maulana Masoodi, *Azan*, July 1968.
15. P.N. Bazaz, *Daughters of Vitasta, op.cit.*, pp. 246-47; *Inquilab*, July 25, 1931; Ibid., August 2, 1931.
16. Ibid.
17. Ibid.
18. *Kashmir Ki Jang-i-Azadi*, Published by Directorate of Information, Kashmir, New Delhi, n.d.; *Our Path to Freedom and New*

*Kashmir* issued and published by the Secretariat of the Annual Session, 1945. The All Jammu and Kashmir National Conference, Mujahid Manzil, Srinagar, The Normal Press, Srinagar; P.N. Bazaz, *Inside Kashmir*, Srinagar, 1941, p. 196.

19. P.N. Bazaz, *Kashmir in Crucible*, New Delhi, 1967, p. 35; Sardar Budh Singh, *Jagir Shahi ka Post Morteem*, Srinagar, n.d., pp. 79-82; G.M. Bakshi, *Kashmir Today Through Many eyes*, Bombay, P.C.C., 1946, pp. 16, 17.
20. Observations of the Special Correspondent of *The Globe News Agency*, June 10, 1946.
21. P.N. Bazaz, *Daughter of Vitasta*, *op.cit.*, pp. 247-248.
22. In Kashmiri dialect Kashmir is called Kashir.
23. P.N. Bazaz, *Daughters of Vitasta*, *op.cit.*, pp. 262- 64.
24. Ibid.
25. *Directory of Indian Women Today*, 1976, p. 339.
26. P. N. Bazaz, *Daughters of Vitasta*, *op.cit.*, p. 262.
27. *The Jammu and Kashmir Year Book*, 1972, Sec. III, p. 89.
28. Ibid., p. 181.
29. Ibid., p. 6.

# 27

# THE KASHMIRI ELITE 1885-1947

During the Afghan[1] and Sikh rule[2] mal-administration in Kashmir was the order of the day, consequently learning suffered a decline, and its sequel was poverty and loss of selfrespect. The Dogra rule in Kashmir (1846 to 1947) being feudal in character could not, at the outset, arrest the tide of degradation and degeneration.[3] After 1846 Western visitors and missionaries started visiting the Kashmir Valley, and began taking interest in the local affairs.[4] They drew the attention of the government of India to the scenic beauty of Kashmir, considered as the paradise on the face of earth, and also to the sad and pitiable plight of its people.[5] Most of the travel accounts focus on the deplorable condition of the people of the Valley during the preceding decade. The accounts also gave a cue to the European missionaries to propagate Christianity in Kashmir.[6] Moorcraft wrote:

> "There is no part of India (except Kashmir) where the pure religion of the Gospel might be introduced with a fairer prospect of success".[7]

After the death of Ranbir Singh and accession of Partap Singh, the British Residency was established in 1885, which marked a watershed in the history of Kashmir.[8] With the increase in power and control of the Resident, after the deposition of Maharaja Partap Singh, a steady influx of the European missionaries, tourists, traders and technocrats started.[9] They were responsible in initiating the process of modernising and westernising Kashmir.

Srinagar presented an abominable picture with filth, squalor, difilement, contamination and unsanitation. The lanes and by-lanes of the city were turned into open latrines where the pariah dogs would do the cleaning work.[10] Epidemics of various types like small-pox, cholera, typhoid, and even plague created havoc, and were followed by famine and starvation, facilitaing the attack of consumption. The inhabitants took these calamities stoically as God's will. [11]There was absolutely no medical facility especially in the maternity field. Many women died in labour in the absence of proper medical aid.[12] The missionaries came forward. To quote the greatest of the missionaries, Dr. Ernest Neve:

> "A Mission Hospital is a moral text book which can be read and appreciated by the most illiterate. And we are right in revealing the sources of inspiration. We have a message, the message of peace and goodwill to man through the Saviour Christ."[13]

The Church of England Zenana Missionary Society in cooperation with the Church Missionary Society opened the *Zenana* hospitals in the state. Dr. Misses Butler and Irene Petrie and Robinson laid down lives in the service of the unfortunate victims. The Darbar also gradually changed its stand form initial hostility to hesitant cooperation allowing the missionaries to run the Drugjan Hospital.[14] The Diamond Jubilee Zenana Hospital in Srinagar, received grants from the royal treasury to help maintain its upkeep and establishment.[15] Even the Swiss Missionaries Danial Vounard and Robert Berger were granted permission to involve themselves in the welfare activities in Khaplu Baltistan and Srinagar.[16] Sisters of Mercy were also granted permission to establish a hospital in Baramulla.[17] Besides, the missionaries also established King Edward Zenana Hospital, a female hospital and leper asylum in Jammu, Gilgit, and Srinagar respectively.[18] The missionaries also took up the gauntlet for civilising the Kashmiris, though they could not win them over in large numbers to Christ. Nevertheless they introduced light and learning through the mission schools.[19] They did not only bring with them their religious doctrines and dogmas but culture and life style as well. They deserve the credit for bringing about a socio-cultural transformation in Kashmir. Notable among them are Arthur Brinckman, Robert Throp, Rev.

J. H. Knowles, C.L.E. Burgess, A. B. Tyndale, Irene Petrie, Frances Mackay, Dr. Kate Knowles and Violet Fitze. Robert Throp laid down his life advocating the cause of the oppressed Kashmiris. The missionary work in Kashmir received a shot in the arm with the appointment of Rev. C. E. Tyndale Biscoe in 1890 A.D. and Miss M.P. Mallinson in 1922 A.D., as the Director and Headmistress of the mission schools respectively.[20] The state of education is graphically depicted by Tyndale Biscoe:

> "Can I forget my first sight and smell of the school — on a cold December morning in 1890 ... The appearance of these bundles of steaming, dirty, smelling clothes enveloping each boy with his fire pot, but rather their physical condition. Nearly all of them sat with their mouths open, which showed that their throats needed attention, their breath was most foul, ... caused by pyorrhea and other teeth troubles. They almost without exception suffered from the itch, and their head seemed to be covered with white scales, which I learnt was "scald heads", a most unpleasant sight...."[21]

The Kashmiri people were determined to reject any change from the ways of their forefathers. The society was a byword for its conservatism and obscurantism. It appears whole valley was in a state of stuper. They posed tremendous hurdles in the ways of the missionaries. Parents wrote applications requesting the Principal to exempt their wards from playing games on the behest of their astrologers and priests. Tyndale Biscoe showed great persuasive power and ability to make students cast aside their traditional costumes like turban, *pheron*, wooden clogs, nose-ring and ear-rings.[22] Biscoe tried hard to inject selfrespect in his students. His constant precept, "In all things be Men".[23] In due course the Darbar started taking keen interest in education, and took measures to force or compel (known in Kashmir as *Zabri-talim*) the Muslims to go to the free educational institutions.[24] Technical schools were also opened which paved the way for future technological development and inculcation of the scientific temperament and aptitude.[25] Gradually the education picked up.

The fiscal policy of the Darbar was infact, "guided by no other consideration than that of wringing the last pice out of all trades and manufactures."[26] The agrarian community consisting mostly of the

Muslims was the victim of harassment and physical torture committed by the corrupt revenue officials for merciless exaction.[27] Another bane suffered by the peasantry was the system of *begar*. Under this system thousands of peasants had been driven off every year to toil as carriers of burden on the most dangerous and risky Gilgit Road. *Begar* was such a terror that at the very mention of its name, most of the villagers would leave their homes for "two or three months with the prospect of death from cold or starvation."[28] The New Settlement introduced by Wingate and completed by Lawrence was a boon to the agrarian community. In the words of Lawrence :

> "The State by its justice and moderation has won the confidence of the agricultural classes and Kashmir is now more prosperous and more fully cultivated than it has been in the memory of man".[29]

The system of cash payments was introduced.[30]

Transport system linking Kashmir with other parts of India was totally absent. The only way one could go to the plains was through a hazardous journey on foot or mules or ponies. This was the chief cause of the backwardness of Kashmir.[31] At the instance of the British the Darbar commissioned the services of the British engineers for building highways, namely, Rawalpindi Baramulla in 1889,[32] the Jhelum Valley Cart Road in 1890,[33] the Banihal Cart Raod in 1923[34]. With the completion of these highways Kashmir started emerging out of isolation into a world of growing contacts. For the convenience of the European visitors, Mr. Harry Nedous constructed a hotel at Gulmarg in 1888, and subsequently in Srinagar.[35] The establishment of the Postal Department in 1886,[36] Telegraph Department in 1905,[37] and the tourist agencies in 1886[38] accelerated the process of modernisation through communication with the outside world. The introduction of the motor transport on the Jhelum Valley road in 1923 was a significant breakthrough.[39] The European tourists attraction for hill resorts resulted in the development of Gulmarg and Pahalgam.

The urbanising process in Srinagar had started in 1886 with the enactment of the first Municipality Act.[40] The rickety and ramshackeled buildings in Srinagar presented a desultory picture of a neglected town, as so many of the buildings were in a bad need of repair.[41] The Europeans in Srinagar adopted Munshi Bagh,

Gupkar Road and the present Residency Road as their habitation. This big area gradually developed into a new complex, dotted with artistic structures on European style, like the Church, the Residency, the Amar Singh Club, the European Shopping Centre, the Post-Office, the State Guest House and the Nedous Hotel.

The Advent of the press in British India revolutionised the mentality and outlook of the Indians. It fortified them with a potent weapon to express their grievances and problems.[42] The state of J&K under the autocratic rule of the Dogras did not enjoy this privilege.[43] The introduction and improvement in the means of communication brought Kashmir in contact with the British India, especially Punjab, and the Kashmiris began reading old editions of the newspapers brought by the European visitors.[44] Temperamentally Kashmiris had a taste for news. They also requested Maharajas Ranbir Singh and Partap Singh for printing and publishing newspapers, but the permission was not granted.[45] Until 1924, no newspaper was allowed to be printed and published in the State. Meanwhile Urdu became very popular after being declared in 1907 A.D. as the official language of the State.[46] In Punjab and U.P. most of the papers were in Urdu language, and some of them devoted a space in discussing the problem of J & K State. Prominent among them are *Marselie Kashmir*, Lahore, 1880, *Akbar-i-Aaam*, Lahore, 1881, *Khair Khawah Kashmir*, Lahore, 1882, and *Kashmir Darpan*, Allahabad, 1898.

Press in the state owes its genesis to the Glancy Commission.[47] One of its most important recommendations was the freedom of expression. It was with great difficulty that in 1924 Lala Mulk Raj Saraf managed to bring out a weekly, *The Ranbir* from Jammu.[48] In the Valley, however, the credit for doing the pioneering work goes to Prem Nath Bazaz, who started in 1932 an Urdu weekly *The Daily Vitasta* from Srinagar. Afterwards there was a spate in the field of journalism. To name a few The *Martand*, The *Sadaqat*, The *Haqiqat,The Khalid*, The *Kashmiri Jadid, The Albarg*, The *Bekar*, The *Hurriyat*, The *Nur*, The *Khalsa Gazette*, The *Hamdard*, The *Khidmat*, The *Kesari*, The *Desh*, The *Navyug*, The *Khalid* and the *Mulsim* and *Shandhur weekly* etc. English weeklies were also started, e.g., the *Kashmir Times*, the *Kashmir Chronicle* and the

*Qaumi Dard.*[49] Another media also came to Kashmir in the late thirties in the from of radio sets through which the elite got abreast of the news and progressive movements which were taking shape in those times around the world, although during the period under study Radio station was not established in Kashmir. They created an awareness in people towards social reforms and inculcated an yearning for political emancipation, through representative institutions, besides, being a media for information.

These changes especially in the field of education resulted in the slow and yet steady development of an intelligentsia. They were educated in the state, Indian Universities and a few of them took their degrees from the European Universities.[50] On their return they propagated new ideas and introduced socio-religious reform movements. The prominent elite among the Pandits, Muslims and Sikhs respectively were : Pandit Anand Kaul Bamzai, Pandit Ram Chandra Dhar, Master Shankar Kaul, Master Zind Kaul, Kashap Bandhu, Pandit Amar Nath Kak, Ram Chandra Kak, Madhusudan Kaul, S.K. Toshkhani, Aftab Kaul Nizamat, Prem Nath Bazaz, J. L. Jalali, Gwashi Lal Kaul, Agha Syed Hussain, Hasan Shah Jalali, Moulvi Mohammad Jawad, Syed Shah Sahib, Kathi Haji Jafar Khan, Lal Khan, Munshi Mohammad Din Fouq Syed Ali Shah, Syed Mohammad Shah Jalali, Ghulam Ahmad Mahjoor, Ghulam Mustafa, Khwaja Saad- ud-Din Shawl, Haji Ali Sahib, B.A., Ghulam Ahmad Ashai, Sheikh Mohammad Abdullah, Khawaja Salam Shah, Mirza Kamal-ud-Din Shaida, Sadaruddin Mujahid, Mirza Fazal Beg, Bakshi Ghulam Mohammad, Ghulam Mohammad Sadiq, Begum Zafar Ali, Mahamuda Ali Shah, Sardar Budh Singh, Akali Kohar Singh, Bhai Kanheya Singh, Jathedar Kapoor Singh, and Gyani Kartar Singh Komal etc.

The elite had started socio-cultural reform movements to lift their co-religionists from the abyss of superstition, obscurantism and stagnation. The Pandit organisations were : Arya Kumar Sabha,[51] Dogra Sabha,[52] Dharm Sabha[53], Fraternity Sabha[54], Yuvak Sabha[55], the Kashmiri Pandit social uplift Association,[56] and a branch of Theosophical Society.[57] Under the auspices of the Theosophical Society Women's Welfare Trust was established.[58] The aims of the these associations were to raise the status of women, education among men and women, social upliftment and preserving and helping the growth and development of Hindu culture, art and religion. The main socio-religious reform movements among the Muslims were : Anjuman-i-Hamdard Islam, Srinagar[59], Anjuman-i-Taraqqi, Talim wa Ittihad,[60] Anjuman-i-Tahaffuz-i-Namaz-Wa-Satri-i-Masturat,[61] Anjuman-i-Hanifa[62] and Anjuman-i-Islat-ul-Musalmin.[63] The general objects of these associations were to inculcate among the Muslims preachings of *Tauheed*, a spirit for education for both the sexes, self help, self-confidence, social reforms, help to orphans and needy, and addressing their grievance to the Darbar.

Socio-religious reform movements were also spearheaded by the Sikh elite. The notable organizations established by them were: Chief Khalsa Diwan[64], Khalsa Youngmen's Organisation,[65] Sikh Sahaik Sabha[66], Kashmir Singh Sabha[67], the Akali Movement[68], and the Sudhar Sabha. The Sikhs like the Muslims being an agrarian community, were backward, the associations worked to give them an identity through social reforms, following the principles of Guru Maharaj and to create an awareness in the community for learning.

With the passage of time freedom struggle waged in India found its entry in Kashmir.[69] Among the Kashmiri Pandits with the education the political consciousness came earlier than their Muslim and Sikh counterparts.[70] They vehemently protested against siphoning off the higher government jobs to the non- residents, thereby damaging the genuine interests of the sons of the soil.[71] Their pleas and canvassing resulted in the implementation of the state subject law on January 31, 1927.[72]

The Muslims also became politically conscious and brooded over their deprivation and sequestration.[73] They presented a memorandum to Lord Reading on his arrival at Srinagar in 1924, but without any immediate success. It was in this background that two youngmen of destiny appeared on the Kashmir scene in Sheikh Mohammad Abdullah and Choudhri Ghulam Abbas.[74] The unemployed educated Muslim youths founded the Reading Room Party at Fatehkadal, Srinagar in 1930, and very soon it became a nucleus for ventilating their grievances and complaints against the

Maharaja's government.[75] Sometimes the pentup anger and suspicion against the ruler explodes like a volcano at a trivial incident, making the moment historic or turning point. That is precisely what happened in 1931.[76] On July 13, that year a large crowd of the Kashmiri Muslims collected at the Central Jail, to hear the trial of a non-Kashmiri Afghan, Abdul Qadeer, charged with the sedition. Mishandling of the situation led to an order of firing in which nine people were killed.[77] The day became famous as the beginning of the freedom struggle in Jammu and Kashmir. The incident led to the communal mistrust, ill-will and carnage.[78] Prem Nath Bazaz holds both the Reading Room Party and Hindu indiscrimination responsible for all the unsavoury incidents.

The Maharaja appointed a Commission under B. J. Glancy of the political department of government of India to look into the people's grievances. The Commission reported in April 1932, recommending some basic reforms.[79] The report paved the way for the formation of a political organization in the state to agitate for people's grievances. The All Jammu and Kashmir Muslim Conference was born in October, 1932.[80] The Kashmiri Pandits felt that the Glancy Commission's recommendations were prejudicial to their interests, and started *roti* agitation.[81]

But this was a temporary phase and the spirit of detente returned with the transformation of the Muslim Conference into the National Conference in 1939[82]. Splinter group of the old Conference, however, persisted in preserving the old name and carrying on the programmes meant for the Muslim community alone under the leadership of Mir Waiz Moulvi Yusuf Shah.[83] The secularisation of Kashmir politics and the re-definition of the goal helped to forge close links between the Indian National Congress and the National Conference. In 1944, the National Conference issued its manifesto called the *New Kashmir.*[84] Secular in spirit and socialistic in approach, the *New Kashmir* manifesto has ever since 1944, provided the guidelines to the National Conference's policy to the problems of Kashmir.

The last phase in the freedom struggle was the 'Quit Kahsmir'[85] agitation launched by the National Conference in 1946 to get rid of the twin strangle-hold of feudalism and colonialism. But a section of the Muslims under Choudhry Ghulam Abbas revitalized the Muslim Conference as a challenge to the National Conference.[86]

India was declared free on August 15, 1947, and the subcontinent was divided into two independent states India (Bharat) and Pakistan. On October 22, 1947 two thousand tribals invaded the valley. Maharaja Hari Singh sent an S.O.S. to the government of India for immediate help, which advised him to sign an Instrument of Accession with it in lieu of military help to vacate the aggression, and to call upon Shaikh Abdullah to form an interim government. Maharaja Hari Singh signed the Instrument of Accession at Jammu on October 26, 1947, and the accession was accepted by the Governor-General of India on October 27, 1947. The accession thus became legally and constitutionally complete.

Emergence of the elite was a tryst with destiny. Modern Kashmir is the work of its elite. It has emerged from the narrow confines of its isolation. and is on the threshold of progress and prosperity. The process of socio-cultural transformation has been conditioned by development such as these and is well on its way to moving hand in hand with other states of the country.

## References

1. C.B. Pyne, *A Short History of the Sikhs*, Patiala, Dept. of Languages, Punjab, 1970 (Reprint).
2. D.C. Sharma, *Kashmir Under Sikhs*, New Delhi, 1983, p. 279.
3. W.R. Lawrence, *The Valley of Kashmir*, London, 1895, Indian Reprint, Srinagar, 1967. "Much has been written of the abuses which have prevailed in the administration of Kashmir..... They had been taught for many years that they were serfs without any rights but with many disabilities. They were called *Zulm parast*, or worshippers of tyranny, and every facility was afforded to their cult.... and their position was infinetely worse than that of the *tiers Etat* before the French Revolution".
4. NAI/John Collett to Sir J. Wallace, For Ext. B, October 1887, nos. 223-226, For Sec. E., March-October 1887, Nos. 81-84; Nisbet to the Secretary of Government of India, For, Sec. E., April 1889, Nos. 80-98; Lawrence to Nisbet, For, Feb. 1891, Sec. E, Nos.

295-326; Henrey's Note For Sec. E., March 1883, No. 86; For Sec. Jan. 28, 1848, Nos. 41-42; Despatch to Secret Committee, For. Sec. E, January 22, 1898, no. 10; Arthur Brinckman, *Wrongs of Cashmere, London, 1868, Chapter III;* Rev. Morrison, *Educational Work in India During Queen's Reign*; RNNP, *The Hamdard i-Hind , Lahore, Sept. 16, 1895; Thakur Dass,* A Study of the Christian Pioneers in Education in Kashmir, Chapter II, p. 43 (An unpublished disertation, could be had from the author, teacher in the Biscoe School, Srinagar).

5. A. Brinckman, *op.cit.*; C.G. Bruce, *Kashmir,* London, 1915; Frederic Drew, *The Jammoo and Kashmir Territories*. London. 1875; Frederic Drew, *The Northern Barrier of India*, London, 1877; Margaret C. Morrison, *A Lonely Summer in Kashmir,* London, 1904; William Moorcroft and George Trebeck, *Travels in the Himalayan Provinces of Hindustan and the Punjab in Ladakh and Kashmir*, 2 Vols, London, 1841; Robert Palmer, *A Little Tour in India*, London, 1913.
6. CMS *Intelligencer*, April-May, 1872; *Misssionary Review of World*, July 1901.
7. Moorcroft, *op.cit.*, Vol.II, p.129.
8. *The Englishman*, Sept. 25, 1885, p. 5; D.P., Reel 519, Pratap Singh to Dufferin, Sept. 18, 1885, Encl. 17, To the S.O.S., October 19, 1885; Madhavi Yasin, *British Paramountcy in Kashmir*, New Delhi, 1984, pp. 33-35; Henry Martyn, *Robert Clark of the Punjab*, London, 1907; The Missions of the C.M.S. and C.E.Z.M.S. in the Punjab and Sindh, London, 1904 (Edited and Revised by Robert Maconachie).
9. E.D. Tyndale Biscoe, *Autobiography*, London, 1951; Margaret C. Morrison, *op.cit.;* Tarachand Wazir's Autobiography, unpublished manuscript is with the *N.A.I.*
10. Log Book, *Against the Current in Kashmir*, 1937-38, Church Missionary House, Salisbury Square, London, E.C. 4, p. 6; Also Tyndale Biscoe, *Kashmir in Sunlight and Shade,* London, 1922, pp. 124-25.
11. E.D. Tyndale Biscoe, *Fifty Years Against the Stream*, 1880- 1930, Mysore, 1930, Chapter, XIII.
12. Ernest Neve, *A Crusader in Kashmir*, London, 1928, p. 70; Ernest Neve, *Beyond the Pir Panjal*, London, 1915, p. 291; Henry Martyn Clark, *Robert Clark of the Punjab,* London, 1907.

13. Ibid., SA/J, General Records, Index of Records, Vol. V. Pol. Dept., Permanent Group, year B-13-189, Letter dated May 3, 1900 to the Vice President of the State Council from H.V. Cobb, Astt. Resident.
14. Ashley Carus Wilson, (Mrs.), *Irene Petrie Missionary to Kashmir*, 1900.
15. SA/J, General Records, Index of Records, Vol. V, Pol. Dept., Permanent Group, year 1936, File no. 246/Accounts - 37; Ibid., Vol. III, year 1909, File No. 115/B-13; Ibid., AAR. Samvat 1995-96; Ibid., AAR, Samvat 1980, Ibid., Pol. Dept., File no. 321/E-15/ of 1914.
16. Ibid., Vol. V, Pol. Dept., Permanent Group, year 1934, File no. 239.
17. Ibid., From 1889 A.D. to 1938 A.D., year 1928, File No. 11/212/G.
18. JKA/Srinagar, A.A.R., for the year October 1927—October 1930, 1984-1987.
19. *Fifty Years Against The Stream, op.cit.*, Chapters XVI & XVII.
20. *A Century of CMS Schools* 1880-1980, Srinagar, 1980, pp. 1, 38.
21. Cannon C.E. Tyndale, *Biscoe Log Book*, 1930, CMS Archives, London.
22. *Fifty Years Against the Stream, op.cit.*, pp. 13-14.
23. It is enshrined in the School motto and crest.
24. SA/S, A.A.R., for 1961 (1904-05 A.D.), Ibid., for Samvat 1971 (1914-15 A.D.) and onwards.
25. SA/J, Year 1931, File No. 38/15, Note on the Technical and Industrial Education in the State; *Against the Current in Kashmir, op.cit.*, p. 9; Margaret C. Morrison, *op.cit.*, p. 258.
26. Henvy Report on Kashmir (confidential), Simla Records, For. Dept., Sec. E, Progs., January 1883, Nos. 239-240, N.A.I.
27. W.R. Lawrence, *op.cit.*, pp. 399-417 : A Brinckman, *op.cit.*, p. 14; From Pandit Suraj Kaul to Walter R. Lawrence, Calcutta Records, For. Dept., Sec. E, (Demir-official), Srinagar, June 22, 1889, NAI; KGR, File No. 72/C-57 of 1920.
28. *The Begar*, was the curse for the cultivators from Walter R. Lawrence to Sir Mortimer Durand, dated Camp Bijbehara, Kashmir, June 29, 1889, Calcutta Records, For Dept., Sec. E, Nos.

204-208, (K.W. No. 2), N.A.I.; W.R. Lawrence, *op.cit.*, pp. 412-13.

29. W.R. Lawrence, *op.cit.*, p. 450.
30. Ibid., pp. 243-245.
31. W.J. Cunningham's letter to the Resident in Kashmir, dated Feb. 22, 1890, N.A.I., Sec. E, Feb. 1891, Nos. 295-326; SA/J, J&K (General Record), Pol. Dept., File No. 181A/B-106, year 1906; Francis Younghusband, *Kashmir*, Edinburg, 1909, pp. 47-49; Dermot Norris, *Kashmir: The Switzerland of India*, Calcutta, 1932, pp. 20-21; Fred Markham, *Shooting in the Himalayas*, London, 1854, p. 366; Walter Del Mar, *The Romantic East*, London, 1906, p. 69.
32. W.R. Lawrence, *op.cit.*, p. 244; G.L. Koul, *Kashmir Through the Ages*, Srinagar, 1967, (Eighth edition), p. 108; Walter Del Mar, *op.cit.*, p. 137.
33. The construction of the Jhelum Valley Cart Road, which was 196 miles from Rawalpindi to Srinagar had been commenced in 1881 under the charge of Mr. H.E Stubbs, who was the Divisional Engineer, Ernest Neve, *Beyond the Pir Panjal*, London, 1915, p. 43; It was opened for traffic in 1889 but it was not until 1890 that cart traffic was allowed to traverse on it from Rawalpindi to Baramulla. It was in 1893 that the road was opened for traffic from Baramulla to Srinagar. Before that waterways formed the principle means of transport. The metalling of the Jhelum Valley Cart Road was done in 1894. The maintenance of the road was carried on by Messrs Speding and Co., under their contract until the expiry of the same in January 1895 when Mr. W. Mitchell took over the work on considerably reduced terms, AAR, 1894-95, p. 62, Ripon Papers, Add. MSS, 43613, pp. 74-83, St. John to Ripon, July 22, 1883.
34. Tarachand Wazir, *op.cit.*, p. 139; Gordon Sinclair, *Khyber Carvan Through Kashmir; Waziristan, Afghanistan, Baluchistan and Northern India*, London; W.R. Lawrence, *op.cit.*, pp. 23, 24, 397.
35. M.C. Morrison, *op.cit.*, Appendix 267-81, T.R. Swinburne, *Holiday in the Happy Valley : With Pen and Pencil*, London, 1907, pp. 67-69.
36. SA/J, General and Pol. Dept., File No. 12, Year 1892; SA/S, AAR 1894-95; Z.L. Zala, Social and Economic History of Jammu and Kashmir State (1884-1885) unpublished dissertation in the Iqbal

Library, University of Kashmir, Srinagar; M.C. Morrison, *op.cit.*, Appendix, pp. 267-281, Walter Der Mar, *op.cit.*, p. vi.

37. SA/S, AAR, S. 1894-95.

38. Ibid., S. 1895-96, 1938 A.D.; Messrs Dhanjibhoy and Sons, a Parsee firm at Rawalpindi, held the monopoly of the transport to Kashmir from 1886 onwards. It had its branch at Baramulla also. It had a contract with the Government to carry the mail. It would supply private tongas to the travellers with fixed rates authorised by the Government. The cost of a single seat in a tonga was Rs. 36/- and the whole tonga Rs. 110/- upto Baramulla. From Baramulla to Srinagar it would cost Rs. 7/- per head. The chief means of transport were the tonga, phaeton, bullock wagon and ekka. The tonga was the quickest and generally used mode of transit., T.R. Swinburne, p. 68; Walter Der Mar, *op.cit.*, pp. 151-52; M.C. Morrison, *op.cit.*, Appendix pp. 267-281; JKA/Jammu, J&K Government, (General Records), Chief Secretariat, Pol. Dept. File No. 93/B-3, Year 1901.

39. Shirin Bakshi, Kashmir's Response to European Culture (1846-1947), Unpublished M. Phil. Dissertation, at the Departmental Library of the History Dept., Kashmir University, Srinagar.

40. SA/S, Ganga Nath Report, Srinagar; Ibid., Report on Administration of Jammu and Kashmir, 1946 (1888-89 A.D.) p. 137; Ibid., S. 1969, p. 31; Narsingh Das, *Tarikh-i-Dogra Desh*, p. 709; NAI/For., Ext. A. Sept. 1892, Nos. 102-115; F. Ward Denys, *Our Summer in the Vale of Kashmir*, Washington, 1915, p. 168.

41. C.E. Bates, *A Gazetteer of Kashmir*, Calcutta, 1873, p. 353; Tyndale Biscoe, *op.cit.*, p. 49; E.F. Knight, *Where Three Empires Meet*, London, 1905, p. 49; Sir Richard Temple, *Journals Kept in Hyderabad, Kashmir, Sikkim and Nepal*, 1859-71, London, 1887, Vol. II, p. 288; Prinsep. *Imperial India*, London, 1879, p. 212; Lawrence, *op.cit.*, p. 35.

42. *The Indian Mirror*, August, 1861, April, 1862, August 1, 1863; *The Calcutta Review*, 1850, Vol. xiii, Nos. 25, pp. 144-5; *Bengal Gazette*, Feb. 13, 1875; S.R. Mehrotra, *Emergence of the Indian National Congress*, Delhi, 1971, pp. 110-111.

43. *Census of India, Report on Jammu and Kashmir State*, 1921, p. 118; *The Ranbir*, July 7, 1941; *Kashmir Today* (Srinagar), Vol. V. May, 1961, p. 5; P.N. Bazaz, *Inside Kashmir*, Srinagar, 1941, p. 353.

44. *Kashmir Today*, May 1961, *op.cit.*, p. 5.
45. SA/J, J&K (G.R.) 117/P, 51 of 1904.
46. SA/J, Srinagar, A Brief Note on J&K Adm., 1935; Mohi-ud-Din Sufi, *Jammu Wa Kashmir Maen Urdu Suhafat*, Srinagar, 1973.
47. SA/J, Glancy Commission Report, p. 19; *The Statesman*, June 11, 1946.
48. Mulk Raj Saraf, *Fifty Years as a Journalist*, Jammu, Raj Mahal, 1967; P.N. Bazaz, *Inside Kashmir*, Srinagar, 1941, pp. 353-54.
49. J.L.K. Jalali, Freedom of Press in Kashmir, *Kashmir Times*, Vol. 5, No. 6, May 1961, pp. 56; Balraj Puri, why I was arrested, *Indian Express*, February 1, 1974; M.K. Tikku, Kashmir's First Periodical, *Vidura*, Vol. 9, No. 6, December, 1972, pp. 403-409; Copies of *Martand* are available at Sheetalnath Sathu, Srinagar ; Copies of *Ranbir* are at the University of Jammu Library, Jammu Tawi; Copies of *Khidamat*, are at Aabi Guzar, Srinagar; Copies of the most of the newspapers are available at the Information Office, Srinagar; P.N. Bazaz., *The History of Struggle for Freedom in Kashmir*, New Delhi, 1954, p. 165.
50. Tarachand Wazir, *op.cit.*, pp. 77, 144, 186-189, 273-74. The first to go to Europe was some Zutshi, followed by T.C. Wazir, Hakim Ali, Des Raj Dogra, Ved Lal Wazir, Dr. Shama Kaul , R.C. Kak.
51. SA/J, File No. 26/IC-28 of 1971, G.D.; Ibid., File No. 262/27-C of 1918, G.D.; Interview with Dina Nath Nadim, a prominent educationist, poet and freedom fighter, June 1886; Interview with Damodhar Hanjora, a prominent social reformer at Karan Nagar, Srinagar, March 1981.
52. Hafiz Mohd Ismail, *op.cit.*, October 14, 1926, item 4 and October 15, 1926, item 1.
53. Census Report of 1901, 1, p. 24; SA/J File No. 52/L-11 of 1898.
54. Interview with Mohan Krishan Tikoo, Former Law Member of Jammu & Kashmir Assembly, at Sanatnagar, Srinagar, September 15, 1985.
55. Interview with Pt. Kashap Bandhu, May 1885, at Tral.
56. Ibid.
57. Interview with P.N. Bazaz, doyen among the social reformers, journalist, historian and freedom fighter at Jawahar Nagar, Srinagar, June 1977.

58. Ibid., Interview with Damodhar Hanjora, *op.cit.*; Interview with Gwasha Lal Kaul, Journalist and writer in 1981; *The Ranbir*, December, 5, 1932.
59. Hafiz Mohammad Ismail, *op.cit.*, October 16, 1918, item 2; *The Zamindar*, Lahore, August 3, 1928.
60. SA/J, File No. 240/P-136 of 1918, Education Minister to Chief Minister, August 16, 1918; Ibid., File No. J-88 of 1924.
61. SA/J, File No. 439 of 1923; Ibid., File No. J-88 of 1924; *Akhbar-i-Kashmir* July 25, 1925, Feb. 21, 1929.
62. JKA/Jammu, File No. 274 of 1925.
63. Interview with Padmshri Begam Zafar Ali, an Educationist and Social Reformer, M.L.A., May, 1986. The First Muslim woman who matriculated and came out of the house to serve as a teacher; Mohammad Yousuf Shah, *Musalmanan-i-Kashmir-Ki-Tarakki-ka- Raj*, Urdu, Lahore, Ahl-i-Hadis, January 15, 1926.
64. JKA/Jammu, File No. 216/A-92 of 1918.
65. JKA/Jammu, File No. 439 of 1924; Ibid., File No. J-44 of 1924; File No. 216/A-92 of 1918; *Khalsa Akhbar Lahore*, Lahore 28, 1918.
66. JKA/Jammu, File No. 259/62 of 1920.
67. JKA/Jammu, File no. 439 of 1924; Ibid., File No. J-44 of 1924; Ibid., File No. 8-89/A of 1924; Ibid., File No. 435 of 1924; Ibid., File No. 389 of 1925; Ibid., File No. G-104 of 1925.
68. *Khidmat*, January 28, 1947, March 15, 1948.
69. SA/J, File No. 9 of 1920; NAI/Home Dept., Progs., Pol., July 1920, No. 105, Bannerman to Johnwood, July 16, 1920; Ibid., Home Dept., Progs., Pol. June 1921, No. 12; Ibid., Home Dept. Progs., Pol., August 1921, No. 18; JKA/Jammu, File No. 73 of 1922; NAI/Home Dept. Progs., Pol. April 1921, No.42; JKA/Jammu, File No. 55 of 1922; NAI/Home Dept., Pol. Jan. 1930, File No. 18, Fortnightly Report for first half of January; Rasheed Tasser, *Tahreek-i- Hurriyat Kashmir*, Srinagar, 1968, p. 140.
70. SA/J, File No. 40-S-18 of 1904.
71. NAI/Home Dept. Progs., Pol., Jan. 1922, No. 18; JKA/File No. 21/F - 219 of 1909; Ibid., Memo by A. Mitra, May 23, 1910.
72. 'Definition of State Subject : A Historical Review', *The Ranbir Weekly*, Jammu, May 20 and 27, 1935, p. 3 (Copy available at the University of Jammu Library, Jammu Tawi).

73. NAI/Home Dept. Progs., Pol. June 1924, File No. 25; Ibid., Nov. 1924, File No. 25; Ibid., Dec. 1924, File No. 25; G.S. Raghwan, *The Warning of Kashmir*, Allahabad, Pioneer, 1931, p. 63.; R.L. Handa, *History of Freedom Struggle in Princely States*, New Delhi, 1968, p. 249.

74. F.M. Hassnain, *Freedom Struggle in Kashmir*, New Delhi, 1988, p. 19; Mohammad Yusuf Saraf, *Kashmirs Fight for Freedom*, 1819-1946, Lahore, 1977, Vol. I, pp. 335-388; P.N. Bazaz *History of Struggle for Freedom in Kashmir*, New Delhi, 1954, p. 138.

75. JKA/Jammu, File No. 830 of 1922; *India Quarterly*, April- June, 1931, Vol. 7, No. 2.

76. Kashmir's Journey to Freedom, A survey of Political Events in Jammu and Kashmir State since 1931, Jammu and Kashmir, Mujahid Manjil, Srinagar, Kashmir.

77. NAI/Home Dept., Pol., July 1931, File No. 18. From the Resident in Kashmir, No. F-9-C/30, dated July 17, 1931.

78. JKA/Jammu, *Report of the Srinagar Riot Enquiry Committee*, Srinagar, 1931, p. 133; *The Mussalman*, July 30, 1931, p. 6, National Library, Calcutta.

79. JKA/Jammu, Glancy Commission Report, Jammu, 1932, p. 54.

80. *Alfazal*, October 25, 193; Jalali, Kashmir's Political Movement, *Kashmir Scene*, Information Dept., J&K Govt; G.M. Hamdani, *Kashmir : Kahan se Kahan* (urdu), Srinagar, 1949; Freedom Movement in Kashmir, *Atlantic Monthly*, March 1950; Rashid Taseer, *op.cit.*, pp. 171-261.

81. Rashid Tasser, *op.cit.*, Vol. I, pp. 230-237, F.M. Hassnain, *op.cit.*, p. 71; Veena Zutshi, *Role of Kashmiri Pandits in Freedom Struggle of J&K State*, An unpublished dissertation for the M.Phil. at the P.G. Dept. of History, Kashmir University, Srinagar.

82. M.Y. Saraf, *op.cit.*, pp. 527-529; *Al Islah*, June 16, 1939.

83. Rashid Taseer, *op.cit.*, Vol. II, pp. 207-208; F.M. Hassnain, *op.cit.*, p. 110; M.Y. Saraf, *op.cit.*, pp. 688-696; P.N. Bazaz, *Freedom Struggle, op.cit.*, pp. 264-265; H.L. Saxena, *The Tragedy of Kashmir*, New Delhi, 1975, pp. 381- 82.

84. New Kashmir Manifesto published in 1944, Mujahid Manjil, Srinagar.

85. S. Budh Singh *Jagirshahi Ka Postmortem*, Srinagar, n.d., pp. 79-82; Ghulam Mohi-ud-Din, *Farce of Dyarchy*, March, 1946; P.N. Bazaz, *Kashmir in Crucible*, New Delhi, 1967, p. 35.
86. A.S.R. Chari, *Kashmir Problem*, New Delhi, 1965, p. 33.

## ABBREVIATIONS

| | |
|---|---|
| Annual Administrative Report | AAR |
| Church of England Zenana Missionary Society | CEZMS |
| Church Missionary Society | CMS |
| National Archives of India | NAI |
| Report on Native News Papers | RNNP |
| State Archives Jammu | SA/J |
| State Archives Srinagar | SA/S |
| Samvat | S |
| Secretary of State | SOS |

# 28

# AN INTERVIEW WITH MADAR-I-MEHERBAN – AKBAR JEHAN BEGUM

Seeing Madar-i-Meharban is a sight in itself in the picturesque valley of Kashmir. But she is something more—not only East comes to sight, but a synthesis of East & West also, in her being the daughter of Harry Nedous and a pretty Gujar girl of Tangmarg.

It is unbelievable that one is seeing a relentless freedom fighter, who had been in the fray for thirty odd years until 1947, as there are no scars, no tensions, no frayed temper, or an arrogance of a rescuer from bondage. Dressed immaculately and tastefully, she exudes a refined taste, and her innocent face wins the confidence of the audience and beholder.

Being a born fighter, after 1947, she is fighting for the emancipation and promotion of woman's status in the society with no respite. In herself she is a perfect woman who has played to her credit the roles of a daughter, sister and wife. She is now the accredited mother of the people of the state.

## INTERVIEW WITH MADAR-I-MEHRABAN

Q. 1. Madar-i-Meharban, I would like to know about your early life i.e. ,birth, parentage, and education etc.

A. My father Harry Nedous came from a family of commercial magnates, of United Kingdom. He at first started leather factory at Puna (modern Pune), afterwards came to Kashmir, and settled here after marrying my mother, who hailed form Tangmarg. He left the leather business and opened a chain of hotles at Srinagar and Gulmarg. He was the founder of the present Nedous Hotel. I was born in 1916. My parents took great care of the education of their children. My mother was especially very keen in my education, and always encouraged me. There was a lot of competition in getting good marks in the examination between my brothers and myself. I studied at the Presentation Mission School at Shimla. I passed Senior Cambridge Examination with distinction at the age of seventeen.

Q. 2. What were the influences which shaped your early life (relatives, teachers, and prominent political personalities)?

A. I was very much influenced by my parents. My mother was a God fearing woman, who instilled in all of us a religious bent of mind—Religion not of a fanatic, but a religion whose cornerstone is love and mercy, compassion and forbearance. From my father I inculcated the spirit of philanthrophy. I used to see that before going to the hotel, he used to distribute free medicine—this dedication and devotion to the poor left an everlasting impact on me.

In my educational career, I was very much impressed by Mother Magadalen, who was not only a disciplinarian, but also devoted to the cause of education.

Like many others of my times the life and total abnegation of Mahatma Gandhi had a great impact on me. Jawaharlal Nehru's political ideology and modernism had appealed me. When Gandhiji came to Srinagar, he stayed at Gogji Bagh in the house of Seth Kishori Lal, forest lessee. He invited me to attend prayer meetings. I attended with my brother Colonel Ghulam Qadir. Gandhiji requested me to recite the Quran, and I did. I feel very honoured that both Mahatma Gandhi and Panditji had a soft corner for me.

Q.3. When were you married ? Did you have a notion at the start of your married life that you have married a leader of men, dedicated to their upliftment?

A. I was married in 1933, at the age of seventeen. By this time my husband had already entered into the arena of politics. At that time frankly speaking I had no comprehension that he would rise to such a distinction, but in the beginning of our married life I was particularly impressed by his boldness, stand for truthfulness and determination to liberate the country.

Q. 4. Did you find any difficulty in joining your illustrious husband in his day to day activities ? Did you have any disagreements on certain principles with your husband, as P.N. Bazaz has hinted in his *Daughters of Vitasta*, p. 264.

A. In the beginning I had to face much difficulty. My husband had thrown himself in the vortex of freedom struggle. He had already left his employment as a teacher...hence financial constrains were there. The children were born, naturally I had to look after the household and rearing up children, so as to spare my husband from the domestic front. Even when my husband was not in jail, the children did not see him for months together. All that time my main support was my parents, who helped me in every possible way. Afterwards, when my husband acquired the office of prime minister (Now it is called chief minister) things eased out for me. I had at no time any difference of opinion with my husband. This is a political journalists' flight of imagination.

Q. 5. During your young age the political life in India was surcharged with patriotism and sacrifice. When did you take part in the freedom struggle of Kashmir.

A. Of course the freedom struggle was going on in full fury in India, and its repercussions were naturally felt in Kashmir also, which was passing through the trauma of Anglo Dogra oppression. Until 1945, I behaved like a traditional wife looking after the children, who needed protection and attention. Actually until then I played the role of 'two in one' i.e., both of the mother and father.

I was fully aware of the facts of the freedom struggle, as its venue was my own house, but actually, I threw myself in the struggle during Quit Kashmir Movement, when my husband was arrested in May 1946. I waged a double struggle simultaneously, rejecting the veil and joining the Movement. I led the anti- government demonstrations, made speeches, and boosted the morale of my husband's followers during absence. During the tribal raid, I was in the forefront of the Women's wing of the Peace Brigade, which fought the invaders. I did my best to rehabilitate and soothe the victims of the communal frenzy.

Q. 6. How were you drawn to social activities and programmes regarding the upliftment of the women, handicapped and welfare of the child — also to the weaker section of the society ? I would also request you to throw some light on the *Markaz-i- Bhaboodi Khawateen*, so as the common man should understand it.

A. 'Service above Self' is in my grain. I have already told you that my father was a philanthropist in his own way. Suffering of the people also inspired me. I know how they became the victims of the money lenders, because I had a personal experience. My husband during the heyday of the freedom struggle used to borrow money, and in a short span of time the interest became four times more than the capital. Besides, I knew that the illiteracy in general and particularly in womenfolk is a bane to the progress of the country. I believe in the adage, 'Educate a woman, you educate a family'. For the healthy growth of society education is a must. But I do not believe in literary education, it should be a job oriented one. I also realised that there is a percentage of handicapped people in our society; I want them to live a respectable and decent life, and learn to earn.

About the Miskeen Bagah Complex at Srinagar, the idea to start this type of centre came to my mind when I had visited every nook and corner of the valley during the freedom struggle, and saw pitiable condition of the women. I do not go for the academic degrees for the women in general, which is impossible also, but I wished that they should be trained in basic education, arts, crafts and an aptitude for social service be inculcated in them. This type of training would be a source of earning to them and would also be helpful in making them efficient housewives, good citizens and talented social workers.

My dream was realised after a long time in 1975, when the Hon'ble chief minister Janab Sheikh Mohammad Abdullah converted Miskeen Bagh Guest House into an institution exclusively meant for the welfare of the downtrodden women of the State. I was given the honour of being the Chairman of the Society. The

Miskeen Bagh complex started with the admission of 200 girls in August 1975, with God's grace the complex is progressing with galloping strides. Its branches are rapidly being spread all over the state of Jammu and Kashmir in urban, semi-urban and rural areas. It has imparted an identity of their own to the Kashmiri Woman, who by nature are freedom loving, but the circumstances had forced her to be contented with the status of a domestic servant.

At the complex various trades are taught e.g., carpet weaving, sozni, papier-mâché, crewel embroidery, leather embroidery, *tilla*, machine knitting etc. Training in stenography, printing press unit, and a condensed course of Education for adult women (Matriculation) are on its agenda. Quality goods are produced and marketed. In this way the arts and crafts of our rich heritage are being revived.

This complex fully realises that the work and wage is the main problem of destitute and needy women and orphan children. Therefore, it has taken up a number of schemes sponsored by the Central Social Welfare Board for setting up production units, especially from the industrial sector. Smt. Indira Gandhi, the prime minister of India, Begum Abida Ahmad, Ms. Ragu Ramaya, Begum Ali Yawar Jang and Ms. VardhaPan and other prominent ladies have visited the complex and were very much satisfied with its work.

The complex has established a Home for destitute women, a Hostel for working women, and a Home for orphan children (Gulzar- i-Atfāl), where about 50 orphan children are looked after under S.O.S. programme. On May 24, 1982, Dr. Hermann Geminar, Director General S.O.S. Kinderdorf International, visited the Miskeen Bagh complex, and was much impressed with its working. The Jammu and Kashmir State Council for Child Welfare was founded in 1974, and since then this institution has been doing commendable work in trying to create an awareness among the people of the State for the care and all-round development of the child.

My people have bestowed upon me the title of Madar-i- Meharban, and you know that to a mother her weak child is the favourite, and thus I am very much solicitious about my six lakhs of the most backward and nomad population of Gujars and Bakarawals. I am doing my best to bring them to the mainstream of social progress and civilization. Special patronage is given to them in education, employment and other fields. At the Miskeen Bagh complex Gujars and Bakarwal girls are given free lodging and boarding, besides, free training facility. I am also looking after the welfare of the Harijan and other downtrodden people and trying my best to create an awareness in the people to shun the prejudices against caste and creed. Nishat Destitute Home and Cheshire Homes are also running under my supervision and care. I am so busy that I have hardly any time for myself. But this has brought fulfilment and contentment in me.

Q. 7. These time consuming activities have an additional burden on you—How do you reconcile the activities inside home and outside home ?

A. Sometimes I do feel overburdened but it is not without pleasure of doing something to achieve a mission. I also feel pride in it as it is the woman who can accomplish the responsibilities of home as well as outside home. Where is a will, there is a way.

Q. 8. What do you think to be the greatest duty of a woman?

A. To me woman accomplishes her fulfilment through marriage. But after marriage she must devote the spare time in social service. This is my personal opinion as a wife and a mother. Even otherwise I am seeing many of my girls who have totally dedicated their lives to their respective fields of activities as scientists, doctors, aeronauts, educationinsts, teachers, journalists and nurses, i.e., in all walks of life they are acquitting themselves remarkably well. They are serving the society in their own way.

Q. 9. The women, who are working are they neglecting the demands and interests of hearth and home? Do you think that a synthesis between the two spheres of activities is possible?

A. I do not think that the working women are neglecting their homes. Work means worship, and worship is not 'neglect'. I do think that the synthesis between the two spheres of activities is possible, if there is a right aptitude, and right division of time between the home and sphere of activity.

Q. 10. The qualities of love, piety, sacrifice, dedication and service, which are attributed to women—whether these qualities are the result of compulsions due to a 'MAN RIDDEN SOCIETY' or are essential characteristics of womanhood ?

A. Yes, these are essential characteristics and intrinsic qualities of women since the creation. The male dominance came afterwards, but even in her worst days, she had clung to these virtues.

Q. 11. What works women can do to serve her community keeping in view the limitations of the womenfolk? Whether such programmes and works may be beneficial to the society as a whole or is it confined to women?

A. Women should be educated. Training in arts crafts is necessary. They should be taught to take up social service. Woman is an intrinsic part of society, she is the real home, and thus the society as a whole is benefited by the educated and accomplished women.

Q. 12. How do you like your office as an M.P. ? What is your contribution as an M.P. ?

A. I had contested the election to do something for the country. I had plans in my mind. It was the period of Janata regime, and much precious time was wasted in the appointment of Commissions and *vendetta*. But I did speak whenever I got the opportunity. I spoke forcefully in favour of Preventive Detention Act against Misa. Man's basic rights should not be violated under a democratic set up. On various occasions I directed the attention of fellow parliamentarians about the pitiable conditions of the various segments of the people of my state, a fact which was not known to the members before.

Q. 13. What is your message for the women of India ?

A. The women should remain feminine—modesty and sobriety would add lustre to them. But they should fight against injustice—it is they who are to be blamed for their tribulations. My heart bleeds whenever I read about bride burning on account of dowry. Law will not come to their aid, it is the women themselves who have to take cudgels against this cruel practice. They should work for the cause of their country, social justice, human rights, and amity.

# 29

# AN INTERVIEW WITH PADMA SHRI BEGUM ZAFAR ALI

In Kashmir as a prelude to foreign rule for centuries together, there took a general decline in the education, especially that of women folk. During the Dogra period a breakthrough was made towards the emancipation of the Kashmiri people by the Christian Missionaries. The condition of the females was appalling. To ameliorate their condition on the behest of the Kashmiri Missionaries stationed in the valley, the Church Missionery Society of London sent young girl missionaries. Notable among them were Misses Irene Petre, Frances Mackay, Violet Fitze, M. P. Mallinson and Kate Knowles.

In due course the Kashmiri social reformers came forward to help themselves. The first woman who pioneered social reforms and education in Kashmir is Begum Zafar Ali. She was elected as an M.L.A. in Sheikh Mohammad Abdullah's government on March 28, 1978. The President of India, in an investiture ceremony awarded her Padma Shri in recognition of her educational and social services.

Here is an interview with Begum Zafar Ali.

Q. : Begum Sahiba, What was the condition of the women folk during your time ?

A. : I am now 86 years old. In my time there were no schools for the girls, even the education of the boys was in its infancy. My father Agha Syed Hussain was the first Matriculate form Rawalpindi (now in Pakistan). In 1910, when my mother had expired, I was only ten years old. Social conditions were totally different from the present times. Women were kept in strict *purdah*. The Muslim women were taught only Quran-i-Sharif, which they learnt like parrots. They were allowed only to recite and cram but not permitted to write even alphabets. Such was the fundamentalist society. They were not allowed to go outside the four walls of the house, not even to the compound, lest they should come to the gaze of male servants and gardeners.

Q. : How you became educated, when the society was so averse to female education ?

A. : The girls of the Muslim aristocratic families could be allowed to learn three Rs. through European governesses. But it was not a common feature. My father engaged for me Miss Odoiver, an Irish lady. She had been formerly the governess of the Nizam of Hyderabad. There was a strong protest in our community against my education. Our family was vigorously boycotted for this sin. At the age of ten the governess taught me to wear saree. I was also taught to play badminton. The society even could not tolerate my going out in a burqa in a covered carriage. But my father withstood all opposition with rock like firmness. Thus I was taught house-keeping, hygiene, health care, physiology and domestic science etc. I never took any examinations.

Q. : How your early life was shaped ?

A. : I was totally isolated, except my father, two brothers and foster mother, I never saw anyone. The governess never preached against the *purdah*. I was not allowed to wear saree, as I would look beautiful in a saree than the traditional *Phiran*.

Q. When you got married ? Whether your married life gave you any inspiration for the social and educational work, which you took later on ?

A. : I was married in 1915 at the age of fifteen to my second cousin Agha Zafar Ali, who was studying in the Xth class. Within six years of marriage I had three sons.

When my husband was transferred to Gilgit, I also accompanied him, leaving my youngest son to the care of my parents, who had adopted him. Gilgit, where I had spent three years of my impressionable age was the formative period of my future career. There I had a chance of going out and meeting women. What I saw was simply staggering and stunning. The abject poverty had dehumanised the human beings. The women never washed during the winter season. To meet the ritual exigency of bathing, they kept knots and they would fulfill all the obligations of leftover baths in one single day.

The poor illiterate and low-paid fourth class employees were exploited by the officers. They were given only half of the salary, as cheap fruit was available in abundance. Begar was also enforced upon them.

Even the wives of officers were also ignorant of the basic needs of cleanliness and motherhood. They simply whiled away their time in gossip. When, I saw all this, I started a Craft Centre for the officers wives, as I could not bear the neglect of the children. Though I had started teaching them knitting and needle work, yet my basic project was to make them good mothers. That was the first Social Welfare Centre in Gilgit.

When I came back after three years, a missionary lady Miss Violet Fitze had opened the Memorial School C.M.S. at Fateh Kadal. It was attended by the Muslim girls from weaker section. Pandit (Hindu) girls were strictly prohibited by the society from attending the schools. At this time Girls Guide Company was started at Sheikh Bagh. Miss Churchil Taylor, who was a frequent visitor to our house, introduced me to Miss Mallinson. I was still in strict *purdah*. She persuaded me to come out and help Miss James in running the Guide Company. I was twenty-four. My husband encouraged me to take up this honorary work as it was once in a week, but my father was dead against my going out and joining the Guide Company. I took up the work with the permission of my husband.

Q. : How you got involved in the teaching line, when you had no examination certificates ?

A. : Meanwhile the Maharaja had started Girls School at Fateh Kadal for this he requisitioned the services of Miss Bose, the chief inspectress at Lahore, as the lent officer. The parents refused to send their daughters to the school. The Maharaja Hari Singh was in great predicament. He sent Smt. Watal, wife of his Finance Minister and sister of Rameshwari Nehru, to my father, who was the High Court Judge (the first Kashmiri Muslim to adorn this office) to allow me to take up the job as a teacher, so that the parents should send their daughters to the schools. Father refused. I was longing to go out and help the girls to come out and breathe freely. The condition of the women in the valley was same as that of the women in Gilgit. They were born, lived and died in *pardah*. They could not even peep through the window. Superstitions were rampant. When sick they instead of medical doctor would visit *pirs*.

My father's refusal had greatly perturbed Miss Bose. After some time Miss Mallinson came to my home and persuaded me to take up the job as a teacher. She took me to Miss Bose who was delighted. Afterwards she took me in her own Tonga to the first Girls High School, at Fateh Kadal, the heart of Srinagar. I was appointed as the third teacher. The staff consisted of Miss Chanar B. Sc. (Oxon), Principal, teaching IX and X Classes all the subjects. Smt. Mahe, a Hindu teacher from Jammu was Vernacular Middle pass, teaching VI, VII and VIII Classes. Smt. Pesaro Devi, a Hindu teacher also from Jammu was Vernacular Primary Pass and was taking Primary Classes. This was the total staff of the first High School at Srinagar. I had to teach Urdu, Physiology, English and Domestic Science. I had to take seven periods daily.

Q. : What was your reaction and experience as the first Kashmiri women teacher without any formal educational background ?

A.: Yes, the new job was challenging. I had never been to school, never seen the class. The students of IX and X class were about my age. I felt shy and nervous, and did not know how to start teaching. The first day when I returned, I went to see my father. He was sitting in the garden. I sat near him and started crying, from the guilt conscience in not taking his permission, and also for the inability to teach. Father was no longer annoyed with my judgment.

He understood my difficulty and demonstrated how to teach. I said 'I have to learn myself before teaching'. Therefore, an old male Muslim teacher was engaged for me to teach the subjects, which I had to teach in the school. I felt the need to pass an examination. I prepared for the Martriculation Examination. The teacher told me that Maths would be a stumbling block in the examination. With the permission of my husband, father and father-in-law, I sat with my children and learnt arithmetic from their tutor. Within seven months I learnt and appeared for the Matric Examination. I passed in the second class. I was awarded a Gold Medal, being the first Kashmiri matriculate woman.

Q. : How you managed to win over the inhibition of the parents/guardians of the female students ?

A. : It was an uphill task. After gaining confidence as a teacher, I started on the mission of cajoling over unwilling parents. With the Hindus the problem was that of orthodoxy, as they thought that the education would make their daughters immodest and shameless but with the Muslims it was that of dogged dogmatism. I also carried on my mission with matching determination. I started another Guide Company in my school. I used to wash the girls and cut their nails, thus imprinting in their minds the lessons of cleanliness and hygiene. At that time my father had become Law and Education Minister. With the help of my father I resorted to incentives. I requested him to award merit-cum-poverty scholarships to the girls for Primary, Middle and High Schools. My father agreed. Thus ten scholarships were sanctioned, Rs. 10/- for High School, Rs. 4/- for the Middle School was Rs. 2/- for the Primary School students. Rs. 10/- were sanctioned for the soap to wash the clothes of the students. The education was still confined to the weaker section of the Muslim Society.

Q. : How you started your movement for the emancipation of women?

A. : Sheikh Abdullah by 1933 was fully involved in the freedom struggle. He asked me to preside over the First Women's Meeting held at Pather Masjid. This gave me an opportunity to see general Kashmiri Women. They were wearing very dirty clothes.

In fact they never washed clothes and wore it till they were torn out. They wore trinkets and gaudy head-dresses. Their Children were half-naked, underfed and underclothed. I am not a politician. The filth, ignorance and poverty of womenfolk acted as a motivating factor to it. I made my speech in Kashmiri and told them not to wear all of their *Phirans* together, with dirty Phiran over them. I advised them not to waste money on trinkets and ornaments. I told them to come to Zanana Park, which the Maharaja had presented to the women, and I will teach them knitting and sewing. They could knit jersey, while selling vegetables. Thus I got interested in the social work. Sheikh Sahib thanked me in a letter.

For the recreation of the officer's wives a Ladies Club was started. Maharani Tara Devi was the Chairperson and I was the Secretary. One hundred ladies were enrolled as members. It was established for the purpose of taking women out of their homes and for recreation. It was generally attended by the non-Kashmiri Hindu ladies. I saw poor women and poor children coming to the park and looked wistfully at the Ladies Club. Nobody paid any attention to them.

Maharaja was also thinking to start a club for the have-nots section of the Kashmiri women. With the help of the municipal authorities, I converted the gardener's room for Poor Women's Club. Really I am very proud of this achievement, for I taught the poor women knitting, sewing and embroidery. To their little children I taught reading and writing. I felt sad about their lot. They must have an identity of their own. They should be made economically viable to gain self-confidence. I started Adult Education Centre with this aim. There were no funds for it. I also did not seek any government grant for this project. I begged and borrowed—not big sum, but small and not even in the shape of money, e.g., if anyone could spare some wool or other material it was accepted gratefully. After some time it became a Literary Centre for Girls and Adult Women.

Afterwards I needed government aid and attention for this Centre. Who could better understand **Women problem** than a woman. I took an appointment with Maharani Tara Devi, wife of Maharaja Hari Singh . I started with these line :

*"Dekh Kar Darbariyon Ka Libas".*

The actual lines are :

*"Phir Zamindaron Ki Phati Chadaron Ko dekhana".*

But I changed them to :

*Phir garib riaya ka hal dekhna.*

After seeing the dresses of the Courtiers, see the conditions of the poverty stricken masses.

I requested Maharani Sahiba that in the Ladies Club she had 100 members, if one woman goes for one day to the Poor Women's Club, it would be much useful. At the same time the members would not be subjected to any additional labour, as the turn of each member would come after 100 days. Maharani appreciated my suggestion, and asked the members of Ladies Club to help me in the centre. Many dignitaries visited the Club, including Lord Linlithgo, the Viceroy of India.

Q. : How you came into contact with the All India Women's Conference ?

A. : I explained the working and object of this Centre to lady Collector Buck, lady Dalal and Smt. Rameshwari Nehru. They got so interested that they expressed their desire to see the Centre. I told them that they were welcome. They should come and Maharani Sahiba would inaugurate It. Rameshwariji said "Begum Sahiba this is a wonderful idea. Why don't you have a branch of All India Women's Conference here as well". Honestly speaking I did not know about this organisation. The abject poverty, ignorance and illiteracy among the Kashmiri women had dragged mé into this endeavour. I was only interested in the welfare of orphan girls and widows. Rameshwariji encouraged me that opening of the Branch would also help me in receiving grants etc. for my social work. Thus, a Branch of the All India Women's Conference was opened at the Zenana Club, and I was its first Secretary and Rameshwariji was the President.

We started with the jail reforms. We saw in the jails that the boys about 11 or 12 years were housed with the hardened criminals or murderers. These boys were charged with small thefts, e.g., one boy was imprisoned for stealing Khwaja Ali Shah's *katora* ( a small bowl). I was appaled. Such boys needed reformatory jails. Housing with the criminals was to turn them into criminals. A young man was imprisoned for several years for killing a cow. Lady Collector Buck said in agony "of course the cow is more useful than you". We also saw the prisoners in the summer making *munj* mats in the compound. No shade. They were perspiring profusely. I also saw a solitary women prisoner in a high walled dark room without even a mat. She was accused of killing her two daughters.

After seeing all this, we met Sir Gopala Swami Aiyanagar, prime minister of Kashmir. I made following suggestions :

1. For the woman I suggested (I was the Inspectress of Schools) I could spare a teacher from nearby school for one hour (3 p.m. to 4 p.m.) to teach this woman knitting etc. and also to impart some religious instruction, to save her from getting mentally deranged.

2. Those men who labour and work so hard should get wages. These wages should be collected from them, and when they were released from the prison they should get this money to start some business.

3. The Co-operative Societies should help the prisoners in the rehabilitation. I requested Aiyanagar Sahib to plant trees so that they should work in shade. He replied : *Agar app vahan hotin to lagwata, yeh kud jayenge*. He said that instead of the co-operatives the panchayats would be entrusted with the job of helping the prisoners.

The reforms suggested at that time have been implemented after a long delay. Now the criminals get the wages, half of it they sent home and half they keep for themselves which they get after release. Now they can appear in the examinations, play games and get medical treatment. They could also celebrate Eid. During the government of Sheikh Sahib I requested for the expeditious settlement of the suits.

Q. : What educational reforms you carried out during your inspectorship?

A. : For the children coming from the weaker section, I started mid-day meal scheme. For this I started poultry farm, kitchen gardens, weaving of dusters, and mufflers so as to be able to make out income for the mid-day meals. During my inspectorship, I got constructed buildings for sixty primary schools. I also made each school to create a fund of mid-day meals.

Two Model Schools were established. One at Baramulla and other at Shahidganj, Srinagar. Many educationists visited the Model Schools, e.g ., Zafar Sahab (from Lucknow) and K.G. Sayeedain. They said, "you have done no less than a miracle".

I would not exaggerate, but I would tell you that I had a keen eye in spotting out the genius among the girls, and to give them all encouragement and inspiration, which they needed. Such genius I located in Sajida Begum (who later on became the secretary of education in J&K govt.), Miss Mahmuda Ali Shah, the noted educationist, and Sufia Hasan Shah to name a few. Meanwhile I did my B. Ed. from Lady Maclagan College, Lahore.

I would relate one episode. It was before 1947, I has gone to Muzaffarabad for holding a refreshers course for the teachers. Sheikh Sahib happened to be there. I asked for his permission to meet him. He the great man as he was himself came to my room. I told him : "Sheikh Sahib, you could not succeed in uplifting the people until there was education and awareness, especially among the women. The awareness towards the importance of female education, which had come to the Pandits was totally lacking in the Muslims. As an Inspectress of Schools I had seen that there was not a single private school or even a Maktab for the Muslim girls, though the Muslim population in the Valley was 95%. The educated girls were coming only from the Pandit community." Sheikh Sahib understood what I meant.

In 1948, I was promoted to the post of Chief Inspectress of J&K State. At that time there were only 9 Muslim matriculate female teachers. The Muslims female education had missed the mark, whereas the Hindu female education was making good progress.

I made a great effort to get Sheikh Sahib's sanction for 15 scholarships each for Middle class pass and Marticulates to further their studies. The irony of fate was that the sanctioned scholarships were 15 but we had only 9 teachers. Fifteen teachers were sent to the college for higher studies on their full pay. Every year two teachers were sent to Lady Irvin College, New Delhi, for the training in Home Science.

As Inspectress of Schools I had started Teacher's Club to improve upon the attainments of the teachers. Each Saturday at the same Zanana Park 200 Teachers were taught Methodology of Teaching. The All India Educational Conference under the Secretaryship of Syeedain once made a surpise visit. They were impressed. I still remember Mr. Vyas, one of the members words: "We are happy to come to Kashmir, We will take this original and wonderful idea to all parts of India." He quoted Tagore : "That teacher is best who is a student himself". Here we see with our own eyes—''200 teachers working as students. We congratulate you."

I also saw the exploitation of the women engaged in industries at the Chattabal Co-operative Craft Centre for Spinning and Weaving. Women used to spin beautiful pashmina, but the middle man paid them only 2 Annas per day. With the help of my brother Aga Syed Ahmad, who was the Registrar Co-operatives, their income per day was raised to 14 Annas per day, later on to Rs. 4/-. When I was the Vice-Chairperson of the Central Social Advisory Board the team of the Board including Durga Bai Deshmukh, Mrs. Sen, Tara Ali Baig visited the Co-operative Societies. A grant for Rs. 70,000 was sanctioned for purchasing 30 looms. However, it lapsed as it was not taken in time. In course of time fourteen hundred women got enrolled.

Q. : What is the role of the women in this male oriented society?

A. : When I opened the Ladies Club, I quoted following verse :

*Aai Maon Bahno Betiyo,*
*Duniya ki zinat tumse hai,*
*Tum ho to gulshan hai watan,*
*Tum bin veran hai chaman,*
*Gamgin dilon ki shadian,*
*Dukh sukh mai rahat tumse hai.*

(O' Mothers, sisters and daughers, this world is beautiful because of you. With you country is like a garden, without you flowerbeds are desolate. In marriages of poignant hearts, you are comfort in joy and sorrow.)

What could I say about the importance of women, except 'can a bird fly with one wing'? The educated woman is a must for happy home. The hand that rocks the cradle rules world. But the hand should be the hand of an educated and disciplined woman.

Begum Zafar Ali has most deservingly been honourered with the award of Padama Shri. When she was questioned by TV interviewer, how she felt? Her reply was : "I am very happy". It means that she is happy because female education in Kashmir has grown by leaps and bounds. At last the Kashmiri women regained their identity and confidence. Her life mission has been fulfilled.

# 30

# SHEIKH MOHAMMAD ABDULLAH AS AN EDUCATIONIST

A small boy of a tender age seeing suffering, injustice and oppression around him asked his mother the reason for all this. The widowed mother imbued with a fatalistic approach towards life gave the answer. "Wish of Heavens". The reply failed to satisfy the young boy who was gifted from the very beginning with a scientific temperament and was destined to be the first Kashmiri Muslim boy to take his M.Sc. in Chemistry from the Aligarh University in 1930. The boy turned out to be Sheikh Mohmmad Abdullah, the 'Father of Renaissance and Reformation in Kashmir. One swallow does not make weather; one M.Sc. boy was not the panacea for the widespread mass illiteracy and ignorance. In the words of Sheikh :

> "From Aligarh I came with the ideology : never yield before anybody on righteous course"

For a short time he worked as an officiating second master in Islamia High School with credit, before jumping into the whirlpool of the political agitation. But the teacher in him never died. Like Sir Sayyid Ahmed before him, he had fully realised that the only way for the regeneration of the Kashmiri Muslims lay in Education and Technology which is reflected in NEW KASHMIR, the charter of the Kashmiri emancipation and liberty.

National education was the pivot around which new educational policy was woven. When on 5th March, 1948, a regular National

Interim Government was formed with Sheikh Abdullah as the prime minister, he had only two basic priorities, education and end of feudalism in Kashmir.

**Primary and Secondary Education**

The new prime minister took up the cause of education as was envisaged in the NEW KASHMIR in right earnest. Rooting out of the mass illiteracy was not only the main plank of his government, but to bestow on the Kashmiri people a new identity and sense of self-respect so as to enable them to take their rightful place in the new social setup. Forty centres were opened for training the illiterate adults. The visionary in him fully understood that to attract the people, the entertainment programme with rural orientation ought to be arranged. Thus a festival of folk music and dance was held in the Nagrota Relief Camp—a mini *Apna-Ustav*.

He laid importance to practical and job-oriented education. The literary education was knit together with practical education by introducing subjects like wood-work, papier machè, embroidery, weaving, spinning and agriculture as optionals for the matriculation examination.

Inculcating pride in cultural heritage in pupils and public so as to develop an integrated personality was the chief aim of the new government. For this the beginning was made to impart primary education in Kashmiri. A committee of experts evolved the script of Kashmiri, which was a great landmark in the cultural history of the Kashmiri people. An exhibition of Basohli School of paintings was organised in Jammu. A museum was established to preserve arts and crafts of the Jammu province.

Various other measures for the promotion of education were the publication of the new text books, introduction of the Refresher's Course, and opening of the Children Schools on the Indianised pattern of Montessori system. Private enterprise was encourged to boost education. To encourage reading habits in the people, book-weeks were held both in Jammu and Srinagar. Research and Archaeology Department was also activised. Professional education was still not established in 1948, therefore, liberal stipends and loans were given to the candidates in the veterinary education, engineering and medical discipline to accomplish them in various universities of the country and abroad.

**Women Education**

Sheikh Sahib knew fully well the importance of female education in building up Naya Kashmir. He wanted that the women should come out of illiteracy, ignorance and superstition to take their rightful place. His discerning eyes found a capable educationist in Begum Zafar Ali. In her words. "In 1949 when Sheikh Sahib took over charge of Education Department, the condition of education was appalling. There were few school building and these were ill-equipped. The teachers, generally, were untrained and half illiterate. I was asked to take over as Chief Inspectress and we began to translate the dream of 1933 at Pather Masjid into practice. There were only nine matriculate lady teachers in the State Schools. The untrained and unqualified teachers were deputed either on full pay or stipends to complete their education."

For women aspiring to earn and supplement their domestic budget, he opened a centre at Miskeen Bagh, where women are learning various arts and crafts under the trained teachers. The Centre is placed under the charge of Begam Sheikh Mohammad Abdullah, who is equally devoted to the welfare and social uplift. Polytechnique-Institute for women, which has started is training to various crafts and vocations was also initiated by him.

Women's college at Maulana Azad Road, established in 1950, is an everlasting momento of Sheikh Sahab's contribution towards women education. Started with about fifty students and six faculty members, it has now become one of the leading colleges of the state. Sheikh Sahib took special interest in nurturing it and looked into its smallest details. In those times when women emancipation throughout the sub-continent of India was in its infancy, he sent young girls to United Kingdom and other states of Europe for academic pursuits. Notable among them were Begam Zafar Ali, Mahmuda Ali Shah, Sajida Begam and Begam Quareshi to name a few. He never believed in the dictum that women are a decorative piece, and instilled in them the courage and pride, which are the characteristics of Sherè-i-Kashmir himself. Modern Kashmiri girls owe their liberation to this great leader. Fortunately for Sheikh Sahib, his dream proved true during his life time.

What Iqbal sang, Sherè-i-Kashmir translated into reality. His millions of daughters believe in the dictum of Iqbal:

*Ai tairey Lahuti Us Rizk Se Maut Achhi*
*Jis Rizk Se Aati Ho Parwaz Me Kotahi*

O celestial bird, death is better than that food, which clips the wings.

Today the women doctors, engineers, scientists, academicians, artists, and musicians etc. of the state are the embodiment of Iqbal's poetry and Sherè-i-Kashmir's vision. His dream to found women's University on the pattern of SNDT of Bombay was left unfulfilled.

**University Education**

Soon after assuming power during his first stewardship of state, he enacted the Jammu and Kashmir University Act, under which the Jammu and Kashmir university was established. Shri A. A. A. Fyzee, the renowned educationist, was appointed in 1957 as the first full-time Vice-Chancellor. Subsequently, two separate & full-fledged universities came into existence. The University of Kashmir is situated on an idyllic site known as Amar Singh Bagh, a gift of the former Chancellor, Dr. Karan Singh.

Jammu University situated in a busy road was starved of space. In the words of the ex-Chancellor of the Universities of J&K, Shri L.K Jha; "He (Sheikh Abdullah) himself selected sites for expanding the Kashmir University and for developing a wholly new campus for the Jammu University. He looked at the plans prepared by the architects in order to ensure proper landscaping and beautification of the areas and to improve the living and teaching facilities for students and teachers. However busy he was otherwise, he always found time to attend to student problems and issues pertaining to education."

During his absence, the malaise of mass-copying, hooliganism infected the colleges and universities. As soon as he returned to power he made a bid to remove those ills. The students had already heard about his tenacity and discipline from their parents. He used to visit examination halls unannounced, and the result was that the evils disappeared as if they never existed before. The student unrest had led to the suspension of the annual convocation. With Sheikh Sahib at the helm, it again started.

Unemployment of the educated youths worried him most. He understood the need of restructuring of the educational system. The education should be highly productive. Thus various centres such as the Centre of Research for Development (CORD) was established in 1979 to undertake research on scientific and technological problems connected with the economic development of the state. Visionary as he was, he understood fully the importance of Kashmir's intellectual contact with the Central Asia. For this in 1979, the Centre of Asian Studies was established. The students of this centre are going to different states of Central Asia and are acquitting themselves well.

To enable the students to pursue their education privately, Institute of Correspondence courses was set up in 1976. Besides, the Centre of continuing Education and State Resource Centre were established in 1978.

He took special interest in the all-round development of the Kashmiri language. Sheikh Sahib said, "When we achieved independence in 1947, the Government, as promised, prepared the basis for the growth and development of the Kashmiri language, but as the whole of our life was disturbed in 1953, our mothertongue was also buried in the lap of oblivion. I wish that the language should be given the status which it deserves and which has been guaranteed for it in our Constitution". The department of Kashmiri was upgraded as a full-fledged post graduate teaching department and a publication and research centre.

During the brief tenure of his chief-ministership, he rode like a Colossus in every sphere of activity, especially in education. He wanted to be a doctor but could not get seat. The establishment of Sher-i-Kashmir Medical Institute fulfilled his ambition. Similarly, Sher-i-Kashmir Agricultural University is translating his dream for a better future to the peasantry in increasing their harvest by the use of modern technology.

He is fittingly buried in front of the Kashmir University campus—his life work, on the bank of Dal and near Hazratbal Shrine, where he used to make his important decisions. Webster has truly said, "If we work upon marble, it will perish, if on brass, time will deface it, if we rear temples, they will crumble into dust : but if we work upon immortal minds and imbue them with principles, with the just fear of God and love of our fellow-men, we engrave on those tablets something that will brighten all eternity".

# 31

# SIDE LIGHTS ON KASHMIR PROBLEM

The happy valley is again unhappy. Only a couple of years back it was quiet, peaceful and prosperous. Tourists from all the parts of India and abroad flocked to this place to enjoy the sylvan beauty of this emerald green valley. Tourists never complained of the molestation of their womenfolk or theft. When lawlessness is the order of the day in some parts of North India, Kashmir was the shining example of peace and rectitude. Gandhiji has seen a ray of light in Kashmir, in its tolerance and secularism.

## ORIGINAL SIN

Beneath this veneer of placidity there was a dormant resentment against the government of India, which was bequeathed from one generation to another. Freedom of expression, the privileged right of democratic societies was denied to them. Whenever they wanted to express their resentment, they were labelled as the Pakistanis, which meant traitors. These people, mostly youth were put behind the bars, and were tortured. Sometimes hot iron was pressed upon their cheeks. These excesses led to the heart searching among the Kashmiris that if this was the result of their freedom struggle against the Dogras, then their freedom struggle has not ended. They should continue it now against the government of India, which is treating them as a colony. This feeling is fanned by the status of Kashmir as a disputed territory. It is really surprising that such a peaceful people, whose weapons used to be stones and

*Kangri*, now its youth generally in their teens are roaming with Klashnikavas in the streets and bylanes.

Original sin was committed when at the direction of the Governor general, Mountbatten, the then prime minister of India made at 08.30 p.m. a broadcast on October 28, 1947, that a plebiscite would be held in Kashmir under the U.N. auspices, and going to U.N.O with a complaint of aggression against Pakistan towards the end of 1947. These two events proved to be unmitigated blunders.[1] V. Shankar says :

> "that commitment has ever since been a millstone round our necks and has been responsible for a great deal of embarrassment to us both with the U.N. and countries close to us."[2]

Mountbatten had come to India with a covert mission, Churchill, the leader of opposition, had advised him :

> " I am sorry that you should perform the grievous duty. I am not going to tell you how to do it, but I tell you one thing — whatever arrangement you may make, you must see that you don't harm a hair on the head of a single Muslim."[3]

Jawaharlal Nehru, the prime minister of India came under the sway of Mountbatten through Lady Mountbatten and Krishna Menon. He repented this afterwards and wrote to his sister, who was then India's Ambassador in U.S.A. on May 10, 1950 :

> "The most difficult thing in life—what to do with one's friends."

The impact of this decision could be realised by this urdu couplet :

> "वह वक़्त भी देखा है तारीख की गहरायियों ने,
> लमहों ने ख़ता की थी सदियों ने सजा पाई"

The prime minister had a weakness for Sheikh Abdullah, who advised him to force Maharaja to abdicate. The Maharaja abdicated most unwillingly on June 29, 1949, in favour of his son, Karan Singh, a young boy of 18 years. Had Maharaja been allowed to continue as a constitutional head, he would have exercised a sobering influence upon the young ebullient Sherè Kashmir. The state had acceded to India on a federal basis and delegated to the union defence, communications and finance.

Again the incorporation of the Article 370 was the result of diplomatic manoeuvering between the government of India and National Conference, in which the latter had checkmated the former. The article in itself is not sacrosanct as its provisions could be amended by the parliament of India. It provided Jammu and Kashmir with the special status.[4]

**Sheikh Abdullah**

The architect of Kashmir's accession to India is Sheikh Mohammad Abdullah, the tallest among the National Conference leaders. He was a synonym for secularism. Even twists and turns in his life did not deviate his faith in secularism. He kept down the hot- heads among his followers with the words :

"Hindu are my relatives because I am from the same stock. If you kill them you are killing my relatives."[5] One of his greatest characteristics was the absence of vindictiveness. Though he was imprisoned for as long as 13 years — perhaps not without justification considering what he said and did to undermine the basis of Kashmir's relationship with the rest of India — he bore no grudge against Nehru. He was on a goodwill visit to Pakistan, when Nehru suddenly died, and he rushed back to Delhi, his eyes swollen by weeping. It was a remarkable instance of forgiveness[6]. Much of misunderstanding was the result of his unmindful speeches, which he made from time to time when being irritated with the government of India. Morarji Desai once so succinectly put it: "the Sheikh first makes a statement and then thinks about what he has said."[7] Essentially he was a Kashmiri not a national leader, whose lifelong ambition was to safeguard the Kashmiri identity of his people. If it was in any way in the red, he was ready to go to the extent of snapping ties with his mentor, Jawaharlal Nehru.

With no apology to Sheikh Abdullah, his ambition was egged on by U.S.A. and Pakistan, who had flooded Kashmir with gold. The flow of money is still continuing and the list of doners is multiplied, The prominent among them are Lybia and Saudi Arabia. Thus the clue to kashmir tangle lies in understanding the personality of Sheri-Kashmir. Till his last breath he was steadfast to the accession with India. Now the disillusioned Kashmiri youth are so much bitter against him that they had the rashness to desecrate his grave — who is Baba-i-Qaum and their regenerator.

**IRRITANTS**

The Kashmiri people greatly resented the arrest of their leader, Sheikh Mohammad Abdullah, on August 9, 1953. The Kashmir Conspiracy case brought against him was never substantiated, but it injured the sentiments of the Kashmiris. Again he was arrested in 1965, after his Haj pilgrimage to Mecca and visits of Saudi Arabia, Egypt, Algeria and the United Kingdom. He was first detained in Ootacamand and later in Kodaikanal. In January 1971, Sheikh was externed from Kashmir and his Plebiscite Front was banned. He was not even allowed to participate in his youngest daughter Surayya's marriage. All this added fuel to fire.

Siphoning off the autonomy of Kashmir in stages, affecting the special status of Kashmir. They say to name a few : That in 1959 permit system regulating entry into and exit from J and K was abolished. That in the same year the Jammu and Kashmir Legislative Assembly adopted the Official Bill amending the State Constitution to extend the jurisdiction of the Union Election Commission to Jammu and Kashmir and bring the high court of Jammu and Kashmir at par with other high courts of India. That in 1960 an Ordinance was promulgated by the President of India, which accelerated further formal integration of the state of Jammu and Kashmir with the rest of India. That in 1965 the designations of the head of state and the head of the government in Jammu and Kashmir changed from sadr-i-riyasat to governor and premier to chief minister. That in 1967 an ordinance was promulgated amending representation of the People's Act to bring in on par with the central laws by government of Jammu and Kashmir.[8] The Kashmiris charge India with going back on its pledge to hold plebiscite. Its reply was given by the then Prime Minister, Jawaharlal Nehru, to the Parliament of India on August 7, 1952 :

"There still seems to be a good deal of misunderstanding about Kashmir's accession to India. The other day I said in this House that this accession was complete in law and in fact in October, 1947. It is patent that no argument is required because accession to every

State in India was complete on these very terms by September in that year or a little later. All the States acceded in three basic subjects, namely, Defence, Foreign Affairs and Communications. Can anybody say that accession of any State in India was incomplete simply because they acceded in only these three subjects? of course, not. It was a complete accession in law and in fact by the end of October, 1947. It is not open to doubt or challenge. When United Nations Commission accompanied by legal advisers and others came here, it was open to them to challenge it. But they did not because it was quite clear to them and to their legal advisers that there could be no question about the legal validity of the accession."[9]

Leaving apart above legal implications, it is a general belief that 'if a plebiscite had been held within a year or two of the UN-imposed ceasefire, Pakistan would have clearly lost.'[10] The Kashmiris as a whole are very allergic to the demand of scrapping the Article 370, which is voiced by the leaders of B.J.P., as they take this article as a bed-rock to protect their special status. They were disillusioned when the Colossus of Kashmir involved himself in the family dispute between his son and son- in-law over the succession to the chief ministership, and not leaving the issue to the people. The Kashmiris have hoary ties with the Punjab due to geographical proximity. The Rawalpindi road was the heartline of Kashmir before 1947, being the supply route. Its closure to them means snapping of their traditional ties which had bound them with the Punjab. It has got so much emotional appeal to them, that the dying Kashmiris instruct from father to son that when this line is opened come to their graves and whisper this message.

## GRIEVANCES

The Kashmiris say not without truth that all the high offices in the state including that of the c.m.'s are appointed by the government of India. Thus they look upon c.m.'s as the stooges of the government of India. The Kashmiris love a leader so long he opposes government of India, but dislike which could be stretched to hatred when he occupies chair, which they think with the crutches of the government of India.

Rigging, malpractices, bribery, and muscle power is the common practice in the elections. Only during the Janata government's rule elections were free and fair. The Kashmiris take the elections as a fraud and farce. When the last elections were held in 1987, the rigging took place on a mass scale. Had the elections been free and fair and MUF would have come to power as the Kashmiris say, this present insurgency would not have taken place. The torture, harassment and imprisoning of their workers was the last straw on camel's back.

They say that the governors are not impartial, and are the agents of central government. They cite the example of toppling of an elected chief minister in 1984 and instituting as a chief minister, their henchman. Widespread corruption, jobbery and nepotism in the administration is another charge, which is also a fact. Their grievance is that because of the rigging in the elections with the connivance of the central government, deprives them of the legal means to get rid of the corrupt government, and institute another.

There is no planning. New colonies are coming up without roads or means of sanitation. Short supply of the electric power is the major grievance. During winter when temperature goes to freezing point the power is cut for two or three days in a week, making their life a hell. Even when light comes it is of such a low voltage that its light is just like a thin candle. Continuous and ceaseless meddling of the central government in the state in the role of king makers, e.g., in 1986, it brought back the dismissed chief minister, and foisted upon the people a coalition government comprising of the National Conference and Congress. The result was that both pulled in the opposite directions and paved the way for the present insurgency.

The communal flareups and carnage in India also scares them, and they do not want to leave the valley even if they get a good appointment. This does not mean that they are insular. They are going and prefer to go to any part of the word. They think if they are independent and declare Kashmir an islamic state, the money from the Arab and gulf countries would flow in Kashmir.

**Role of Pakistan**

The government of Pakistan is more interested in Kashmir, than their own, as they call it the 'Juglar vein of Pakistan'. Using religion as a trump cared since 1947, they are provoking the Kashmiri masses to revolt against the government of India. They have moreover never forgiven India for the break up of East Pakistan and emergence of Bangla Desh as a sovereign republic. General Zia-ul-Haq formulated a plan code named as 'Op Topac' to get Kashmir liberated in phases, which was reported in IDR of July, 1989.

The military training camps were opened in Pakistan and Azad Kashmir to train the educated unemployed Kashmiris. They were going and returning with arms and ammunition and the Intelligence Department took no notice of it. They have become so formidable, that they are ruling the state behind the cover. They openly kill whomsoever they suspect as the agent or spy of the government of India — he or she, Muslims or non-Muslims. Pakistan gloats over its creation of gun trotting and blood spilling youth, who otherwise would have been pursuing their studies. 15th August and 26th January under their dictates are celebrated as 'Black Days', and people willingly or unwillingly comply to their dictates.

The killings of the innocent citizens — many of them get killed in the cross-firing, between militants and security forces under, the deployment of B.S.F. which the Kashmiris take them as a badge of servitude around their neck. They hate them, in the downtown area they are spat upon and called as 'Black Dogs'. The Kashmiri are also scared of them — so much that when the children do not drink milk, mothers say : "Drink, otherwise security man will pick you up, and children readily drink milk."

They are equally terrorised by the militants. There are so many outfits, and each demands money from the middle class families. Sometimes in a single day more than four or five outfits demand money, from the same person and threaten with dire consequences if money is not paid.

**THE OTHER SIDE OF THE MEDAL**

It is said that secularism was the hall-mark of the Kashmiri character . But now the communalism has become the order of the day. Services are the monopoly of the Mulsims irrespective of merit. So long it was practised against the non- Mulsims, it was borne by them with sullen resentment. But now it is practised against the qualified Muslims of havenots section, and it has led to the deep-seated resentment against the government of India, Generally for every wrong or even for natural calamity the government of India comes under fire.

Whereas the Kashmiri Pandits being denied of opportunity in kashmir, go to the other states of India, the Muslims in general are scared of crossing Banihal pass. If given to them, the Muslim government employees would not have gone to Jammu during the *Darbar* move.

The government of India has spent billions in Kashmir, but anti- Indian feeling is daily mounting. The money has not percholated to the masses, but remained in the pockets of a coterie, with the result that the rich have become richer, the poor, poorer.

The government of India always encouraged defection, and rewarded them. When these people went out of favour of the government they cried hoarse for plebiscite or self-determination.

For Kashmir affairs the government of India relies upon a coterie, and it is they who are responsible for such a pass. Had the government relied upon some objective and impartial intelligence agency, many of the blunders would have been avoided.

The concept of *Hindu Rashtra*, frightens them. Even among intellectuals there is a general feeling that the government wants to eleminate Muslims in Kashmir. The scare is so much that if the Kashmiri Muslims would go outside valley for educaion they would prefer Muslim Aligarh University or Osmania University than any other.

There is a general feeling in India that only Hindus are the targets of the militatns. But the fact is otherwise. Muslims are equally on the hit list. Many of them are staying there, with no means to quit the valley, but those who have got the means have left the valley along with their family members. But their travails and sufferings are not highlighted by the media. The Sikhs are also suffering and some of them have left the valley.

## THE WAY OUT

The government has to win the confidence of the people, which is totally shattered. Undoubtedly it is an unhill task. But nothing is IMPOSSIBLE. The intelligence system should be geared up, and impartiality should be injected into the system. Crackdowns and interrogations should be stopped. They convert pro-Indian Kashmiris into India baiters. The unemployment problem is to be solved not as carrots, but as a matter of policy. The government of India should abandon its policy dabbling in the politics of Kashmir, and pave way for a free and fair elections. Special status of Kashmir should be left untouched. State centre relations should be guided on federal principle. Article 370 should be retained till the Kashmiris themselves think it redundant and scrap it. Erosion of Kashmir autonomy should be stopped. Pakistan should be specifically told not to interfere and act according to Shimla Agreement of 1972. The policy of making time to time Accords e.g., Nehru - Sheikh Abdullah Accord of 1952, Indira Gandhi - Sheikh Abdullah Accord of 1975, and Rajiv – Farooq Accord of 1986, should be abandoned. They make both the parties a laughing stock.

Still everything is not lost. A pragmatic and national approach can retrieve the situation. To learn lessons from the mistakes is discretion and tact.

### References

1. M.O. Mathai, *My Days with Nehru*, Delhi, 1979.
2. V. Shankar, *My Reminicenses of Sardar Patel*, Two volumes, Delhi, 1974, 1975.
3. Larry Collins and Dominique Lapierre, *Mountbatten and Partition of India*, New Delhi, 1982.
4. M.K. Teng, *Kashmir Article 370*, New Delhi, 1990, pp. 76- 78.
5. *Indian Express*, Thursday, September 9, 1982.
6. *The Illustrated Weekly of India*, September 14-20, 1980.
7. *Ibid.*
8. V.R. Trivedi, *Facts About Kashmir*, New Delhi, 1990.
9. *Ibid.*
10. Dina Nath Raina, *Unhappy Kashmir - The Hidden Story*, New Delhi, 1990, p. 176.

# INDEX

# INDEX

## C